'Identity is at the heart of many conflicts that we see in society today and yet one of the most difficult to discuss rationally. This book brings clarity to this sensitive subject with its powerful mix of psychological research, intellectual rigour and personal insight. I totally loved it!'

Professor Binna Kandola, OBE, Business Psychologist, Senior Partner Pearn Kandola

'What is the Self? How is it related to consciousness? This dilemma has entertained some of the greatest minds of human history. This book contributes in a significant way to that history, written by one of today's great thinkers, Geoffrey Beattie. In this unique book, Beattie brings us into his own world of Self-construction. We thus come away understanding what psychology should really be—a discipline that aims to uncover truths about consciousness through the reflections and recollections of the individual. In the style of stream of consciousness writing, Beattie lays out his thoughts, emphasizing how his background had an impact on how he perceived his mission in life and how it directly influenced his own approach to his discipline. He paints a powerful narrative-ethnographic-reflective picture of how the individual copes with rearing, overcomes it (in certain situations), and is able to grasp itself as a distinct entity, rather than as a formless sense of being. This is a book in psychology "from the other side", as Beattie puts it—that is, through the experiences that he went through, from suffering to conflict, in order to become aware of himself and his role in the world. It is required reading by anyone interested in understanding what consciousness is and how it emerges throughout the life cycle.'

Professor Marcel Danesi, University of Toronto

'In *Selfless: A Psychologist's Journey through Identity and Social Class*, Beattie has adopted a clearly different approach to psychology than the mainstream practices of writing on the subject, elegantly integrating such crucial topics as identity, education, social class, and mobility in a down-to-earth, unpretentious, yet deeply moving and encouraging, autobiographical narrative. What can be envisioned is that this book has the potential to contribute to relevant fields of inquiry in the same way Oliver Sacks' books did to neurology and the history of science.'

Professor Hongbing Yu, Ryerson University

T0244358

Selfless

Selfless is a memoir, reflecting on identity, social class, mobility, education, and on psychology itself; how psychology as a discipline is conducted, how it prioritises objects of study, how it uncovers psychological truths about the world.

Geoffrey Beattie takes the reader on a journey through his early life in working-class Belfast, his Ph.D. at Trinity College Cambridge and subsequent academic and professional career, to explore fundamental issues within psychology about social class and social identity. Beattie discusses the difficulties inherent in this process of education and change, and how social background affects how you view academic work and the subject matter of one's discipline. This book movingly details a life and how it is changed by the processes of education, the psychological pressures when abandoning those close to you, the dissonance within, and how it feels and operates. The book takes a critical look at psychology from the other side, and examines the process of becoming 'selfless', meaning having little sense of self rather than being overly concerned with the wishes and needs of others.

Showing how our early experiences and their influence continues throughout life, Beattie's emotionally engaging, entertaining, and witty text offers general readers, students, and academics fresh insights into psychology, adaptation, and personal change.

Geoffrey Beattie is Professor of Psychology at Edge Hill University and a prize-winning academic, author, and broadcaster.

Selfless

A Psychologist's Journey through Identity and Social Class

Geoffrey Beattie

Routledge
Taylor & Francis Group

LONDON AND NEW YORK

First published 2021
by Routledge
2 Park Square, Milton Park, Abingdon, Oxon OX14 4RN

and by Routledge
52 Vanderbilt Avenue, New York, NY 10017

Routledge is an imprint of the Taylor & Francis Group, an informa business

British Library Cataloguing-in-Publication Data
A catalogue record for this book is available from the British Library

Library of Congress Cataloging-in-Publication Data
A catalog record for this book has been requested

ISBN: 978-0-367-62976-2 (hbk)
ISBN: 978-0-367-61483-6 (pbk)
ISBN: 978-1-003-11169-6 (ebk)

Typeset in Sabon
by Apex CoVantage, LLC

This book is dedicated to my father, my mother, and my brother, who had faith in me from the start. They always said that I could make something of myself. I just hope that this is what they meant.

Contents

Acknowledgements

This book is about a journey through education and through life, so there are some educational institutions that I must thank (as if institutions can hear you). St. Mark's Primary School in Ligoniel was where I felt most comfortable. My mother always said that she had to take me on the first day of school but after that first day I insisted on walking up there with my chums; friends I later had to leave behind. I then attended Belfast Royal Academy, the oldest school in the city, and this school changed my path in life and for that I have to be eternally grateful. The University of Birmingham was a joy from start to finish, liberating, exhilarating, I felt free, and again I am truly indebted. The University of Cambridge is one of the top academic institutions in the world, and I was honoured that they (and Trinity College – the greatest of the colleges) accepted me to study for a Ph.D. Some individuals from these institutions stand out – I am indebted to Mrs Ritchie (St Mark's), Mr Lord (BRA), Dr Ros Bradbury (the University of Birmingham), and Professor Brian Butterworth (the University of Cambridge) but, of course, I am indebted to so many more.

My family, of course, requires a special thanks. I would particularly like to thank Carol who knew me from the 'turn-of-the-road' gang and witnessed the many changes – both good and bad. I have written about aspects of my life before in various books and papers and I would like to thank Granta for permission to reuse extracts from *Protestant Boy* and to Routledge for permission to use the material on the double bind from *The Conflicted Mind*. In Chapter 4 in particular of the current book, I use extracts originally published in various newspapers and magazines (*The Guardian*, *The Observer*, *The Sunday Telegraph*, *New Statesman*), which were then used in collected volumes published by Chatto & Windus, Victor Gollancz, Heinemann and Orion, and again I thank them for use of this material.

Edge Hill University has great ambitions and encourages original creative thinking, and I would like to thank John Cater, the Vice Chancellor, George Talbot, the PVC for Research and Dean of the Faculty of Arts & Sciences, and Rod Nicolson, an old friend from Cambridge and my head of department. All three are incredibly supportive. This is an institution that is fundamentally committed to equality of opportunity.

I would also like to thank my publisher, Eleanor Taylor from Routledge, and my agent, Robert Kirby from United Agents, both offer much needed encouragement in this loneliest of professions (I mean the writing not the university work!).

And finally, I would like to thank Laura McGuire for her support, encouragement, good sense, good humour . . . the list is endless. She is almost certainly the kindest person that I've ever met, which is incredibly important in this unkind world of ours.

Chapter 1

The turn-of-the-road

Figure 1.1 Copyright Bill Kirk/Belfast Archive Project

> The past is not for living in; it is a well of conclusions from which we draw in order to act.
>
> John Berger (1972: 11) Ways of Seeing

John Berger was an English art critic, novelist, painter and poet, someone experienced with both words and images. In the early 1970s, he presented a television series on the BBC called 'Ways of Seeing', and later the same year he published a short book with the same title.

It was a book that was full of ideas, about the relationship between seeing and speaking, and the way that seeing comes before words, about the relationship between the image and the text, about how to 'see' great art, about visual perception, interpretation, understanding, response. For someone like myself with my social background, it was an important book that gave me the courage to think about culture (perhaps with a small 'c') in different ways. The TV series was genuine public service broadcasting, the BBC at its best. The book even hinted at the vocabulary I might use. The epigraph above is quoted out of context, but that doesn't really matter. Berger here is talking about the interpretation of great works of arts, the portrait by Frans Hals of the Governors and Governesses of an Alms House for old paupers in the Dutch seventeenth-century city of Haarlem. But there is a general point here about ways of seeing both art and life.

The yard wall and other barriers

I was sitting on our bed, the bed with three legs and the dip in it towards the side wall, the wall that was always damp. I was staring out the window at nothing in particular. My head was full of things, ideas jostling with each other, in an excitable sort of way, random thoughts, nothing important. My mother always said that she had to shout for me three or four times to get me to do anything, that I could be very ignorant with people, that I would just ignore them, living in my own little world.

The sky was slate grey, and the rain beat down on the corrugated iron roof of our toilet across the yard, the noise only softened by a thin layer of felt that had gone patchy with wear over the years and had been lifted by the wind. To get into the entry you had to climb up the cracked and splintering toilet door by pulling it open, and then put your left foot on the cross panel on the inside of the door, and next swing your right leg onto the bottom of the slippery roof and then pull yourself up. Then you could jump straight down into the entry below, the entry which smelt as if all the dogs in the neighbourhood relieved themselves there. The chosen place; dog shite everywhere.

The toilet door was a means of escape – there was no backdoor in the yard for these sorts of mill houses. The toilet door was the *only* means of escape, or you could just pretend to climb over but instead sit up there on the roof of the toilet, looking down into the other yards, those private places in our street, watching the world, watching the people and all their little foibles.

'I'm on top of the world, ma,' I'd shout when I was a child, towards my mother in the scullery, mimicking Jimmy Cagney in *White Heat*. 'Top of the world!'

'Get down off that roof before you bloody well fall off,' she'd shout back, mimicking nobody, except herself.

My mother always said that all this climbing had worn the felt down and that we didn't have the money to replace it. She said that this made the roof of the toilet even more dangerous and that one day, my brother Bill or I (or both) would end up in a heap in our yard.

I shared the back room and the bed with my brother, and in the night, he would slowly in his sleep push me into that dip against the cold, damp wall. The bed sheets were always damp, and the springs of the mattress cut through the thin sheets. Sleep was always intermittent and then I'd sleep in late in the morning, long after they'd all gone to work, late for school.

My books were laid out on the eiderdown on the top of the bed tonight – mathematics, physics, chemistry, some Russian literature (Tolstoy, Dostoevsky, Pushkin) – stories of the aristocracy and war, the nobility of the peasant, class, war, deceit, love, destiny, resentment, anger, notes from underground. Lines from Pushkin stuck in my head: 'We're all bound for the vaults eternal/And someone's hour is always near' (Pushkin 1829/1997). Always that feeling, always that, hanging over everything, from such a young age, hanging over even the briefest of joys.

My older brother Bill had left his job as an electrician now and he was away climbing somewhere; he was always away now. He used to practice his climbing technique on our yard walls, around and around the yard, his feet never touching the ground. He taught me his simple technique for getting over the yard wall, and a few of his other climbing moves, but they were always of less interest. I just wanted to learn how to get out of the house quickly by climbing over that yard wall.

I had the room to myself. I was alone and able to think without much distraction. 'I'm working, leave me alone!' I'd shout down the stairs whenever my mother called up for me to go and do a message.

Sharing a bed with a sibling wasn't uncommon in our street, in those dank, condemned mill houses, two up, two down, with no real privacy within them. They sat just a stone's throw from the mills themselves, and there were four linen mills in Ligoniel alone. We played in the streams around the bleaching mill, the stream a different colour each day. The houses huddled together in long lines with paper-thin walls and you could hear conversation through these walls, sometimes the words themselves but always the tone of voice. You knew when there was a row on. And when our next door neighbour was annoyed with us or angry at her husband, Old Jimmy, you would hear her shouting, and in her anger and frustration she'd sometimes throw bricks over the yard wall as you made your way out to the toilet. Bricks just lying handy in her yard from her crumbling yard walls. I'd sometimes sit on the roof of our toilet to catch a glimpse of her, to see what was going on, to catch her in the act. My mother said that she'd gone a bit mad – her husband and his drinking had driven her to it. She was taking it out on us.

Perhaps I was born to be a psychologist, just sitting there on the roof of the toilet waiting to observe the old crazy woman in action; the woman driven insane by her love of a good man, although, to be honest, I'd never heard Old Jimmy described as a good man.

Everybody in our street shared a bed with their siblings – some of the families were very large, the Catholic families that is, and there were quite a few Catholic families in our street, so for them it was top to tail for six, seven, eight or nine children all fighting over the one bed. The beds looked dirty, the sheets unwashed, with large, dark stains that nobody tried to cover with the eiderdown. Some of these houses smelt very bad because of the number of people living in them, and I would hold my nose when I was in the Rock's house – there were eleven living in there. I tried to hold my nose in a way that nobody would notice. I didn't want to hurt anybody's feelings. But if you've got eleven people living in a tiny house with two bedrooms, adults, teenagers, children, babies, with no bathroom, nowhere to wash properly, and no washing machine, it's not going to smell very nice; it's nobody's fault.

If I ever forgot my house key, I would always have to wait for my mother to get back from the mill in the Rocks' house, there was always somebody in. I would take one huge gulp of breath just before I went into their house and then pinch my nostrils through force of will, without using my finger or thumb, and sit there waiting for my mother to get home, trying not to talk because of my lack of breath. I would just nod or shake my head when Mrs Rock, always kind, offered me a jam sandwich, or a slice of white bread dipped in white sugar. We didn't eat bread dipped in sugar at home, we were never that poor. If you had to take a deeper breath, and sometimes it was inevitable, the smell was sharp and acrid, unpleasant and lingering. There were lots of pictures of Christ on the walls, Christ on the cross, crucifixes, bleeding palms, a crown of thorns, all that great symbolism of Catholicism; the colour crimson, it seemed, in every image. I have always associated that smell with the colour crimson. To me, that's how crimson smells. It smells of poverty.

We were very fortunate boys, my mother always said, there were just two in our bed, but it was still very awkward when you became teenagers. We had a geyser in our scullery, and we'd wash by standing in a basin on the floor and we'd flick the boiling water onto us followed quickly by a handful of cold water – the water from the geyser was always boiling hot as the temperature gauge had broken years ago (the tin bath still hanging on a nail on the yard wall had rusted over many years before so baths were a thing of the distant past). It wasn't very elegant washing all over in the scullery, balancing in the basin, and flicking the boiling water onto yourself, and it wasn't a good way of trying to keep clean. The door into the scullery was made of glass, a sort of patterned, frosted glass luckily, so any neighbours sitting in the front room could watch you trying to wash, if they wanted to, if they were bothered trying to work out what was going on in the myriad of shapes refracted through the glass. You could hear them commenting sometimes on how you were developing or how they thought you might be developing. My first proper shower was at secondary school after sport, but I would never have admitted this at the time. I was never shy in the shower; I was used to lack of privacy, I was used to being looked at naked.

We were always very well turned-out though; my mother saw to that, she had a sewing machine in her bedroom, a black Singer, and she made a lot of our clothes when we were young. The Rocks had to wear hand-me-downs that never fitted, some of the children were very thin, some much bigger, and sometimes you would see the younger ones barefoot in the street because there weren't enough shoes to go around, with the clothes hanging off them because they'd been passed down from an older sibling. My mother made our clothes, my father made us guiders and a toy car out of metal for my bother when he was a child that he could sit in and steer. My father and mother were both very handy.

'You don't know you're born,' said my mother, in case we ever forgot this. 'You're spoiled rotten, the two of you.'

When the potato lorry came to make deliveries to our local grocery shop, a couple of the lads would hop onto the back of the lorry, always left gaping wide open, to pinch a couple of potatoes each. One in each hand. They would hop off the back nonchalantly with a big wide wink. Then we'd go up the fields, light a fire, and cook them, digging them out of the embers with long, scorched sticks. I was never that hungry, never really starving like some people, like them at times, but I'd eat with the hungry ones, all sitting around the fire, laughing about how careless the delivery driver was and how he never saw anything. You could rob them of anything.

'I'm starving,' I'd say. I still say it today because it reminds me of something, but it makes people angry. 'What are you talking about?' they say, 'you've never been hungry like that in your whole life.'

I still love the taste of potatoes cooked in an open fire, burned right through with blackened skin, the charcoal flaking off. It reminds me of a happier time.

When you had an apple, one of the Rocks would always ask for your ruts, your apple core, the bit you would throw away. I'd leave quite a bit for them, some of the lads from my street would bite the apple right down to the pips, slower and slower, teasing them, while they stood there waiting patiently for what was left. It was like the way Pavlov might tease a salivating dog.

My father was a motor mechanic for Belfast City Corporation working on the buses, and every Saturday he'd take me round scrap yards on the outskirts of Belfast to look at old cars, to see if he could fix one of them up and get them working. I never thought that we'd ever get a car. That was beyond any of our dreams. Then one Saturday afternoon in Bates' scrapyard just past the bus terminus up in Ligoniel, he found one that he liked the look of. It was a Ford Popular and there wasn't too much rust. He struggled to get the doors open. I got in beside him, into that musty old car, which I can smell in my imagination to this day, and he tried to get it started. He opened the bonnet and tinkered with it for hours, whistling away, as I pretended to drive. As 'happy as Larry', that's what they always said about my father when he was working with engines, and whistling away to his heart's content. Finally, he pulled out the choke for the fifth or sixth time, maybe more, but careful not to flood it, and it shuddered into life.

'We've got our own wee car now,' he said, and hugged me. I'll never forget those words, and he got out to haggle with one of the Bates family, as the mangy Alsatians with the matted coats on the chains around the yard, four or five of them, reared up and barked at him. My father spat on his hand to seal the deal; he always did that. He got it for £14 and we drove back to Legmore Street and parked in front of our house. My mother came out with his hands over her eyes. She screamed when she saw it. 'Oh, Billy,' she said, 'it's gorgeous.' Even our Bill was impressed. The four of us got in and we drove around the streets. My father drove so slowly that my brother always asked whether he was stopping. All the neighbours came out to watch; we were the first in the street to get a car. When we got back, the Rocks ran down the street after the car. I begged my father to give them a spin in it, and Kevin and John hopped in the back. They were on their best behaviour and they waved at everybody as if they were royalty. They were the first of my friends ever to get into the car. Bill and I washed the car, the Rocks helped. It belonged to all of us in a way.

The car changed our life. Every Sunday in summer we'd drive up the North Antrim coast to Ballygally or Glenarm, nestled at the foot of Glenarm Glen, for sea fishing from the pier, or further up to Cushendun or Cushendall for picnics, or down past Bangor to Groomsport, or over to Lough Neagh to sit on a rug on the lough shore and wave the midges away and come home full of bites on our tanned legs and arms. 'We're a great family for the sunbathing,' my mother always liked to say, 'as soon as Old McCormick is out, we're out sitting in it.' She'd cover us in coconut oil until we shone, and we came back with glistening legs with little red bite marks all over them. They were the signs of a good day out.

My father would drive Bill and I to the Six-Mile-Water or Dundrod to fish, and we'd come back with brown trout for dinner, sometimes three or four, sometimes even a rainbow trout, rarely without any catch. My brother was a great fisherman: he'd disappear up the river and stand in the streams in his waders for hours, fly-fishing with his hand-tied flies that would swoop and dip on those deep, hidden pools with over-hanging trees, greener than the rest with lots of reeds, where he knew the trout would rise. I'd sit on the bank near the car just using worms and a hook and a little red hand-painted float that my brother had given to me, with my father beside me, just reading his newspaper, with me dangling the worm and hook carelessly in the water. There wasn't much finesse with my fishing, nor much skill. But sometimes I got lucky and Bill was always shocked when he got back from somewhere up the river and realised that I'd managed to catch something. Once I caught more than him, and I could see my father trying not to smile. And then we'd stand in the scullery gutting the fish for my mother to cook. Bill showed me how to gut them, and I'd set the fish on a plate and run my finger tentatively up inside the fish with its belly sliced open, stopping every time I got to something sharp, with Bill laughing at my slow, careful technique. He would do it with one smooth movement, holding the fish open with his left hand, two fingers of the other hand used as the scooper, letting the fish's guts drop straight into the sink. Expertly.

We were a very happy family and I never once heard my mother and father exchange a cross word, although she did tell us that she once threw an alarm clock at him, but that's before we were born. She couldn't remember why she did it. 'I've always had the Latin temperament and the Latin looks,' she said. 'Your father's very placid.'

When I was about twelve my father got a job as a sheet metal worker in Belfast Technical College and he would drive me to school in our new wee car and some days he'd pick me up as well after school, and we'd drive up the Hightown and I'd kick a rugby ball about, while he read the *Daily Mirror* with his glasses at the end of his nose. But those days of long summers and long, sleepy drives home, all together, were not to last.

I remember my mother saying one Sunday night when we came down that steep hill at the end of the Hightown Road, before you get to the Horseshoe Bend, that she hated the idea of us all dying on our own one day, and that if we had to go, she'd like it to be now, when we were all together, in that car from the scrapyard, after a wonderful day by the sea, with the salt and sand matted in our hair, and our legs and faces glistening brown from the sun. It made me both sad and happy at the same time. My friends all told me that I had the best mother and father in the world. Many of them had a belt taken to them regularly, or the lead for the dog, which was always kept handy for the beatings; sometimes they had to go into the coal hole below the stairs for the beating so as not to upset the other children. I was never hit by either of my parents. My father once pretended to, but it wasn't much of a pretense. He just told me to tell my friends that I'd had the arse scalped off me for running away with the Rocks over the Antrim Road to Belfast Castle without telling anybody where I was. We were away all day and late into the night. I was probably about seven or eight.

My brother Bill became a born-again Christian when he was in his teens, so I shared a room and a bed for several years with a born-again Christian, which is not necessarily the easiest type of person to share a room with. He kept a box on the dressing table with hundreds of rolled-up biblical quotes which he would extract with tweezers and read over and over before going to bed. It took him ages to get into bed. I would kneel to say my prayers aloud at the side of the bed, as he watched, and I would usually say eight or nine prayers, all word-perfect. He studied the Bible, and then he would pray silently; I tended just to memorise bits of it, that's what he said, and I knew a lot of prayers, which I would recite perfectly from memory.

'You have to mean it, you know,' he would say, 'not just say the words to show off – if you want to be saved, that is – if you don't want to go to Hell.' With a born-again Christian in the house, Hell was rarely far from our thoughts, and there was no getting away from Hell in our street. My friends and I would sometimes go down to the local Elim mission hall on a Tuesday night because they gave out lollipops to children on a Tuesday to entice us in, without our parents. They would walk round with a cardboard box full of lollies, before the preacher started. You were only allowed one lollipop each. And then as you sucked the lolly, the great reward, the preacher would start in his loud, bellowing voice. He was shouting at us.

He would elaborate on the Hell that was waiting for each and every one of us, unless we became born again, reborn in Jesus Christ. We were about nine or ten. My pals just told me to ignore what he was saying and enjoy the sticky lolly that tasted of sugar and nothing else; it wasn't much of a distraction to be honest, but it was hard to ignore hearing about your parents burning in Hell, forever. I always laughed to myself to see my friends sucking harder and harder as the pains of Hell were spelt out to them in the most graphic detail. At least we were in this together.

'You'll not recognise your parents in the flames,' the preacher bellowed at us, 'there will be no comfort. Your ma won't be looking after you then, she'll not be running after you to wipe your nose, she'll be screaming in agony.'

My friends tried to act tough, but I could see through them; you could see it in their eyes, that fear, that vivid imagining, when they thought you weren't looking. And they'd dander back home afterwards, with a wee swing in their shoulders, like the hard men from the corner, who we all looked up to, but there was no confidence in that walk at the best of times, none, we were only practicing. And certainly not on the way back from the mission hall.

Those words, sentences, endless threats, were etched into my tender childhood brain. 'Each day, you go down one more step towards Hell, one wee child's step but it makes no difference, you're heading right for the flames. Your ma will be burning right in front of you when you get there.'

Years later, I realised that the first sentence here that has terrified me since childhood, about the steps you take each day towards Hell, came from Baudelaire's *Les Fleurs du Mal* (1857/1995), and it was preserved somehow more or less intact in that bellowing sermon. How it ended up in the Elim with the boys from our street in the congregation is anybody's guess.

Bill was a Christian when my father died; I was thirteen and he was seventeen. That's why the lines from Pushkin about being bound for the vaults eternal have been in my mind since childhood. Never a day has passed since then when I don't think about death.

My father had gone into hospital for a routine check-up in the Royal Victoria Hospital, that's what he told us, but never came round after an operation. He tried to keep his visit to the hospital secret and only let it slip at the very last minute when he was talking to my Uncle Terence: he didn't want to worry the family. We went to visit him on the Sunday, the night before his operation. That was the last day of my childhood.

He never regained consciousness, and lay in a coma for a week and then they brought him home. He was laid to rest in our front room just by the front window where the gas meter was, but with the blind pulled down. He looked just the same but so white under all that powder and so cold and without that loving smile of his. My mother always said that all the neighbours, traipsing in on their own or in pairs, told her that they had never seen such a good-looking corpse.

I'd have to go down past him at nights to get to the toilet in the yard. That's when I cried, when I was on my own, out there in the yard, where no one could hear me, sobbing uncontrollably in the dark, muffling the sound into the crook of my elbow, the sleeves of my pyjamas hardened from my runny nose. And then I'd pull myself together to go in past him again. I knew he'd be watching me, looking down on me, I didn't want to let him down. I had to be a man now, that's what I was told. Not a wee boy anymore.

My father didn't go to church on a Sunday morning with the rest of us and this caused me great anxiety. I couldn't bear to ask Bill what this might mean for his soul. I didn't know if my father said any prayers; I'd never heard him say any. I couldn't bear to think of him in Hell. He was fifty-one when he died, my mother was forty-five. Bill had been baptised as a child, but at the time of my father's death he was baptised again, as a born-again Christian, fully immersed in the water. But it didn't last in the end. Perhaps he didn't like the idea of my father going one way and him going another; perhaps he didn't like the idea of the forced separation of death, and those direct and diverging paths to Heaven and Hell; perhaps he was struggling with his own demons and his own uncertainties.

We had an electric fire downstairs in the front room, that was the only permanent source of heat in the house, and there was a rule about the fire – you were only allowed to have one bar on. If you tried to switch two bars on then the argument with my mother could last the whole night, three bars and it was bedlam. I ran every day more or less from second year at secondary school onwards (the year my father died). It was cross-country mainly, and we didn't have a washing machine, so my wet shorts and vests caked in sweat and mud would be balanced on a pouffe in front of the electric fire, competing for the thin rays of heat. The vest and shorts would be hand-washed once a week, but I ran every day, and twice some days, so the sweat-stained drying clothes would lie there on the pouffe, drying, giving off bad odours for the whole week, blocking the heat from the one bar of the electric fire. They smelt of digestive biscuits after a few days. My mother gave me one of her old tops to wear when I had to run in the rain and cold (we couldn't afford a tracksuit top), and it smelt of stale perfume and now even staler sweat, heated and reheated over many days before it would be washed with all the other running gear in a basin in the yard on a Saturday and then run through the mangle – before the mangle seized up with rust and just lay there in the corner of the yard.

There was a whole vocabulary for those who ever complained about the cold and the fact that the small electric fire never managed to heat this damp house – 'cold crackers' was the most common pejorative term. 'You're a right cold crackers,' my mother would say, 'I don't know who you take after.' This is an expression that I've never used, although I like many expressions from my childhood.

My mother had been born in that house, and her father, George Willoughby, lived there when he returned from the army. He had been in the Royal Inniskilling Fusiliers and he had served in India and in South Africa in the Boer War, 'lovely warm countries', my mother liked to point out, but when he got back to Belfast and that damp little house, he never once complained about the cold or the damp in the house, or so she said. Not like me.

I discovered many years later that the Irish regiments serving in the Boer War called the sun 'Old McCormick' (and as deadly a foe as Old Kruger himself, they said), and George brought that nickname back to Legmore Street with him. My mother would shout up the stairs: 'Old McCormick's out' and Bill and I would run down and strip down to our pants and sit in the yard, glistening with coconut oil from the tin, with our arms stretched out in front of us. My mother would hoik her dress up, and open her top. My father would just roll his sleeves up and keep working away on some parts of a car engine lying in the yard on a newspaper. She had no idea where the term came from, or how negative it was for those who invented it. Our family loved Old McCormick, unlike those who named him when they were fighting the Boers on that parched scrubland with no shelter from the sun or the enemy.

George had joined up at eighteen; he was a rougher in the linen mill before he joined up and a rougher afterwards when he came out of the army. He signed the Ulster Covenant in 1912 like all the Protestants in our street, even though he got on well with all his Catholic neighbours, including the Rocks who, like him, had been there from when the street went up. Like most, he also joined the newly formed Ulster Volunteer Force of Edward Carson to use 'all means which may be found necessary to defeat the present conspiracy to set up a Home Rule Parliament in Ireland'.

'No Surrender!' to a United Ireland they all said as one. He was in the Orange Order and his Orange sash sat in the top left-hand drawer of the dressing table in the front bedroom. In 1914, the UVF brought arms in to the coastal towns of Larne, Bangor, and Donaghadee to resist Home Rule by force of arms. They loaded the guns into cars and in the words of the historian Jonathan Bardon, the motor cars 'sped through the small hours,

distributing them [the weapons] to prepared dumps all over the province'
(Bardon 1992: 444).

My grandfather, however, took no part in the distribution of the guns.
They called for him that night, but my grandmother couldn't wake him up.
'My family have always been good sleepers,' my mother always said in his
defense. 'They just couldn't get him up – he slept through the whole thing.'

'Had he been drinking?' I'd ask.

'How the hell would I know?' she'd say. 'I wasn't there.'

With the outbreak of the First World War in 1914, the UVF formed the
major part of the 36th Ulster Division. Thirty-five thousand members joined
up, all volunteers, 'nobody made them do it, they didn't have to ask twice',
my mother liked to point out. They were part of Kitchener's New Army.
The 36th Ulster Division served at the Somme on that first day of that most
awful of battles. 'The greatest loss and slaughter in a single day in the whole
history of the British army,' according to Churchill.

'Not a single man turned back,' was what I was told when I was a child.
'Not a single man. You need to remember that.' The war correspondent of
The Times wrote this about that day: 'When I saw the men emerge through
the smoke and form up as if on parade, I could hardly believe my eyes.
As the leading soldiers neared the First German line there were cries of "No
surrender, boys!"'

Of the nine Victoria Crosses given to British Forces at the Battle of the
Somme, four were awarded to the 36th Ulster Division. According to the
war correspondent Philip Gibbs, 'Their attack was one of the finest displays
of human courage in the world.'

I was reared on these stories.

But I always wanted to know more. I wanted to know if my grandfather
was there on that first day (or there at all), and if he was, what did he do,
what had he seen? I never met him, he was dead before I was born, so I had
to rely on my mother. But it was always very vague. There were never any
details.

'None of them talked about it,' my mother would say, annoyed at me
for asking again. 'They saw terrible things. Men who never stammered in
their life came back hardly able to say two words. There was this fella from
Ligoniel who just blinked at you all the time. There were men with an arm
missing or only one leg. You couldn't ask anybody anything about that day
when they went over the top. They've all blocked it out. There was one fella
I remember who had only one leg and half a hand missing. He talked about
the war a lot but he never talked about the Somme. He used to sit picking
bits of shrapnel and bits of dirt out of his good leg when he was reminiscing.
It was like a wee nervous habit. The problem with his good leg was that,
because there were so many wounds in it, all the dirt of the day seemed to
get caught in it. You'd just see him sitting there, picking away, even when
he'd got all the dirt out. He couldn't leave it alone.'

My mother's father was in the army, and her oldest son was now a mountain climber, bivouacking in the Hindu Kush in Afghanistan – bivouacking in his sleeping bag outside the house in the middle of the night in the snow rather than rap us up – and I would sit in the front room, not moving, studying, concentrating, thinking, tormented by Yeats' 'ravens of unresting thought' (1900/1990) (which I have always assumed is really a metaphor about thinking rather than a metaphor about birds; ravens are, after all, dark, noisy things, sometimes terrifying, untamed, like thoughts themselves), surrounded by books for hours on end, complaining about the cold. I sometimes understood why she got annoyed at me.

There was a paraffin heater for the back bedroom but only for when it was very cold, and it was only brought out in late December, at the very earliest. Getting the paraffin heater out was a big event in the year. The paraffin heater projected the most beautiful kaleidoscopic patterns onto the ceiling, and I loved that warm, comforting smell. The room smelt damp, and the nylon blankets were damp to the touch, but the fumes of that paraffin heater smelt lovely. I felt woozy and enjoyed the sensation; it was like getting high.

The Troubles were now raging, and you could hear the shooting at nights from somewhere out there in the dark and the rain, and sometimes a bomb that would make the windows shake. 'Jesus, that one was close,' my mother would say, and then she'd apologise for taking the Lord's name in vain. When she still cared that is, before it all got so much worse.

'All the women around here are on nerve tablets,' she'd say, 'and many of the men just drink – that's their way of coping with it.' My father had died three years earlier, and my brother was off climbing somewhere: it was hard to keep track of his movements, the Cairngorms, the Alps, the Rockies, the Hindu Kush, somewhere far away from here. He would turn up unannounced and unexpected with things I had never seen before or heard of – fondue sets, bottles of green spirits in small, exotic bottles, ('Chartreuse,' he explained), and ski sweaters from Chamonix (he was a ski instructor as well), and numerous tales of other lives. He was my hero, he showed me that anything was possible. You didn't need money to have a different sort of life, a life of glamour and travel, which was just as well as he never had any, you just needed the will, the will to see the world and enjoy the good life – the life that is out there, somewhere.

Sometimes he would have lucky escapes in the mountains or on the rock faces, but he never seemed to worry about the dangers. Some of his climbing friends seemed to have very short lives. I used to ask him when they were born so I could work out how old they were when they died. Their short, truncated lives always worried me, but he dismissed such negative thoughts. He lived moment-to-moment without worry or much planning it seemed. I was always studying – for the future, whatever that might be, or a future. It was vague and cloudy, like the thickest of fogs.

As a child, Bill had been impossibly good-looking, and my mother, 'the best-looking girl in Ligoniel', my father always said, 'like Gina Lollobrigida', would take him out in dresses to show him off in prams made by my father. The whole neighbourhood would stop my mother to admire his angelic and, it must be said, very feminine looks, and now he climbed jagged peaks in countries they had barely heard of. But he was now rugged and good-looking. My mother looked like a film star in clothes she made herself. 'Always a great one for the style,' my Uncle Terence would say. So when she was out pushing a pram with Bill in it, it must have been quite a sight.

My father's description of her might not have been that inaccurate. Years later when I started doing some journalism, and long after my father had died, I was in Belfast during the Troubles visiting my mother and at the same time (and much to her consternation) writing an article for *New Society* about life during the conflict. I thought that it would be a good idea to get some shots of Crumlin Road jail and the courthouse to illustrate the article, so I decided to go down there early in the morning on New Year's Day because the streets would be empty. I got out of the car and started taking some photographs, and suddenly, in a matter of seconds, an unmarked car pulled up beside me, and two men in plain clothes jumped out, grabbed my arm, and told me that I was under arrest. 'What for?' I asked. 'You've been photographing prison warders' number plates,' was the reply (there had been a host of bomb attacks on prison warders' cars in the preceding months). They took me to some bare room somewhere in the complex to interview me. I'd no means of identification on me: I had dressed in a hurry; it was a spur of the moment type of decision to go down the Crumlin to take some photographs before flying back to Manchester. I explained that I had a flight that day to Manchester – they said that I wouldn't be flying anywhere that day. Several official-looking people wandered in to take a look at me, someone from the army, an RUC man, neither of them saying anything directly to me, and then a man in plain clothes who came in and sat to my side, so that I couldn't see him, but I could tell that he was having a good look at me.

After a few minutes, he started to speak. 'You're not related to Eileen Willoughby, by any chance, are you?' he asked (Willoughby was my mother's maiden name). I explained that she was my mother.

'Oh, I know Eileen,' he said, 'she was the . . .'

'Best-looking girl in Ligoniel,' I said, interrupting him, and he burst out laughing. 'That's right. A great one for the style – always dressed to the nines.' He moved around in front of me and we spent some time chatting about my mother and who she had met and married. He told me that I was the spitting image of her. He asked me to send her his regards. They wanted to keep my camera 'to stop me getting into trouble again', but I explained that I'd borrowed it from the university. Eventually, they let me leave with it.

'Give my regards to your mother,' he said again as I left. 'And be a bit more careful around here.'

I told my mother the story when I got home but she was annoyed that I hadn't asked him for his name ('What did he look like then?') and angry that I'd been so bloody stupid to try taking photographs down by the jail.

'You don't know what this place is like, it's not your home anymore. You need to be a bit more careful around here. And I can't believe you didn't ask him his name.'

The gang

There were just the two of us in the house now, my mother and I, with a front door that was never locked ('Sure that's the way it's always been, we're like a wee village up here in Ligoniel, I'm not locking the door for those yahoos with the guns and the balaclavas') and a glass door into the front room that could be kicked open at any time. And if it was to be kicked open there would no escape unless you could climb over the yard wall and jump down into the entry. Only one of us could do that.

My Uncle Terence and Aunt Agnes who had been in our house every day had moved to England a year after my father's death. They moved to Bath and then to Chippenham, miles from home. My Aunt Agnes, my mother's older sister, worked with her in Ewarts Mill in Ligoniel and came down for lunch every single day. My Uncle Terence, her husband, was my father's best friend, and they would go down to the bar at weekends, always together. They had no children and a big treat for me was to go up to Lesley Street at the top of Ligoniel to sleep between them. I would have to bring my corn-flakes with me. That was always the little last-minute joke – 'Don't forget his cornflakes, for goodness' sake, he loves his cornflakes.' My mother missed the two of them terribly. So did I.

The gunfire was like a conversation, or an argument, the taking of turns, you might say, if you were a psychologist interested in those sorts of things: you'd hear one gunshot and wait for the reply, trying to work out whose voice it was, an angry and staccato opening, and the return fire, sometimes much louder than the one before, an amplification of intensity and purpose. That never sounded good in this dyadic exchange.

Sometimes, I'd be upstairs in the back bedroom doing my homework when the shooting would start. I'd go downstairs to see what was going on. My mother would be sitting in front of the TV, the TV that had never worked, ever since she'd bought it second-hand from a neighbour, a TV *engineer* she said, but it was just a local OAP with such bad eyesight that he was nearly blind. 'Joe 90', they called him because of the thickness of his glasses. I always thought that his occupation was slightly improbable.

You could see the grey streets of Ardoyne on the screen, just down the road from us, with some serious-looking journalist in a raincoat and some bullet holes in the front of a house, which he pointed out one by one, in a painstaking and slightly bored way. Then on the news there was another story and yet another atrocity with an image of some wee country road (I wasn't sure where, I missed that bit, they all look the same) with a tree with no leaves and glistening scraps of butchered animals caught in the forks of the tree, the debris of a car, and a dead person covered in a blanket stained with seeping blood, and a hole in the road from the blast. Just a two or three second scan of rural life in our province and a story that was already becoming old and familiar. I wasn't sure whether they were horses or cows in that tree, the camera didn't linger, it just hinted at what was happening to this quiet wee country of ours, full of hedgerows and farm animals and unspeakable acts, and then the tree with the bits in it was edited out of the later bulletins. The stained blanket with the shape underneath was left in.

Seamus Heaney wrote: 'the voice of sanity is getting hoarse' (Heaney 1975/1992), and it certainly was around here.

The TV was still on the blink. 'Hit that a wee skite for me on the way past to get it working,' she said, 'I've been up and down four times.' She needed some distraction. The window pane shook again.

I walked over to the TV and slapped it hard on the side, almost knocking it off its stand. 'Jesus, you've hit that too bloody hard, now the picture's gone off completely. You're so bloody careless.'

I sat for a few minutes in front of the television now with no picture. 'They're at it again,' she said, motioning to the dark and the distant gunfire. She got up and turned the TV down, so she could hear better, now there was no picture and no sound, just some wavy hypnotic lines.

'That's the army firing back,' she said. She'd become an expert on the sounds of gunfire, or so she liked to think. 'You wouldn't know who'd started it tonight. It was one or the other.' There was another loud bang. 'Jesus, it's getting closer. Did you hear that one? That's not far away now.' We sat there in silence, if sporadic gunfire in the far or near distance could be considered silence.

I had heard that somebody had chalked 'Is there life before death?' up on a gable wall just off the Falls Road, and somebody had tried to write the same message up our way, but it had been washed off almost immediately, doused by water. 'Making fun of the Bible,' my mother said, by way of explanation. 'What do you expect?'

I glanced down at my watch and told her that I had to get back to my homework. 'That's right, you leave me sitting here on my own. They'll be firing through the window next, and you'll be up those stairs reading those big books, oblivious to what's going on down here.'

She hated being on her own. Life a few years earlier had been so different in that same little house. 'You father was one in a million,' she'd say. 'We were inseparable.' And I can remember the sing-songs on a Saturday night after the pubs closed: my Uncle Terence had a great voice, he was in a choir, I didn't know which one, and he would always start with the same song. You didn't have to request it; he knew what everyone wanted to hear. They would all set down their drinks and sit in silence, and there would be a pause with no clattering of glasses and no whispering – it was almost reverential, more reverential than church even – and then a voice that I would never immediately recognise, always a moment of doubt about where that voice came from. It would emerge in the silence of that smoky little room where all the men and all the women had a wee puff.

'Oh Danny Boy . . .'

There was a resonance in the voice, as if it belonged to someone else, and somewhere else, as if it didn't belong here, slap bang in the middle of Legmore Street, and my mother would dab at her eyes in a way that she hoped nobody would notice.

Then it was others' songs in the wee front room packed with friends and music and laughter, and my brother going into the scullery to wash himself by standing in the basin before going out for the night. He'd sing some Irish folk songs before he left. 'Bloody rebel songs,' my mother called them with a laugh.

Bill would stand up, taking it all very seriously, dressed for a night out. He didn't have a great voice.

'And now as I lie here, my body all holes, I think of those traitors who bargained and sold, and I wish that my rifle had given the same, to those quislings who sold out the patriot game.'

'Jesus, some of them rebel songs are awful depressing,' my mother would say. Then it was my turn.

'Our Geoffrey prefers Protestant tunes,' she'd tell our neighbours. They'd give me sixpence to sing that great Protestant anthem, 'The Sash My Father Wore'.

'Sing it to your Uncle Terence, he loves that song, he can't get enough of it,' my mother would say, and they'd all laugh, but I never saw the joke as I sang it right into his face. For years I didn't understand it, until Kevin Rock told me, a little spitefully I remember, that my Uncle Terence was a Roman Catholic – he'd seen him going into St Vincent de Paul chapel, his chapel – that was the choir he was a member of – it was a Fenian choir.

I didn't know at the time that my Uncle Terence hadn't been allowed into the house of my Uncle Jack, who was a staunch loyalist (a member of 'the Black' to be exact – the Royal Black Institution, one up from the Orange Order) and married to my Aunt May (my mother's other sister), for nearly forty years. Jack was a very good man and my Aunt May was the nicest woman that I've ever met, but that's blind ideology for you, I suppose. Forty years of exclusion, it makes me weep to even think about it.

So I would sing right into the face of my Uncle Terence, a big relaxed face slightly reddened with the drink, and reeking of porter.

'And it's on the twelfth I love to wear, the SASH MY FATHER WORE!' And they'd all roar at the end of it and applaud my passion, including my

Uncle Terence, who would give me an extra sixpence and rub the back of my head.

'Go on, Geoffrey, give us a wee shout of "No Surrender!" like your grand-father, George Willoughby, a proper Orangeman,' my Uncle Terence would say. I didn't know that he hadn't been able to marry my Aunt Agnes until after George, the proper Orangeman, died.

And they'd all be laughing away. So I'd shout it out at nobody in particu-lar. 'NO SURRENDER!' That great Ulster Protestant slogan echoing around that little room with the paper-thin walls with so much laughter. I was a shy boy but this was my party piece.

And now it was just this. Me upstairs doing my homework and her sitting there on her own, waiting for the next round of gunfire.

I told her that I had lots of homework to finish for the morning. 'Some of your friends will be out on the street as we speak, trying to protect this area. There's going to be roadblocks and all sorts. So, what's so important for you to do tonight?'

'I have to do some Russian,' I said. 'You know that it doesn't fit into my timetable anymore, I have to work on it myself. I'm translating some Rus-sian literature tonight.'

'Well, that's going to be very useful, if the Russians ever land up by the mill dam, you can direct them to all the best joints in town,' she said. 'A lot of bloody use that's ever going to be. When are you going to Russia?'

She was alone and angry, I understood that, and anxious, undoubtedly, everybody was. She was trapped in that house. The Troubles now meant that nobody went out after dark and the shooting was getting worse – more frequent and ever closer. Nobody ever visited, even the minister had stopped calling. Bill was always away, and we looked forward to his visits home with his bottles of absinthe, and cocktails that they might drink in ski lodges in Chamonix. It was like a holiday when he turned up, with his stories about a glamorous life beyond these streets, but I had work to do up those stairs every night with that thick, intoxicating smell of paraffin that made my head light.

Sometimes I would try to work at the yellow card table in the front room to keep my mother company, but if I did, it looked like I was just sitting there, gazing out of the window of the front room. But that wasn't right, I was working – I was thinking – that's work, but it didn't look that way. At school, it would have been hard to explain how bad things were getting around here, around Ligoniel way, around the turn-of-the-road. They would have thought that I was exaggerating or making excuses. That would have been the worst thing. I wanted to get the work done without excuses. I hate excuses; I always have.

Life was changing all around me – roadblocks, bomb scares, random shootings, I saw the change in my friends, boys I had known for years from church and Sunday school, the lads from the corner. It was a slight change in their characters, as they got sucked into the conflict, slowly at first, but faster now. They were getting more serious somehow.

We were the 'turn-of-the-road gang', a long-winded sort of title, but hardly a title at all, more a description, a gang of lads who hung around the rather vague 'turn-of-the road' (vague unless you knew that part of Belfast). Just working-class boys, nothing special, bored, always bored, looking for distraction, time on our hands with nothing to do, getting into the occasional fight with other gangs from other vague sounding places. We never started them

'Skirmishes', we always called the fights.

I looked the word up recently for the first time, and it seems to be accurate enough. 'An episode of irregular or unpremeditated fighting, especially between small or outlying parts of armies or fleets.' They were always irregular and unpremeditated, and we were certainly outliers, and the skirmishes were nearly always reactive rather than anything else, anything intentional or planned, but perhaps that's just me.

We were always being picked on when we left our patch, or that's how it felt, and we had to leave our territory to find something to do – going down the Crumlin to the cinema, going into the city centre, going up the Hightown, making yourself vulnerable, always wary, always watching and waiting, ready to run, ready to fight. The gang wasn't designed to be aggressive to others, it was designed to protect you from the violence all around you.

But there was always a line that wasn't crossed in these skirmishes. I have a very small, almost imperceptible scar on the middle finger of my left hand when a fight broke out at a party somewhere near the Shore Road. I was sixteen. The fight continued onto the street outside, miles from the turn-of-the-road – dangerous territory in this most territorial of cities (we always called it 'Comanche territory'). We started for home and suddenly from nowhere – we never saw it coming or expected this – a car drew up beside us and some man, for he was indeed a grown adult man, jumped out and pushed me to the ground and tried to push a broken bottle into my face. I protected myself with my hands. I was beaten and lay pinned on the ground; he was a heavy, broad-shouldered man, but he never got the bottle into my face, and I pushed him off with the sort of strength that comes from terror and ran off. I'd had some drink, a few pints of lager, so the pain was bearable. A mile away I collapsed on the pavement somewhere on this side of the Antrim Road and oddly and surprisingly a friend from my grammar school, passing in a car with his father, saw me lying there and they carried me to their car and brought be back to their house, and his father plucked the slithers of glass out of my neck and hand with tweezers, as I thanked them over and over again for their kindness. That was just the drink talking though. I'm normally not so effusive.

This scar is a small, embodied memory that reminds me of small wounds that have grown with me over the years.

That was all on the right side of the line, just, but suddenly that line seemed to be disappearing altogether.

I was always studying. That's what my mother would say when the lads from the corner came around to see me. 'He's up in that wee room, studying again. I've told him that he'll be wearing glasses before too long.' I'd come down and chat with them in the hall, three foot by three foot, about nothing in particular, and they would go off laughing, and that would happen a few nights a week until Friday night when I'd wander down to the chip shop, and stand by the hot air vent with the rest of them, as the police patrols drove by aimlessly, and we stood there aimlessly, and I'd catch up with what I'd missed. It was never anything much, until all this happened, until all this new stuff. Now there was more to catch up with, a lot more.

One Friday, Duck arrived, talking with great excitement about what was happening down the road, just off the Shankill. We couldn't miss it; we couldn't miss out.

So, we walked down the Woodvale and then down the Shankill, through the streets of terraced houses between the Shankill and the Falls, streets and houses just like ours, until we got to the invisible line between the two communities – the houses on each side the same as each other, no difference between the Protestant and the Catholic houses, no difference at all between those condemned mill houses. We could hear the crackle as we approached. There was a fire raging and a crowd in front of the flames cheering, a Protestant crowd, we were amongst our own, and there were these punctuated howls from women somewhere in the dark behind the flames, perhaps from the houses themselves, perhaps from the yards at the back of the houses, or perhaps even from the street behind – you couldn't tell. It was like a disembodied emotional commentary on the whole thing, part fear, part anger, part desperation. This odd, disturbing noise that would rise and fall unpredictably, with strange pauses, and you wondered whether it had suddenly finished and whether it was all over, whatever it was. And then it would restart, reminding us that this was not the sectarianism we knew, that we had grown up with – the bonfires on the 11th Night, menacing perhaps to the other side, but purely symbolic – Lundy or the Pope on the top, only in effigy form.

The noise of the flames and the cheers and the howls of the women, wherever or whoever they were, filled the air and I felt sick to my stomach. My friends weren't enjoying it either, I could tell by their faces, this wasn't the excitement that any of us were looking for.

And then I heard a whoosh behind me and I turned to see a man, balding and grey, in the middle of the crowd with a catapult of all things, firing at the houses at some dark wavering shapes somewhere behind the flames. It could have just been shadows, I couldn't tell. That's what I remember most vividly about that night – this grown man, somebody's father, with this big, shiny metal catapult glinting in the dark with thick rubber cords. Perhaps it was a Christmas present (from a few Christmases ago) for one of his sons to fire at shoe boxes, or at rats in the street, now being used to fire marbles at the burning houses. He had brought a big bag of marbles with him; his friend was holding them for him. 'Pass us another one of those wee marbles, try to avoid the wee beauties (the intricately coloured marbles prized by all of us) – my boy loves those – he'd feel terrible if I lost them,' the man said.

He was standing just behind me, to my right – I remember so vividly after all these years – just behind my right shoulder, and I turned round and looked him in the face but he didn't once return my gaze, so intent was he on trying to keep any remaining residents in the burning houses by firing marbles at the windows, before the flames flicked up to lick them seductively at first and then harder and harder with this ferocious passion. The residents of these small mill houses were probably neighbours of his for years, good neighbours, that's what I didn't understand.

I prayed that everybody had got out hours ago: there were just flames and shadows and wood crackling and burning, and this little act of his which I hoped was just a symbolic act, as the crowd roared their approval at him, and the flames roared through the wood and plaster work.

I prayed like I meant it – I wasn't just saying the words.

'Burning them out', that's what they called it then, in the years before ethnic cleansing was a recognisable expression in any part of the world. Each side was now burning the other out. The Protestants had been burned out, now it was their turn or vice versa, nobody knew who started it.

'We'll do it to them, only harder' was the philosophy, the motto, the justification. I heard it dozens of times.

We were just spectators that night, young lads. I was seventeen, inquisitive, excited, fearful. Then CS gas was fired, and we were stumbling back blindly with the old women coming out of those same wee houses as ours with the wet-soaked cloths for our eyes, with the gas still in the air, and I remember how kind and affectionate that felt, almost loving.

'There you are, son, press down hard. The pain will go, it'll only sting for a few minutes. Those RUC bastards, whose side are they on anyway?'

Burning them out, gassing your own, being on one side, being on the other, being a member of your community, becoming a staunch member (no more IRA on the gable walls meaning 'I ran away'), becoming a Protestant Defender. It was a time of perceptible change; we could all feel it.

I had a very strict homework routine: ever since I went to that school, it was instilled into me. We had a homework diary with the school crest on the cover. I would sit with my homework book in front of me, diligently working through that night's itinerary. I never felt resentful; I loved academic work – it was never work. You were only supposed to spend thirty minutes on individual pieces of homework ('times six subjects – that's only three hours per night' our Form Master had explained helpfully in Form 1), but it always took longer. I didn't mind. Our maths teacher always said just work for half an hour maximum on maths but everyone was terrified of him, and in the morning in that high-ceilinged room with the mahogany panels and the chalk dust in the air, he'd ask us all how many questions we had completed one by one and bang our desk with his ruler if he was dissatisfied. For a very tall man he walked softly and quietly around the desks, in a long, lanky stalking motion that built up the tension. You weren't allowed to look around to see where he'd got to, and suddenly he would be beside you. We all spent hours doing maths, and worked through page after page of questions. I was very good at maths, not because of his evident bullying but, I would say, despite it. I suppose that this was a lesson in personal survival, and isolation. Or another level of isolation. I never felt that I really belonged in that school, socially or culturally, that's what I always felt, my intelligence got me there, 'my wee brains', as my mother said, passing the Eleven Plus without the usual preparation.

I was the first in a generation from my primary school in Ligoniel to pass this test, this test that changed my life. I was a celebrity at the turn-of-the-road because of this. I was very shy, but I liked that feeling.

Pro tanto quid retribuamus

It was a Saturday morning; I will never forget that, the excitement of the weekend, music on the radio, and my anxious wait for the results to come. 'You have to be patient,' my mother would say. 'It'll take them a long while to mark all those wee tests.' I was up already that morning, early for me. We liked to lie to lunchtime on a Saturday, the way that some working-class families do. A wee lie in, we called it. We'd sleep until midday, that's what my Uncle Terence always said: 'the Beatties could sleep all day.' He was an early riser. I was jittery with expectation, and the brown envelope came, eventually, clattering through our letter box, as thick and as heavy as a slab of Irish soda bread.

'Is it thick or thin?' my older brother shouted down the stairs, from bed. He hadn't bothered to get up, but I knew he wasn't asleep. He was nervous as well. 'Thick,' I shouted back, fumbling to open it. 'Oh shite, he's passed.'

I can still remember that tone in my brother's voice, that mixture of resignation and despair. His brown envelope had been thin. He was over four years older, but time had not diminished the rawness of the emotion from when his thin letter had arrived. The Eleven Plus was the most dreaded of tests that not only determined your future education, secondary modern or grammar school, but effectively labelled you forever. I knew it even then; I could hear it in my brother's tone. In every conversation leading up to the results coming through, I was reminded of the significance of it, until it was emotionally encoded in my brain.

'Our Geoffrey will pass the Eleven Plus,' my mother kept saying to the neighbours. 'I'm sure of that. He's like me, he's a great wee counter. You should hear him at it. He marks the spellings and the sums of the other children up in St Mark's Primary School. And sure, if he doesn't, it's not the end of the world. Look at his brother Bill. He's getting on fine in Everton Secondary School. He wants to be an electrician. He's not bitter about failing it. Everybody up here fails it.'

I kept tearing at the envelope until I could see the words in black and white. My brother came down and stood beside me. 'Let's see it,' he said. I watched his eyes scan across those few lines on that crisp white paper. I could see sorrow in his face.

'You know something,' he said eventually. 'You'll be studying Latin in a few months' time in a class full of wee snobs. You'll not know anybody, and they'll all just call you "Beattie". That's how they speak to each other in those types of schools. They don't use Christian names; nobody will call you "Geoffrey" any more. You'll just be "Beattie".'

'Don't talk like that,' my mother said. 'Our Geoffrey won't become a wee snob. Will you, son? And you can speak Latin, if you want to, around the house, even though you're a Protestant. Just don't let any of the neighbours hear you.'

She shouted up at my father who was still in bed. 'Geoffrey's passed the Eleven Plus. Bill says he's going to have to speak Latin to us all.'

I was told that I was the first person to pass from St Mark's Primary School in Ligoniel in fifteen years or more. There was no preparation for the exam at my school. Other primary schools had pupils practice on these kinds of tests, but there was no special preparation for the Eleven Plus at St Mark's. One morning they simply announced that the Eleven Plus was to take place the next day. Some children didn't seem to have heard of it. One boy, Albert, thought it was a medical examination – 'to see if you're well enough developed to go to Everton Secondary School'. He didn't even bring a pencil the next morning, but he was wearing clean underpants. I had six new pencils and two new rubbers. I wasn't taking any chances. Some of the boys from St Mark's went on to university, eventually, but they all had to go to the local secondary school first. Albert never made it very far in the end, and he became a bin man, although as my mother always said, if you're not frightened of a bit of dirt, it's a very good job – 'good pay, short hours, and plenty of little perks'.

But I did know about the exam, and I asked my father to go to the education offices in town to get me a couple of past papers, so I could see for myself what was involved. It almost felt like cheating. And my father and I sat together and went through the questions one by one. My father wasn't academic at all, at that time he 'worked with his hands' as a motor mechanic at the Falls Road depot. At primary school we had a lesson on Belfast's Latin motto – 'Pro tanto quid retribuamus' from Psalm 116 Verse 12, meaning literally 'For (Pro) so much (tanto) what (quid) shall we repay (retribuamus)' – as part of getting us to think about how we might honour God. The motto featured as a metal plaque on the sides of buses in Belfast at that time, and we were all encouraged to make a sketch and bring it to school with us. My father went one better and brought me home an actual plaque to bring to school and I carried this big, shiny red, sheet metal object with me the next day, which drew the admiring glances from all the other children in my class. I was the centre of attention, but I was terrified that I might bend it – it had to go back the next day.

My father didn't understand the types of questions on the Eleven Plus, but he encouraged me gently and effectively nonetheless: 'I bet you can do this one as well.' And I would try to show off and gaze on his pride, which was the greatest incentive I ever had.

When I passed the Eleven Plus, neighbours would press sixpences into my hands when they saw me on the street. Everybody seemed to have heard the news. I was very shy and would put my hands behind my back to try to refuse the money; they would have to force me to take it. 'You're a very odd boy,' my mother would say.

My teacher, Mr Lamont, told me that he personally would have been very disappointed if I hadn't passed. I had always felt a little different from my friends, ever since I started St Mark's. At first, I thought that it was just something to do with my memory or even my neatness, neat hand writing pinned on the walls of the class and a funny sort of memory. I would memorise any sort of list that was presented to me – short books of birds and their habits, short books of historical facts, short books of famous authors. I would get my father to turn to a particular page in my Ladybird Book of British Birds and their Nests, and I would recite whatever fascinating information was on that page about the brambling or the whitethroat or the red-backed shrike or the stonechat. Birds that I would almost certainly never see and birds that I wasn't really interested in.

And I could count very quickly, faster than anyone I've ever met. At university, I used to race any student who would take me on. They would count with a calculator; I would do it in my head. I always won. I can still do it today, it's odd to watch, as if I'm not really counting at all. More scanning than counting.

'I'm a good counter as well,' my mother always said. 'You take after your mother. You have to get your brains from somewhere,' she liked to say. She ran the Christmas club in the mill where the women put money away each week for Christmas presents for their children. They trusted my mother with numbers that would add up and with their hard-earned cash. The house was full of scraps of paper and cigarette packets turned inside out with pounds, shillings and pence totalled up in soft black eye-brow pencil. She never made mistakes with these rows of numbers, and all her friends from the mill knew that.

She was the teacher's pet in her class, chosen to sit at the front, and then a generation later it was my turn. Mr Welshman, the headmaster, remembered my mother: 'a very pretty and clever girl, who could have been something if she had been born somewhere else'. I thought the same might be true of myself, and that this was his coded way of telling me.

I had chosen the poshest-sounding school on the list the Local Education Authority had sent out – Belfast Royal Academy. There were a few other schools with 'Royal' in the name as well but this one sounded the poshest of the lot. It was to me at that time just a name, not a real institution, nor even a real building as seen from the outside. I had never actually seen it. It was just a typed line on an A4 sheet of paper, but it had a great sounding name like the Taj Mahal or the Empire State Building, and it could have been as distant. I didn't know where any of the schools were. None of them were anywhere near my part of Belfast, this little loyalist 'ghetto' in North Belfast. I put 'ghetto' in inverted commas because that was how it came to be referred throughout the history of the Troubles (and then 'Murder Triangle'), and quite a famous ghetto at that for all the wrong reasons. At the time it was just the 'turn-of-the-road' to us, as vague and yet as specific as that to anyone who knew Belfast.

After I passed the exam, and not before, the school asked to interview me. My mother took the day off work from Ewarts Mill, in Ligoniel, to go with me to the interview. My father gave us directions to what he always insisted on calling the Royal Academy School. I wasn't sure whether it was the same place as Belfast Royal Academy or a completely different institution. I had this notion that we might arrive at the wrong school and wait for hours to see a headmaster who wasn't expecting us. 'Don't let me down,' my mother whispered as we got off the bus. The bus driver wished me well. He could see that I was apprehensive, as well I might be. He knew my father, who worked as a mechanic on the buses at the Falls Road depot. It was us versus them – 'Show them what you're made of, sonny,' he said as I got off. I thought this was the last thing I wanted to show them. This day, more than any other, I knew I could not afford to be myself.

The headmaster himself interviewed me; apparently this was quite significant as he normally didn't do the interview. I remember that he was a short, balding, grey-haired man with a very large black gown that trailed the ground. I'm not sure that he knew exactly where Ligoniel was, he had probably never made it to that ghetto, even though he did look very learned. He wore a black gown that flapped as he came into the room, with chalk rising from the gown into the air; the flapping sound was like the sound of some great and slightly frightening bat. I found him intimidating in many ways, and not just because he reminded me of a great, blind bat unsettling dust into the air as he moved. He asked a few simple and friendly questions and I provided a few simple and truthful answers, sometimes I directed them to the floor, sometimes to the chalk rising from his shoulder as he talked and gestured, to avoid eye contact, and very occasionally directly into his watery, sad eyes. I was a very shy boy, especially with strangers, and here I was trying to be accurate and truthful in my answers, and not 'too cheeky' as my mother would have put it. So, I would stare sometimes at the shoulders and hope that my interlocutor couldn't tell the difference between that and something more forward, a gaze at the eyes themselves, looking into the gateway to their soul, and affording them with a gateway into mine.

I was truthful all the way through the interview, until, that is, he asked me about the last novel I'd read. Now let me get one thing clear – mine was not a deprived home, it was a condemned mill house, granted, damp and squat, almost shaky on its foundations, with no bath and a dark, black toilet in the yard. You had to leave the light on in the scullery when you went to the toilet, so that you could find the latch on the toilet door. And once you were inside you had to pull the door shut behind you if you wanted any sort of privacy and sit there in the total darkness. We used newspaper rather than toilet roll. 'Far too expensive,' my mother said. Everything was far too expensive. I can remember the electric light installed into the outside toilet by my brother who was a spark at the time, before he started climbing professionally, and the difference that made when you had to go to the toilet after dark. And this was Belfast in the 'swinging' 60s and decadent 70s and power-suited 80s, not Victorian England or the England of the 20s or 30s. The house was not exactly comfortable, but it was not a deprived home.

There were books in the house, lots of them, and novels, invariably obtained as prizes from St. Mark's church or Sunday school usually for 'excellent attendance', but sometimes merely for 'good attendance' (and what a disappointment that was; my mother felt that we had let ourselves down with merely 'good' attendance). Our whole life revolved around the church, twice on a Sunday, Sunday School, the Church Lads Brigade (CLB), the church youth club, the badminton club, jumble sales (and sorting through what we collected to see what to keep for ourselves, that's where our first gramophone player came from and a pile of 78s, in the Belfast of the 60s, the modern era, when things had moved on from 78s). And there were lots of cups and prizes from the CLB – for uniform inspections, for marching, for drills, for physical training, for gymnastics with box work and floor work. My mother always said that all of our neighbours said that there was no point in going to the annual CLB prize-giving because the Beattie boys won everything. The first time I was ever in the local paper was for doing a handspring over a box at the CLB. Later, Bill Reynolds and I were selected to be part of the CLB physical training demonstration team for Northern Ireland, but I couldn't do it because of my homework routines and he said that he wouldn't do it on his own. I knew that he was disappointed, but my homework had to come first.

Bill never went far in the end, he never moved from there – he was murdered in the Troubles just where we'd always hung out. He was the manager of the Village Pool Hall just at the turn-of-the-road (the pool hall wasn't there when we were young, there were no distractions like that). It was half-past ten in the morning and he was playing pool with some local lad, just passing the time. Some man, not even bothering to wear a hood, walked in and said to Bill, 'Alright, mate?' and then opened fire with a sub-machine gun and then, for good measure, shot him six times with a revolver. Bill went down 'like a sack of spuds', I heard. The graffiti went up just a half mile down the road in the Catholic Ardoyne area a day later. 'Freddie Reynolds snookered' it read, not even bothering to check the name of the person they had just murdered. Life had, by then, become very cheap.

We had books at home, but the novels in our house were always just that – prizes that just lay there – to be admired for what they told you about our character and discipline. I didn't read novels, but I took encyclopaedias to bed with me every night – encyclopaedias of science, encyclopaedias of art, encyclopaedias of sport, encyclopaedias of pets, encyclopaedias of fish, encyclopaedias of famous men, the Everyday Encyclopaedia, the Encyclopaedia for the Younger Generation, The Living World of Science, the Wonder World of Nature. My knowledge of literature was very restricted, I'd never read any, but I had read many encyclopaedias, and I did happen to have an encyclopaedia of famous authors. So, when he asked me about the last novel I'd read, my heart sank abruptly, like a fishing float pulled under water. But luckily, I'd been to the King George V Memorial Hall the previous Sunday to see the film Gulliver's Travels and from my encyclopaedia of famous authors, I knew it had been written by Jonathan Swift (1667–1745). The only problem was that my mates and I had been chucked out shortly after the interval for messing about. We were always messing about in the cinema and being kicked out wasn't that uncommon. Our messing about had a pattern; it was always half-planned.

When we were a bit older, around fourteen, and went to see the X-certificate horror movies at the Park Cinema on the Oldpark Road, we'd take old rags to first soak in the toilet, then throw down from the upper circle during the midnight movies. It was funny sitting there in the dark, in the front row of the upper circle, watching Duck get the first wet rag out, showing it round to all the suppressed giggles and then there would be the little underhand throw, and then the silence as we waited and listened to where it would land. Maybe one or two would go astray and land in the aisle or an empty seat, but soon they would hit their target and you would hear the frightened yell from the darkness below you, as the monster from Frankenstein took hold of some unfortunate blonde victim on the screen and the wet smelly rag slipped down across their face in the pitch dark, with everyone else around the target going 'shooooosh', on the assumption that somebody was just too scared or worse just making a racket to spoil the film for all the rest of us.

'Keep it quiet down there,' my friends would shout out, muffling their hysterical laughter, 'we're trying to watch the film up here. Not like you clowns down there in the cheap seats, down there in the basement where you belong.'

Sometimes we threw marbles from the balcony. That night with Gulliver's Travels, it would have been a few marbles that caused the commotion. We were rounded up and led out. A few of us got a clip around the ear for our troubles. I didn't throw anything, but I still got a clip and I went home with one of my ears red and stinging.

But that day in the interview, it had to be Gulliver's Travels: I was short on plot – I had missed a lot of it because we had to leave, but I was very good on visual description – how the characters looked, the scenes, the action sequences, all very graphic in my account of the novel. I got to the point where we'd been chucked out and said, 'Would you like me to continue?' The headmaster said that he'd heard enough. He was already impressed by my visual imagination – by my ability to conjure up complex visual images and detailed scenes full of description and action from the written word. I was in. My world was about to change.

I went to the official school outfitter to be kitted out – official school blazer, tie, white shirt, grey flannels, cap, rugby shirt, cricket flannels, athletics vest, shorts. A cap! Everything was very expensive and had to be bought from this one shop. My brother pored over the details of the school uniform when they were sent out as if they were for him – one kit for winter and one kit for summer sports – he was transfixed, and there were some garments that I had never heard of, like flannels. 'What are flannels?' I asked in that excited way of mine. 'Trousers,' said my brother, 'they're just grey trousers with a crease in them. They're nothing to get too excited about, you know.' My brother tormented me endlessly by saying that all the pupils would refer to each other by their surnames only, like some great English public school. 'That's how they do it at Eton and Harrow, you know,' he said. 'It's all "Smith, put your flannels in your cricket bag" and "Jones, help him pack the wickets", all Smith this and Jones that. You're not allowed to use Christian names. Nobody will even know that you're called Geoffrey down there. You'll just be Beattie to them. Just Beattie.'

It was a brave new world I was entering, and it scared the life out of me. On the surface at BRA, or 'great BRA' as we sang in the school song, we all looked very much the same. Below the surface, everything was different. I could never understand how anyone could be so unworldly as to write a school song praising a great bra. I used to snigger at the words, and my school friends told me not to be such a 'pleb'. I didn't know what a 'pleb' was. 'Plebeian, Beattie,' they would explain, 'you're just a plebeian.' I, fortunately, was none the wiser.

And at nights my father would ask me my Latin and I would recite my verbs to him, 'amo, amas, amat . . .' and explain how 'dominus' declines, and how the nominative case differs from the accusative. And he would sit in our front room in his oily overalls, looking at me with so much admiration in his eyes, not understanding a word of what I was saying. But I loved his encouragement and his interest and his pride in me.

I hardly mixed with my fellow pupils; they went one way, I went another after school, back to my grey street, and the lads from my street that I grew up with, who all went home together, laughing and joking, squealing with delight about mitching off again. They were always mitching off.

At lunch times, after the first year or so, rather than queue up for the tuck shop, I went for a run on my own every day around the waterworks, and ate alone in the school dining room, served by a neighbour of ours from the turn-of-the-road, who always saved two apple crumbles for me. I was always late back to the physics lab to set up the equipment. Less talking, less interaction that way, but I never did learn how to assemble the equipment for a physics experiment. It became part of my general uselessness with practical tasks: my dad was a motor mechanic, my brother served his time as an electrician before he became a climber, my mother worked on the machines in the linen mill, and I wrote numbers down on pages and added them up quickly and effortlessly with this odd gift of mine. Not necessarily a very useful gift. But it was a gift shared with my mother. She, however, never got the chance to develop any of her skills. She went straight into Ewarts Mill in Ligoniel when she was fourteen and worked there most of her life. Her older sister worked in the carding room. 'Wee millies,' they call us, 'everybody looks down on us. And when I was a young girl, and I told people that I worked in the mill, they thought that I'd be a good thing. Everybody was out to take advantage of you, one way or the other.'

The backroom was my little cell – not a prison cell, nobody was holding me there, more a monastic cell. I'd make my way up there straight after dinner, without being asked to, without any order or cajoling. 'Your brother was never like that,' my mother would say. 'I don't know who you take after.' And when Bill was forced to do some homework in the bedroom, he'd have to take the mirrors off the dressing cabinet because he said that he was too good-looking and didn't want to be distracted by his own reflection.

As darkness set in, I would hear the lads from my gang – Duck, Craigy, Jackie, Kingo – outside, running up and down the entry, squealing. It was kick the bucket one year, then kicking the doors and running up the entry to get away the next, shouting back at the old neighbours, too infirm to run up the entry after them: 'Charlie Chuck married a duck', 'Charlie fucking Chuck', 'Squeak . . . Squeeeeeeeeeeak'.

Squeak wasn't strictly a neighbour, nobody seemed to know where he lived; he lived rough generally, sometimes in an abandoned lorry, but his shoes, ripped and torn, made a squeaking noise when he walked, so the torment began. Duck said he deserved it because Squeak had polished off a full pint of buttermilk with one gulp in the Mayfair sweetshop and then belched right in his face. He didn't do it on purpose, even Duck admits that, Squeak just turned to the side and belched the sour taste right into Duck's face. Duck got even for this, and not just with a bit of name calling, he went and did something in the abandoned lorry where Squeak was sleeping. I heard them up the entry, laughing about it: I wasn't sure what it was.

One night we tormented Squeak at the park gates, I wasn't name calling, I never did, not because I was a goody-goody, just because I didn't agree with this level of torment on one individual – but I did enjoy the chase, or I'd grown to enjoy it. Those heart-pounding moments had once just been fear, but now they could be excitement for at least part of the experience before the fear itself kicked in again. They broke the boredom. The next minute a policeman on a motorbike came roaring towards us along the pavement by the park railings. We all ran in opposite directions and I ran down Ligoniel Road, along Limepark Street, and down Lavens Drive and into the grounds of the Elim Pentecostal Church. The policeman roared after me the whole way, my heart-pounding was now just undiluted fear, and he trapped me against the wall with his bike, the front wheel of his bike caught my leg, and he pushed the bike in against me, trapping me more forcefully. 'If you try to run away, I'll run you over,' he said, full of threat. I must have been eleven or twelve. He told me to take him to my house.

It was a summer Sunday evening, and, ashen-faced, I walked towards our house, with him pushing the bike beside me, one hand on the bike and one on my collar, lifting me slightly. The front door of our house was unlocked, and I walked straight into our front room. I felt deeply ashamed. My father and mother, Aunt Agnes and Uncle Terence were all sitting there, watching Sunday Night at the London Palladium. I think that was the first thing I noticed, what was on the television, as if by way of distraction, before I told them that there was someone outside who wanted to see them. They all looked very surprised, trying hard to imagine who might visit the house on a Sunday evening when Sunday Night at the London Palladium was on, when everyone in the street would have been settled down in front of the telly. My father got up to turn the telly down. The RUC man came in, tall and stern, he smelt clean, I remember that smell, like carbolic soap. He explained what we'd been doing and how Mr Kyle had complained to him as he had been passing, and how I'd tried to escape. He said that it would be my one and only warning and that if it happened again, I'd be in serious trouble. 'Do you want to end up in Borstal?' I shook my head, 'No, sir,' I said, without looking at him.

My mother recognised the policeman from our church. 'He's a good boy, you want to see the way he sits down to do his homework, you never have to force him, or threaten him, not like all those other boys.'

'Well, Mrs Beattie, you just need to keep an eye on him,' said the policeman. 'Mr Kyle has just had enough of those boys shouting names at him and you'll never guess what one of them did. They went to the toilet in his bed, where he sleeps, and I don't mean just a . . .' there was a very long hesitation, '. . . not a wee wee, but the other thing.'

'Oh, my God,' said my mother, 'Billy, did you hear that? Those boys wouldn't do that. Surely to God.' My father didn't reply but I noticed that he was quietly shaking his head.

My Uncle Terence spoke up. 'How do you know it was these boys? That sounds a bit unlikely to me. Are you saying that they waited until they had to . . .' there was another hesitation '. . . spend a penny and then thought, I know I'll go and do a shite in old Squeak's bed, and just hope that he's not in the bed while I'm doing it because it's dark in that old lorry, isn't it?'

You could see that the policeman saw this as a little confrontational, especially because my Uncle Terence didn't go to our church (I hadn't yet been told that he was a Catholic, or 'Roman Catholic' as my mother always said, 'we're all Catholic'; it was the biggest shock of my young life, I refused to believe it for years). The policeman was big in our local church, St Mark's – Church of Ireland, Protestant. They were both physically big men, who would stand their ground. My Uncle Terence had stood up, so that the policeman was no longer towering above him. 'Answer me that,' said my Uncle Terence, who had a fearsome reputation when he was younger as an amateur boxer in our local neighbourhood.

'It couldn't have been our Geoffrey,' added my mother, 'because . . .' And now she hesitated.

'Because what?' said the RUC man.

'Because he's always constipated, he just does these wee hard lumps. When he was a child he did one in the bed and his brother thought that it was a Malteser and tried to eat it, he'd be there all night in John Kyle's bed just trying to go.'

Nobody laughed, and I didn't know whether to laugh or cry. I'd forgotten about the Malteser; I didn't want to smirk which I often do when I'm in trouble, so I just kept my head bowed. My leg was sore where the motorbike had run into me to stop me getting away, but I wasn't going to mention it. The whole conversation had moved away from the name calling to this other unsolved and potentially more serious crime. I thought of Duck's smirking face, and felt ashamed, and ashamed for my friend, if that makes sense, ashamed for the gang.

'Just keep an eye on this boy,' said the policeman as he was preparing to leave, and he tipped his peaked motorbike helmet and left.

There was a silence, only broken by my mother. 'What have you boys been getting up to when you're out? You all need to catch yourself on or you'll be getting into serious trouble. Would you like to end up in Borstal because that's where you're heading?'

My father spoke for the first time. 'It wouldn't be our Geoffrey. It would have been one of those other boys,' and he pulled me down onto the settee beside him and put his arm around me and turned the TV up.

'You should have said something, Billy,' chided my mother. 'Only Big Terry spoke up and he was right to.'

'I think John Kyle dirtied himself when he was drunk and tried to blame these wee boys, they would never be cruel like that, no boys their age would,' my father replied. My father always liked to see the best in people.

But I agreed with my father in a way, it was a strange sort of cruelty and maybe not a cruelty at all. It was 'funny' rather than cruel, a cruelty that did not involve imagining in any detail the real consequences of your action apart from Squeak's comic face when he realised what had happened, and maybe thought that he himself might be the culprit, for a split second at least. This was a cruelty more focussed on how the rest of the gang might respond to the latest stunt, to get attention and break the boredom, get a laugh and guarantee inclusion deeper and deeper in the group. That was always the concern – how to be part of something bigger than yourself, us, the boys from the corner, the turn-of-the-road gang, everything else was secondary, cruelty was instrumental, incidental, an act with no deeply imagined consequences, a necessary evil to get a laugh.

Perhaps, the idea wasn't that original anyway, perhaps it had come from Moke. We would walk for an hour to Grove Baths on the Shore Road on a Saturday afternoon, and every time we jumped into the water, after a few minutes, the whistle would sound, and everyone would have to get out. Moke had gone to the toilet again, he thought that it was hilariously funny, and they had to scoop it out and close the pool for the rest of the day. But it was never funny, not even for an instant, and the waste of a very long journey. Moke ended up being barred from the baths. In boredom, we all walked home along the Shore Road and one afternoon we climbed into a sealed-off park with a high fence for the tractors of articulated lorries. I was last in; I was twelve. It was Duck's idea again. He had been in there before and he knew his way around. We called the tractor parts of the lorries 'Mousies', although I've no idea why, it was what Duck called them. The keys were in the ignition and they would drive around in them. We had been doing it for maybe half an hour, or they had, I was just watching – I was a few years younger and had no idea how to drive anything – and suddenly the transport police arrived in cars through the big gate, now flung open, and we ran for miles to get home, hiding in entries and under cars; I could hear whistles blowing from different directions. I arrived home covered in engine oil, hours later, sweating, white as a sheet, heart thumping. I can still feel the terror of that day if I just close my eyes and drift back.

By a very strange coincidence, on that Monday morning, a boy I knew very well at the Academy told me that his father worked for the transport police and he told me the whole story from his father's perspective. He had no idea that I might be involved, and needless to say, I didn't tell him. He said that the break-in was going to be in the papers. I felt sick.

So, it was back to my bedroom, and the homework, back to my other life. Slipping out of the street in the morning and only putting my school cap on with the royal crest on the front when I was getting off the bus and saw the other Academy boys arriving at the school gates in pairs and groups, laughing together. And changing back out of my school uniform as soon as I got home.

I was 'Geoffrey' but usually 'Beattie' at school (my brother was partly right) and 'Beats' in my gang. Two personas that I had to try to keep apart. The boys from the corner never asked about the schoolwork, but they'd known me from St Mark's Primary when I would sit in the middle of the hall at a desk on my own and mark their spelling and arithmetic, embarrassed by the forced separation. I was moved from P4 when I was eight to P7 because I was seen as gifted, and I stayed in P7 for three years, marking the work of the other children in my last two years at primary school. I would sit there at my own desk in the middle of the room in the church hall between the two classes on either side. I couldn't wait to cross the divide and get back with the gang. So when the headmaster found some barley from a pea shooter in the school playground one day, and got the cane out, and asked who had been using a peashooter at lunchtime, I stepped forward with the rest of my mates, the guilty ones that is, and we stood in a line and got caned, one hard whack on each hand, right on the base of the thumb. I had to mark their spelling that afternoon, while struggling to hold the pencil with my swollen hand. But I could tell by how they looked at me that they admired my action: I was one of the gang, all facing the music together, I wanted to be part of it, to fit in; I'd fight any of them when I had to. I had a peashooter with me that day, the casing of a biro, but I hadn't brought any barley, so I couldn't have been responsible for the barley in the playground.

I rarely got caned, some of them were caned all the time. They knew that I was good at schoolwork, just as they were good at climbing trees or using their feet in a fight; they seemed proud of me getting to the new school but told me that I was missing out by not going to Somerdale with them. 'Don't you miss the craic?' they would say. 'What's the craic like at the Academy? I bet they don't know how to have a good time.'

But I was still part of the gang, just not every night, and sometimes I could see where the craic was heading. BRA was a different world. It took two buses to get to my new school, or one bus and a long walk, whereas all the friends from my street could dander together down to theirs in their little clump of a gang.

But great BRA did broaden my horizons. I met children who had been to America for their holidays. I met a girl who had been to Saudi Arabia. I'd never even been across the water, as they say in Ireland. And when I opened my mouth, I stuck out a mile. My accent was as thick as buttermilk. But it wasn't just my accent, it was my whole style of speaking. I wasn't linguistically deprived or anything like that, but I was still surprised to hear eleven-year-olds say, 'He's such a sarcastic and ostentatious person.' I used to look the words up at night in my Little Oxford Dictionary and practice them the next day. 'Don't be so sarcastic, Henshaw,' I'd say. 'Why, Beattie?'

'Because I'll stick my toe right up your arse. That's why,' I'd say. The polite 'ass' instead of the much more common Belfast-sounding 'arse' came much later. My mother thought that I was starting to talk awfully proper. 'With our Geoffrey it's always "ass this" and "ass that", these days,' I heard her tell one of her friends. 'He'll be saying "bottom" next if he's not careful.'

My linguistic habits were deeply ingrained – my accent, my vocabulary and my whole style of speaking – even at eleven. Now, one marked feature of the Belfast dialect is the regular occurrence of the expression 'you know' (the equivalent of 'like' in Scouse). At times 'you know' almost seems to act as a universal punctuation mark: 'I have to get a couple of buses here in the morning, you know, sir, that's why I'm a bit late, you know. Sorry sir, it won't happen again, you know.' Both pupils and staff tormented me about this, rolling their eyes every time I said 'you know'. One day, during a history lesson and in front of the whole class, the master decided to rid me of this irritating, nasty little working-class linguistic habit once and for all. 'I know that I know, Beattie. Would you kindly stop saying you know? It's you who doesn't know what you're talking about.' The more he insisted, the more I kept saying it. My anxiety was going right through the roof. He told me to get a grip on myself, and I tried, you know, I really tried. I learned to hate the sound of my own voice.

Years later I wrote an article about my background for *The Guardian* and I mentioned this incident. I was shocked to get a letter from the master concerned. He said that he remembered me fondly as 'a boy with warm, soft, smiling eyes'. He asked me who the teacher was, he said that he thought he could guess – was it Mr O'C.? he asked. He never realised it was him. Perhaps he'd just forgotten, a small, everyday incident in the lives of all masters to teach some recalcitrant boys a lesson, a small lever of change for boys from less privileged backgrounds, a nudge in the right direction. I never replied to his letter, which is a little shameful and makes me slightly embarrassed, and now it's too late.

It's interesting the way that some small communicational events with a slightly emotionally harmful tinge to them are remembered much better by the recipients of the message than by the senders (Helion et al. 2020). This is the source of so much divergence, and so much difference in understandings and recollections of place and time. And indeed of history itself.

But I was aware that my speech set me apart – I could never be part of the BRA crowd, one of the BRA boys, if I continued to speak like that. It was visible for all to see – fellow pupil, teacher, headmaster – there was no hiding it. It wasn't a passive blemish either, which could be covered up with suitable cosmetics. It was active, moving, and dynamic; it drew attention to itself. I just had to open my mouth and there it would be – out of its cage, circulating the room, with everyone staring up at it. I would be asked to give an oral account of Gladstone's contribution to British politics, and even the stupidest and least imaginative boy in the class could snigger at my attempt, because of how I spoke. I suppose that's one important aspect of language – it invariably marks you out as the same or different. Unless you stay silent, of course, and that's often what I chose to do.

Finding a voice

When we had to write essays at school, about what we did on our holidays, and other pupils wrote adventurous, and true stories about meeting members of the Saudi Royal Family in Saudi Arabia, I wrote about going to Portrush about sixty miles from Belfast, because that's what I did. The other pupils asked me if a trip to Portrush was really the best I could do. So, I started using my imagination, and I started making things up, trying to forget who I was and where I was from. One year I went to Egypt for my holidays, or so one of my third form essays says. I was quite good at the description of the place, because, after all, there were photographs of the Sphinx, and the bazaars of Cairo, in my Boys World atlas, but I wasn't so good at what the 'natives' were like (the Boys World atlas was always a bit thin on its description of actual people). The next holiday, according to another essay, was to Hollywood. I used to read my mum's *Titbits* and tried to imagine the place from a thirteen-year-old's point of view. 'We saw Frank Sinatra, but only in the distance, unfortunately, he was driving off in his limousine.' I had to add this for good measure – in case anyone should ask me a detailed question about him, beyond the scope of a *Titbits* exposé. One boy from my English class had genuinely been sent to Hollywood. His father was, I believe, a top executive in Emerald Records. My essays were second rate, or worse, third rate, because it wasn't at all clear whether the journalists who wrote these magazine articles had been there in the first place.

However, one day I decided that enough was enough, and this happened very suddenly; it was right in the middle of one of these essays one long Sunday afternoon in our front room. I quite literally stopped writing an essay about my favourite uncle who was (according to the essay) a big game hunter, just back from Africa, one and a half pages in, and ripped it up and I threw the pages all over the front room. I was disgusted with myself and my pretence. My mother ran into the room, I have no idea what she thought that I was ripping up. 'I can see you've lost the head today. You'll be ripping all your books up next and I'll have to pay for them.' But I was calm, and I started the essay again, on a clean sheet of paper, this time about a real uncle, my Uncle Terence, who went down to the bar with my father every Saturday night, and was mauled not by any lion, but by our fox terrier, Spot, when he came home later reeking of drink, the thirteen or fourteen pints of Guinness oozing out of his pores as he and the dog wrestled on the settee in the front room, the dog yelping and snarling as my uncle threw him from the settee to the chair and back.

'That dog only goes for him when he's had a drink,' my mother always said. 'He must be able to smell the Guinness off him. He always tries to give him a wee nip when he's just back from the bar.' It was always 'a wee nip', by the way, she never liked to say that our wee dog had actually bitten him because that would have been a very serious matter. 'If that dog ever bit anybody, I'd have him put down,' she would say. 'Is that blood coming from your neck, Terry, what caused that? It couldn't be the wee dog, it never bites; Spot only nips people in a playful way when they've had a drink. That dog is clairvoyant; it can always tell when you've had a wee drink.'

I tried to describe what a fight was like, because on a Saturday night when I was waiting for my father and my uncle to come out of the bar, I had witnessed the RUC, black and sinister, their truncheons already out, pulsating in their hands with anticipation, lay into some drunks outside Paddy's, our bar at the bottom of Barginnis Street. I call them 'drunks' but they weren't drunks (which sounds like a full-time pursuit or an occupation), they were just my neighbours out on a Saturday night – it was John's da from up the street, and Jim's uncle from down below the baker's, and that man with the thin grey hair who lived up the Hightown on his own in a wee shack of a house, staggering out of Paddy's at closing time. Not drunks, just neighbours, a little bit past merry. This was the real thing, or a real thing, and I had never seen it written about in terms of how it really presented itself, the shouting without saying much, all slurred and profane, the swearing that went on and on, then quick sudden movements of black sticks in the night, and not even that many staccato movements. These things were always over very quickly, and more shouting: 'You're beat . . . I'm far from fucking beat', then silence and low moans, a split head or two seeping blood into the rain on the pavement. And the torrent of accusations and recriminations and more swearing, and deep voices stepping back into the shadows, and my heart pounding in my chest as I stepped back into the doorway.

And then women with their coats thrown over their shoulders arriving to take their men home after their night out, and these sad, sheepish, sorrowful expressions on the men, who knew they were in trouble now alright. It was not like the *Titbits* version, there was nothing at all glamorous about it, there was no real narrative to it; sometimes it hardly made sense, just a wee spot of bother, a wee scrap, and I found that I was good at describing it, but only because I'd been there, standing in the shop doorway, waiting for my father and my uncle in the rain, just some terrified child, waiting expectantly for those he loved. I understood those involved, I knew them.

Writing about my real life and my real uncle seemed risky in some way, as if I was confessing too much, but my English teacher liked them.

I was in the 'A' set for every subject on the curriculum except English, in which I was in the 'D' set, which never really made sense to me in terms of my pattern of exam marks, which were always excellent. I had always performed as well in the English exams as in any other subject. I always assumed that it was something to do with my accent, as if they couldn't bear Shakespeare being read with my strong Belfast accent. But after this essay and the one that followed it about this majestic dog I looked after from down the street, called Keeper (Keeper was half-Alsatian and half-Collie), I was moved to a different class.

Keeper was faithful and protective of me, and vicious with all other animals, but only when provoked – I'm defending him even now. He was intelligent but half-wild because his elderly owner had Parkinson's disease and couldn't look after him properly. So, I looked after him and took him for runs up the hills that surround Belfast, never with a lead, and he followed me to the bus stop every day and stood until I got on the bus and then made his lonely way back to our street to wait for me. He never came into our house, he just sat outside and waited for me and went home to bed when it got late.

But on one of these runs one Sunday afternoon he spotted a sheep down below in the next field and sprinted after it. He wouldn't respond to my calls, something had taken over his instincts. I couldn't control him. This was the first time this had ever happened. The noise that the sheep made was awful; this squealing that's still in my head if I pause and reflect. I couldn't get Keeper off, he was shaking the sheep like a rag doll, his teeth in its neck, the blood splattering Keeper's thick, luxuriant black coat. He kept on until he was tired and then looked up at me, as if he wanted approval. The sheep was long dead. I turned and started trotting along with Keeper beside me, and then faster and faster, to get away. He looked happy, as if we had both just done something important and good, something about survival.

I wrote about this incident and what might have happened next if anyone had witnessed it. I knew how serious it would have been. But I would never have let anybody harm my dog, even though it wasn't really mine. I would have seen to that. In the story, Keeper and I run away from our street, hide in the glens, in the wee dens that we would make for ourselves, and we would be outlaws, living wild, eating berries, killing rabbits. Keeper would be good at that, biting through their necks: I would try to kill them in my own way.

My English teacher saw something in these essays, he asked to speak to me and said that he was very puzzled why I had ever been in the 'D' class for English and I was suddenly moved mid-term and mid-week into the 'A' set without any real explanation.

I repaid his kindness. One night a few years later I spotted my English teacher in town; he'd had a drink and was swaying gently as he walked along Royal Avenue. One of my friends spotted him as well and wanted to roll him: 'He's fucking pissed,' he said, 'he's got that walk, he won't know what's fucking hit him.' But I stopped him, without saying who he was. If I'd told my mate that this was my teacher, this would have been another reason to drop him. But it was my way of repaying my teacher, I suppose, a way of expressing my gratitude. Privately.

I suspect that this recognition by my English teacher that there was something in these essays changed my life as much as anything before, and for that I am extremely grateful. I stopped trying to describe or explain my experiences to Solomon, and the like. They went their way, I went mine. Not necessarily inferior anymore, just different and in my seven years at the Academy I didn't once invite any Academy boy or girl to my home, with the toilet without a light and the backroom with little wallpaper because the walls were too damp for wallpaper.

One friend did, however, come uninvited on one occasion, but he just wanted help with his homework and he didn't stay long. One of my mates Rob took an instant dislike to him and set fire to his school blazer by popping a lit cigarette into his pocket just before he left. His father retuned about half an hour later with the scorched jacket and stood in the middle of my front room, tense and irate ('Steaming,' Rob said, 'fucking steaming!'), as my mother categorically denied that it had happened in *her* house, and that he was wrong to make such accusations. She had genuinely seen nothing and assumed that his accusations were the result of some sort of prejudice on his part and little more. I hadn't seen the butt of the cigarette being flicked into the pocket, but I had seen the momentary smirk of one of my mates soon after and I knew that this flickering smile meant something; it was as clear as day. I became an expert at reading these small, nonverbal signs. This was part of my survival strategy and interestingly it is something that has stayed with me – I've even made a living from it, and written books on it (Beattie 1983; Beattie 2016).

I still don't know why he did it after all these years, perhaps just for a bit of excitement. He craved excitement and got bored very easily, perhaps he felt resentful of the school, and that gold crest on the blazer pocket, and maybe he resented the opportunity I'd been given. Perhaps he didn't want me too bond too closely with the Academy boys, and this was his way of making sure that this didn't happen.

When I went once (and only once) to a Christmas disco at the school, he and a friend followed me down to it. A school prefect on duty that night came in to tell me that there were two lads outside asking to speak to me, and I could tell that he was nervous. 'They're not very nice,' he said. 'They told me to pass this message to you. I hesitated slightly to be honest and they asked me if I'd too many teeth. Tell them that I did what they asked.' I walked out and there they were, stamping up and down to keep themselves warm, pleased to see me: I wasn't so pleased. We stood outside that ancient building in the freezing cold. 'Get us in, Beats,' Rob demanded. I explained that there was no way 'on this earth' that this could happen. We were only there a few minutes and then a few boys from my class came out to see Rob and my other mate, who they'd all heard of. My friends from the corner were, after all, youths now with reputations as genuine hard men in this small city of ours. There was some small talk and then out of the blue one of the boys from the school was hit over the head with a milk bottle, which had just been sitting there neglected on the school steps. There was no argument or disturbance, no row, no cross words, no negative comments, just this random surprising act. But the truth is, I wasn't that surprised. The blood trickled down the boy's white-faced head. I thought that he might cry and hoped that he wouldn't. My friends from the corner wouldn't have let me hear the end of it.

Rob just looked at me and smiled. 'We're all barred now, let's go fucking home. I didn't want to get in anyway, it was always going to be shite.' So, we trudged home, with me hardly talking – I'd had better nights, Rob tried to cheer me up by following close behind a drunk man walking home alone. He always said that when people are drunk and they're staggering they always make one step to the left and then two to the right to correct themselves, it's as regular as clockwork. You just have to get in step with their drunken plodding march. And sure enough we watched him do these movements in perfect synchrony with the drunk himself. Of course, he wanted to roll him as well but I stopped him.

A few years later when I went off to university, I discovered that Rob was murdered up some entry in Belfast; he was stabbed fifty-eight times and had his throat cut. The number of times that he was stabbed has always stuck in my mind as an unnecessary and extravagant display of evil, if ever there was one, and not even sectarian evil, he was murdered by a fellow Protestant. But you could sense that something bad was coming, and not just for him.

I was, justifiably, sometimes a bit wary of members of my gang, and could sometimes feel what was around the corner. But these were my mates, my oldest friends in some cases, and there were obligations and bonds.

'Are you going to back me up?' That expression still makes me slightly anxious to this day. 'Back me up' always meant trouble, always; it meant that it – something – was just about to start. But they backed me up whenever I asked. Without any reflection or hesitation. That was the way it was. It was always somewhat asymmetric and for that I'm both grateful and a bit guilty.

But I never really felt part of that great school. My running at lunchtimes didn't seem that lonely or that unusual, at the time, except perhaps in its frequency and except perhaps looking back. I ran every single day, which with the passage of time seems very significant indeed.

I thought that the teachers always implicitly regarded me as quite different from the rest (but, of course, this could have been my imagination). In a chemistry class one day, and it was the 'A' class for A level chemistry and therefore full of serious students, I remember once laughing too loudly at a letter that our old spinster teacher (and very proper) was reading from an ex-pupil that had gone to Cambridge. The letter was meant to be an inspiration to us all. Maybe, we could make it to Cambridge one day if we tried hard enough. There was a word in this letter that I found hysterically funny; it was the word 'scholar'. It was an unfamiliar word, or unfamiliar in that context at that time. It sounded funny at the time, don't ask me why now. I laughed out loud. It was a sudden, uncontrolled splutter of laughter, a plebeian sort of sound if I'm honest. It was only me who saw the joke and this lone and very loud and solitary sound seemed to echo in the wood-clad laboratory. Maybe I had expected others to laugh at this word, prompted by my anticipatory guffaw. The teacher paused almost mid-word and hesitated, as if fighting for control, then exploded in a rage at me. She was so angry that spit was coming out of her mouth, from between her bad teeth, as she shouted; she slammed the letter onto the bench of the lab and stormed off. I can see her now in my mind's eye, an odd sort of flashbulb memory, all of the detail preserved for all time. I was very surprised by her reaction, by the intensity of her anger, and I knew that it might well have serious consequences. I had genuinely upset her, I could see that, and I didn't mean to. But I could also see something in her eyes as she glanced back, just the once, which said something about boys like me from that part of town, from the 'turn-of-the-road', from that loyalist ghetto that bred such disgusting manners and such resistance to change to more genteel ways. No matter how you try with them, that was what her eyes were saying, no matter how hard you try, and Lord, I have been trying. She asked to speak to me outside, after she had calmed down, just in case I didn't understand the implicit messages, and she said slowly and calmly: 'Beattie, you come from the gutter, and that's where you are going to end up, mark my words. I'm never wrong about these things.'

These words have been burned into my memory for decades. I stared back at her with resentment and a fury that I really felt inside but didn't dare express. I could have hit her, that's what I felt like doing, and that's what some from my street might well have done, or cried, like an Academy boy for sympathy and leniency, but I didn't do either. I just nodded my head in sharp little movements with every word she said and stared at the ground and kept control. She never really looked at me again in class, she never tried to engage me, perhaps she was slightly embarrassed by what she had said, but I did extremely well in chemistry A level even with this barrier between us. We had both lost a degree of control, but in different ways, and for different reasons.

The truth is that I punish myself for remembering this incident so vividly because this school and indeed this teacher did so much for me. But sometimes moments, unguarded and uncontrolled, tell you a great deal about life and about people and she hurt me deeply with her comment. But she was wrong, I was never from the gutter, my mother and father saw to that. That's what upset me most about her comment. She couldn't see beyond the rows of terraced housing, all identical, with the same bad brickwork and the damp, misshapen walls sinking down into the ground, and the images of the men staggering home from work having drunk their wages, and their women screaming at them as they came through the door. She couldn't see beyond the bad boys looking for a bit of excitement at somebody else's expense. She couldn't see the father sitting in the front room with his son night after night, listening intently to the meaningless lines of Latin or French, or the mother working every hour that God gave her in that mill, where the flax dust in the air kills you prematurely through bronchitis and asthma, to support her son through school when all the other boys his age from that street would be out working and helping to support her, a widow woman. My teacher couldn't see any of that.

One other day, the headmaster caught me brazenly displaying a symbol (unintentional or not) of my lower-class background. It was my socks. He said that he was going to send me home for wearing socks that were too gaudy – they had black and white diamonds on them – rather than being plain grey or black, like those provided by the official school outfitter. I was breaking school rules flagrantly and deliberately right in front of him. Every boy has many pairs of plain black or grey socks, he said, but I was deliberately choosing not to wear them. But, in reality, I had no spare socks to change into, that was all I thought to myself; I wouldn't have worn these particular socks to school if I'd had a choice, the other two pairs of socks that I actually owned were wet and had been left trying to dry in front of the dead fire that gave off no heat. I knew that I had nothing to change into that day, so I walked to the school gates and went home and took Keeper out instead. We walked up the Hightown and past the quarry and onto the top of Napoleon's Nose at Cavehill, so I could sit looking down onto the Antrim Road and the houses of the boys from the Academy and the playing fields of this great school with their white rugby posts standing out like some optical illusion, and this other world that seemed to be passing me by.

I once had my hair cut very short – we had to have our hair cut short (we had regular haircut inspections), so I had it cut very short. A teacher called me the 'shaveling'. I didn't know the word. He knew that I didn't know it. 'Joyce, boy,' he said. 'Joyce.' Or it could have been 'Just, boy, just', until he said it all again a few days later, enjoying his little joke. My scholarship was sometimes very thin, on a knife edge. He knew that as well. I learned the course material well; they couldn't fault me on that. We didn't have Joyce at home, or anybody else like Joyce for that matter. Joyce wasn't on the course, so I didn't know anything about him or his fancy language. I looked up 'shaveling' and Joyce when I got home in my dictionary and encyclopaedias. It is strange trying to work out the discourses of everyday life from a dictionary. 'Derogatory – a priest or clergyman with a shaved head. A young fellow, youth.' He might have been insulting me, it was hard to tell. Dictionaries never give you the whole story. It depends on how he meant it. I couldn't be sure exactly which meaning he was implying. It's hard trying to learn your own language from a dictionary – it's like learning a foreign language. You can only get so good at it in the end. He told me that if I got a haircut like that again he would send me home until it grew. I should have a proper schoolboy's haircut, and not one like somebody from the criminal classes. As if only certain classes produce criminals. I thought they were to be found in every walk of life myself.

The shaveling did, however, get twelve O levels with top grades, and Rob would bring random people to my door and ask me to tell them how many O levels I'd got. 'Holy fuck,' they'd say. 'I've never heard anything like that before.'

I studied maths, physics, chemistry and Russian, which I had to do in my spare time as an additional subject with minimal formal tuition at A level. I chose Russian as this additional subject – not because of any great social-ist or communist ideals, but because I thought that this Slavonic language suited my own harsh Northern Protestant sound in a way that French didn't (I regarded reading French aloud in class as one of the worst punishments imaginable and this punishment was often administered. I have never felt comfortable trying to speak French as a consequence). It must have been an odd sight as my mother's friends popped in to see her, and I sat in the front room, declining Russian verbs, partly in my head, partly out loud with this low guttural sound, on this low yellow card table in front of them. 'That boy should be out on the street corner with his friends, not stuck behind that wee table in the front room with his mother, or locked away in that back bedroom,' said Minnie. 'That's not natural for a boy his age. Not a bit of wonder he talks to himself.' It must have been an odd sight, in this wee house, with the slimy, damp walls (you could run your hand over the walls and they were as wet as if you had put them under a tap), with the wallpaper hanging off, not just at the corners but halfway down, and me just sitting there in a school blazer with a crown on the crest, learning a language from a country that I would never visit, reciting Dostoevsky and Gogol, Pushkin and Turgenev. Looking back, I am sure that it was a wonderfully strange sight, but I always thought, despite everything, it must have been a wonder-fully positive sight for the casual onlooker.

But I am reminded of what W.I. Thomas wrote about the psychology of race in *The American Journal of Sociology* in 1912:

> Booker Washington [that great foreteller of the Civil Rights Movement in the U.S.], who has been wiser than we in the education of his own race, says one of the saddest sights he saw during a month's travel in the South was 'a young man who had attended some high school, sitting in a one-room cabin, with grease on his clothing, filth all around him, and weeds in the yard and garden, engaging in studying a French grammar.'

Thomas' prefacing comment on Booker Washington's observation is: 'Our education for white children in the past was atrocious, and when we transferred this, including English syntax and sometimes even the dead

languages, to the lower races we got results logically to be anticipated.'
This leads into a quote from Petrie (1895): 'The harm is that you manu-
facture idiots. Some of the peasantry are taught to read and write, and the
results of this burden, which their fathers bore not, is that they become
fools. . . . His intellect and his health have been undermined by the forcing
of education.'

Here in these short, convoluted sentences the 'lower races' and the 'peasantry' are all rolled together into a neat little bundle, a bundle of despair,
who should not have to suffer the 'burden' of education. Perhaps I, too,
might have been a sad, pathetic little sight for any educated visitor, but what
should I have been doing instead? Maybe hanging around the corner with
my mates every night, like Minnie suggested, maybe trying to dry out the
walls, with blotting paper stolen from school, so that the wallpaper might
stick to them for a few hours more, maybe contenting myself with my social
position in this damp little mill house? Maybe hiding upstairs out of view,
which I now did more and more, reading, thinking, studying in the backroom, my attic, my cell, my prison.

Childish things

So, I stayed there every night in the backroom, trying to concentrate, listening out to the world on the other side of the yard, and the noises would
start: a laugh, a bark, the clatter of shoes with metal on the heels (to save on
repairs) and on the tips (to be more effective in fights). And, if I stood on my
toes, I'd see the gang getting into scrapes, chasing the lads from Ligoniel up
the entry. 'Go on, run away, you wee Fenian fuckers.' Then I'd watch them
climbing up the yard walls onto the rooves of the other sheds and toilets,
they'd wave at me, and I'd wave back at them. Later they'd bring girls up
the entry to lumber and touch; you could see the shaking, trembling hands
indicating some hidden delights. And I'd be sitting there, watching the kalei-
doscope make more shapes, breathing in the fumes, slightly intoxicated with
the smell, keeping my head down, embarrassed to be seen, stopping myself
going out until the weekend, bound by some drive – certainly no clear ambition, just wanting to do well, to not let people down.

It kept me in that room like a prisoner. I'd join them at the weekends,
and the fights and the skirmishes would start up suddenly and without
warning everywhere we went. It's odd to say this, but every time we went
out as a group, something happened, something bad, perhaps it was the
expectation – a sort of self-fulfilling prophecy – a prediction that directly or
indirectly causes itself to become true. As the sociologist Robert K. Merton
wrote in 1948:

> The self-fulfilling prophecy is, in the beginning, a *false* definition of
> the situation evoking a new behavior which makes the original false

conception come *true*. This specious validity of the self-fulfilling prophecy perpetuates a reign of error. For the prophet will cite the actual course of events as proof that he was right from the beginning.

We were always aggressively on guard, you might say, because we expected to be attacked, and no doubt that aggressive anxiety was itself perceived as threatening by others and contributed to the violence inflicted on and against us. There would be fights at the corner, or on buses, at parties (we didn't get invited to many), or on walks, and this percolated outwards.

I was beaten up on my very first date, walking back from a Wimpy bar in the centre of Belfast with my first girlfriend Carol. I knew her from the church badminton club, and after a long time, I had plucked up the courage to ask her out. I was delighted when she said yes. I was never very forward with girls, indeed my mother always said that I was a bit 'backward' in this regard. I never like the connotations of this term. 'You'll never get very far in life being like that,' she said, so I'd plucked up the courage to ask Carol out, eventually. Carol had beautiful, big grey eyes and a dark fringe. Two lads walked towards us that night as we strolled along Royal Avenue in the city centre eating our hamburgers. I paid them very little attention. They stopped us quite suddenly, and one said that he recognised me. 'Hey boy,' he said, 'you're from Silverstream, aren't you?' I had no idea who they were, and I must have looked puzzled, just some sixteen-year old with a girl with large grey, surprised eyes. Out of nowhere, one punched me in the face, a right hook from the side, I never saw it coming, and my cheeseburger fell from my hand and rolled across the wet pavement. I stumbled slightly backwards and was kicked in the head, but just the once. He had a metal tip in his shoe, so it left a dent on my forehead. 'They told me to take that back to Silverstream with me.'

I wasn't from Silverstream, but some of my friends from the turn-of-the-road were so I suppose that it was close enough for them. I stood there in the drizzle, looking at Carol, in an intense state of embarrassment. I didn't say anything. My cheeseburger had rolled onto the road and Carol went over and picked it up and tried to rub some of the oily dirt off it. 'If you're still hungry, it's not that bad,' she said, 'the dirt's only on the one side.'

To save the embarrassment of talking about what had just happened, I turned the cheeseburger around and bit into the clean side. It was hard to chew because the inside of my mouth was starting to throb. I wanted to act nonchalant, as if to say that this sort of thing happens all the time, if you're part of the 'turn-of-the-road' gang. I was hoping that she hadn't seen the dent, which I could feel swelling on my forehead. We walked to the bus stop in silence. I think that she had lost her appetite as well.

My friends and I went to a party, and there was a fight: I've no idea what it was about, Craigy lost half his hair, somebody had got hold of it, and a black eye, and he also left his coat behind. I could sense the fight coming and had picked my coat up before it all started. The house was wrecked with bodies being thrown into tables and china cabinets. Craigy came around to my house the next day, half bald, and asked me to walk back over to the house with him to retrieve his coat. 'My ma will kill me if she finds out it's gone.' I told him to leave it. 'Look at the state of you. What state are they going to be? They might not be very pleased to see you again.'

But where did the ambition that kept me in that bedroom come from? 'You won't need to work with your hands,' my mother would say, repeatedly. 'You could be a wee clerk and work in an office, like the men in the mill; they've got it easy, with all these girls to chat up.' Perhaps that was it; an easy life just around the corner. But I think not. I just loved academic work.

My father was out, night after night, in the street in all weathers on a cut of wet, sodden carpet underneath a neighbour's car. He was never paid for the work; he never asked for anything. 'Your dad's a good man,' my mother would say, 'far too good but far too soft with them, he lets other people take him for a ride.'

He would be working on a car engine in the scullery, I don't know who it belonged to, they would have struggled to get it in, it was a big job even for him, working on it for hours, oil everywhere. You couldn't get anywhere near the kitchen sink to wash yourself. He was always working.

The last time I saw my father in the hospital before his operation, I tried to cheer him up by telling him that my favourite albino guinea pig Beano had died. It was a little routine of mine – I'd tell someone some bad news and then say that I was only kidding to cheer them up. But he looked really distressed and puzzled when I said that it was just a joke, as if I was now lying. 'It's only a joke, daddy, don't look sad, please.' He knew how much I loved Beano. This was the last thing that I ever said to my father, except bye-bye as I left his bedside.

My father was in a coma for a full week. I was doing my school examinations at the time, and every afternoon as the Ligoniel bus swept past the bottom of Barginnis Street, I'd glance up at our house to see if the blinds had been pulled down to indicate a death in the family. My heart would be in my mouth, I was trembling with fear, but I still managed to excel in every examination; no excuses. That, I suppose, is my discipline, the discipline that I had to have to get through all of this.

He died on a wet, rainy, cold night in the Royal Victoria Hospital. My mother was at the hospital with him. My Uncle Terence was meant to pick up my Aunt Agnes and me, but he was late, so we got the bus instead. My Aunt Agnes was angry the whole way there. We saw my Uncle Terence – the 'Big Fella', everybody called him that – walking towards us. I don't remember what he said exactly, but I saw it in his face, and I remember lowering my head so that I was looking at the grey puddles of the uneven tarmac with the rain bouncing off them. It's like an embodied memory. If I want to recall those moments better even now, I just have to stand out in the rain and the cold, and lower my head, to hear that squeal from my Aunt Agnes, as if she had just been stabbed in the neck, and see the glassy red eyes of my Uncle Terence, the Big Fella, fighting for control, still trying to be a man when he'd lost his best friend, trying not to cry in front of me.

It was always vague what exactly had happened to my father; it must have been some sort of stroke during the operation. All my mother said was that the doctor had told her that he would have been a vegetable if he had survived, and she always said that 'your da wouldn't have liked to have been a vegetable', as if I should have found this reassuring. I've never tried to get a more accurate understanding of the operation or what went wrong. What would be the point?

My mother always said that she had never met a boy who loved his father so much or who wanted to spend so much time with him. In the year before his death he had a new job. He no longer worked as a mechanic on the buses, he was working at the tech in Belfast, and gave me a lift to school and even picked me up some days so we could go up the Hightown Road and sit out and read, or I'd kick a rugby ball about, then he'd ask me my homework. I'd do my Latin declensions in front of him or recite lists of mathematical and physics formulae and he would just smile away, understanding none of it, with that warm, soft smile of his, so proud to have a son that clever.

'Did I get any wrong, daddy?' I'd ask. 'No, son, you got them all right again. You'll be top of the class at that Royal Academy School of yours,' he would say without understanding a single word of what I was saying. It didn't matter, I knew when I made a mistake. I never tried to correct the name of the school for him.

We walked every Sunday together, just the two of us, up the Horseshoe Road and turn down by the wee shop with the orange Fanta bottle and down into Ligoniel. That little stretch of path just by the wee shop was our special place. The 'White Brae' they call it locally. The White Brae was our little walk, just the two of us, stopping for a drink in that little mountain stream just before you got to the Fanta bottle.

When I got into Belfast Royal Academy he made me a little scratched engraving saying 'Royal Academy School' done on a spare bit of scrap metal at work. It was a loving gift. Then when he died, my Uncle Terence said that I 'just pulled the shutters down', the psychological shutters, that is. Thirteen is an important age, the end of the age of innocence, my gang playing different games, and I had no role model, no father figure, no protector, but I had the gang around me, they were my role models, my protectors and my greatest danger. I was always going to be guilty by association, always a target for somebody, like that night in Royal Avenue.

I never spoke about my father with anyone. My best friend Duck came to his funeral. He said that I never looked up the whole time. My daddy called him 'little high heels' because he wore Cuban-heeled boots. He was a cheeky boy, but funny, always in trouble with his humour, and his fooling around, but that day he didn't try to make me laugh. He just walked quietly behind me. He had lost his father a few months previously, so he knew what it was like. I needed him to be with me that day, just behind, so that I knew he was there but without having to look at him, without him seeing my eyes.

My brother was now away climbing and skiing most of the time. As soon as he finished his apprenticeship he gave up his trade and vowed that he would make a living from climbing, and he did. So, it was just my mother and me and she would talk to my father every night, softly at first, then sobbing, crying out his name. I found it disturbing but I didn't know how to comfort her. I never mentioned the crying to anybody. She would try to give me treats. On a Tuesday, she'd send me down to the sweetshop for two snowballs and two bags of smoky bacon crisps. This was our regular Tuesday treat. Just the two of us at home now. One boy from my school, the same one who told me that his father was in the transport police, told me that if you split open a snowball and sniffed it, it smelt of vomit, so this ruined the treat night. I told my mother that I was getting too big for these childish things.

I would think of my father when I was alone in that room, endlessly; to cheer myself up, I'd evoke positive memories, to remember him better. I only visited my father at work once; my mother needed him to sign something. He told me that he was going to bring something home for me that night and I waited for him for an hour at the bus stop at the top of the street. It wasn't my birthday; it was just something that he had made for me in his spare time at work. I saw him in his oil-stained overalls with his glasses on, getting off the bus with something large wrapped in newspaper. He was a slight man and he could hardly carry it, but he was smiling, because he knew that I would be very pleased when I saw it. He tottered as he held it in front of him. He wouldn't open the big, untidy parcel until we got into the front room. Our dog Spot was jumping all over the furniture, sniffing the paper and barking excitedly, tearing at it with his sharp teeth. I had never seen anything like it before. It had brown metal ramparts with zigzag steps shaped out of a single piece of aluminium and a hardboard base. The whole thing was solid and well put together. It must have taken months to make in his spare time at work, every bit of metal had been shaped by hand. I had received an expensive Christmas present that year – a Cape Canaveral-type base with missiles that fired. But the fort was different. In these rows of identical mill houses all crouching in that hollow below the hills that ring Belfast, street after street of them as far as the eye could see, all with their cheap, identical flowery settees bought on credit from the same shops at the bottom of the Shankill, and the same pictures on the wall of foxes, fawns, infants, in fact anything with big eyes professing innocence and adoration, there was something individual and unique about the fort, made by and for love. And made for me.

I had hundreds of soldiers in a large rusty circular tin that stayed in the damp back room – cowboys and Indians, Confederates and Yankees, knights whose legs and arms moved and could be swapped over, called 'Swap-its', Russian soldiers with a red star in the middle of their grey winter hats. The knights on horseback were so intricate and such a delight to look at that my mother put them on display with all the best china in the china cabinet. Two knights, the Red Rose of the House of Lancaster and the White Rose of the House of York, were on parade on the top shelf. We weren't allowed to go near the china cabinet, or feed the gas meter, which was just behind it. And when you wanted to play with the knights you had to ask for the key and remove them with a very steady hand from the glass cabinet, which always seemed to tremble and shake with all that china. I can still remember the smell of the china cabinet. All the smells that I have experienced in this life, the lavender in the quiet fields beyond Sainte Maxime, the close-up smell of drying sea weed on those wild gull squawking shores north of Santa Barbara, the fragrant smell of leather in the market in Hammamet with mint tea in the background, but I can still smell the inside of that cabinet with greater ease and with greater clarity than any of them, as if I have just leaned into the cabinet and breathed again. Don't ask me to describe the smell; it must have been some kind of cleaning material that had evaporated in the glass container over many years.

All the soldiers eventually found their way into the fort. It was a generic sort of fort though it looked like Fort Laramie, from the Wild West on the black and white television. But my mother told me that her father George had been to a fort like that in India when he was in the army. My father knew of George's days in India and this might have given him the idea that guided his craftsmanship. British soldiers of the Raj patrolled that fort at night in the corner of our front room, but no shops seemed to sell models of the enemy, whoever the enemy were. But that didn't matter to me, a boy with a fertile and vivid imagination, in a damp, crumbling mill house, who could spend hours on the floor just playing.

But one Thursday in July when I was about eleven we were going to my Uncle Terence's and my mother told me that I was now too old for the fort and the soldiers. She was tired of cleaning my kneecaps with Vim because of the amount of time I spent on the floor. 'You're too old to be on your hands and knees all the time. Too old for that sort of childish nonsense.' It was all done in a matter of fact sort of way, as if it was no big deal. The fort got in the way in such a small house. We kept it in the back room, where the wallpaper hung in great damp swathes from the slimy green wall with the damp running down in rivulets. The fort was going rusty like the metal container with the soldiers, like the tools we kept there, like everything else in the house. It had to go, and it was loaded into our car. I don't know who loaded it into the car, perhaps my brother. I was told that the poor children up Ligoniel would love it. I was told that I had had my enjoyment. It was somebody else's turn. I was assured that the children up in Ligoniel weren't as well off as we were. They had no missile sites, or garages with lifts that could be wound up, or forts made at work by their fathers in good jobs. I knew that they were from big families, families sometimes with no work, Roman Catholic families. 'Too bloody idle,' our neighbours liked to say when Big Terry wasn't about, but I didn't really understand at that time why they only said it when he wasn't there.

There was a steep hill at the end of the Lesley Street; we called it 'the dump'. It wasn't an official refuse site; it was just where people dumped all the stuff that they didn't want. I remember old settees with rusty springs sticking out and black bags full of open tin cans with large black crows picking at the bags and hardly bothering to move when you approached them. My mother told me to leave the fort out on the dump. She told me that it would be found, and that one of the boys from Ligoniel would have a childhood filled with imagination because of that fort, the fort that my grandfather had fought in, and my father had made by hand.

My uncle came with me as I laid the fort out in the middle of a hill of refuse. Dust and hairs, human and dog, filled all the cracks in the hardwood base, the hairs ingrained and dense like thread. But it was well looked after. That's another expression my family liked. The fort, the car and the front step that my mother would wash every couple of days on her hands and her knees, a white froth on the pavement outside the house swept away by basins of cold water. All well looked after, all cared for. Loved, if you like. It was a very Protestant way of thinking about these things.

So, I carried the fort and left it in the middle of this long slope filled with human debris. A beautiful, handcrafted object that had been at the centre of my childhood, indeed still was at the centre of my childhood. That per-haps was the problem. My mother decided that at eleven I shouldn't be scuttling around the front room on all fours with Cowboys and Indians and Russians.

We all sat in my uncle's front room, my Aunt Agnes, my father, my mother and Terence's mother. There was a crucifix on the wall as you came in. I had only ever seen one in the Rocks' house. I never understood what it was doing in my Uncle Terence's house before Kevin Rock explained to me years later. My mother always said that it was something to do with Terence's mother. I didn't know what though. But I couldn't stop thinking of the fort. I was always told that I was spoiled compared to some of the boys in my street, and especially compared to the boys at the top of the Ligoniel Road, from the big Catholic families. I knew that I had more toys than any of them, but I didn't want to give the fort away.

I don't know where I got the hammer from; it must have been from the toolbox in the backroom of my uncle's house. It was a big heavy claw hammer. I hid it up inside my coat and said that I was going out. The fort was still there, just as I had left it, in the middle of the dump. No deprived child had got there yet. I sat down on the slope beside it. I suppose that it was almost like playing again. The first blow flattened two or three of the metal ramparts. The second removed one section of the metal steps. I sat on the dirty stones amongst the piles of rubbish and hammered away. I wasn't emotional about what I was doing. It was a cold act. I was just determined that no child, no matter how deprived or how needy or how hungry, would get my fort where my grandfather had fought for the British Empire, where Davy Crockett, whose father came from County Londonderry, had held out against the Mexicans at the Alamo, where my dreams of lands far away from cold, damp mill houses that turned everything to rust had been nurtured.

I was obviously engrossed in my little frenzy of destruction because what I remember next is my father and uncle standing over me. My father looked almost puzzled, perhaps a little hurt that he had a son who could be like this. I looked up at them. I felt ashamed and embarrassed. I needed to explain my actions, to justify myself. I remember what I said quite clearly. 'It's dangerous,' I said. I remember those very words just coming out. 'Those sharp metal ends, they could hurt somebody. You can't just leave it here. Somebody might cut himself on it. I was just making it safe for them.' I was led away by my father and my uncle, who didn't say anything at first or even look at each other. 'Let's just leave it here the way it is,' said my father eventually. 'But it's ruined now,' I said. 'It's ruined.' I was crying by now, sniffing loudly, wiping my nose on my sleeve. I remember looking down at the trail of smeared snatter along my sleeve, there was just so much snatter. It was a whining, imploring sort of crying that accompanied my excuses. But why I was crying I don't really know, perhaps it was being caught red-handed, the guilt of the whole thing, the fact that there was no way to hide my shame. Or perhaps it was just my way of showing them that I was still a child, who needed to dream, whose time had not come to leave these particular things behind.

I can remember vividly the look on my father's face to this day. It would be nice if the most vivid images involving my father were all positive but after all those years of trying, his look that night on the dump is the most powerful visual image that I am left with, no matter how hard I try to change it. That's the point about human memory, we are not in control of its content nor its retrieval; rather, it seems to enjoy controlling us.

'Too old for childish things', that's what I told my mother in order to stop our Tuesday night treats with the snowballs; 'too old for childish things' was her reason for making me get rid of the fort, with this act occasioning so many negative memories associated with my father, and his disappointment with my selfishness and my spoiled nature. That's the thing about certain powerful, emotional expressions, they seem to just come out unannounced, without reflection or forethought; it's as if we store them unconsciously, over years if necessary, cocked and ready to go, ready to fire when the time is right – ready to kill the thing we love, the memory, the image, even the person itself.

Inner and outer speech

Many years after I left Belfast, when I became a professor of psychology at the University of Manchester, I interviewed Alex Ferguson, the ex-manager of Manchester United, for a radio series on Radio 5 Live called 'Head-to-Head' (Beattie 1998). He was a fascinating interviewee, a master motivator of his players, a master lay psychologist, playing little games with his squad to keep them focussed, to keep them striving for greater success. This is how Ferguson explained one of his motivational techniques.

'After we'd won the League for the first time I said, "There are the names of six players in this envelope who I think may let us down this year. I will review those six players at the end of the season, if we lose the League." So, all the players were saying, "It's not me, it must be you, it couldn't possibly be me."'

'So, whose names were in the envelope?' I asked.

'Only my own,' he replied.

Ferguson was a well-known workaholic, first to arrive at the training ground, last to leave. He always liked to be in control – of everything – the team, the players and their lives, both professional and personal, the club. He said that he found holidays difficult – he preferred working holidays, popping in to catch a game when he was abroad, going talent spotting for his club. I asked him why he was so driven. Why did he have to work so hard, who was he most trying to impress? He had made it. Why couldn't he just relax?

There was a long pause, not so much for thinking, because I believe he already knew the answer, it was more an embarrassed sort of silence. Then he started to speak quietly, almost reverentially. It was his father, he said, that's who he was trying to impress, his father Alexander Ferguson, the plater's helper in the shipping industry from Govan. His father who had died of lung cancer when young Alex was in his twenties, before his unrivalled success as a football manager was realised. Alexander senior never got to see the young Alex in all his glory at Old Trafford with Cantona and Beckham and Keane. Young Alex never got that affirmation: 'You've done it, son, you've come a long way from the tenements in Govan, you've made it, you can relax now.'

Alex was still searching, still fighting for the one thing that he could never receive after all those years. It sounds daft, he said, but he knew what was behind it, and he was the manager of Manchester United for twenty-six years, always 'driven'. That's the word they used about him, and this tells you something about the depth psychology behind it. Pundits said that Ferguson had a hunger for success, but it was a hunger that could never quite be satiated because the one critical component in achieving that flow of satisfaction, that reward, had been removed. I suppose that's what some loss and separation can do to you, it can make some individuals strive and strive relentlessly.

I know that I worked harder after my father died, I was still desperate to please him, as desperate as only a thirteen-year-old can feel trying to please a dead, silenced father. My mother told me that I was an orphan now and that things had to change. That was the word she used, 'orphan', I was shocked. I thought that an orphan was someone who has lost both parents.

I took this to heart, and the change in me was quite literally instantaneous. I woke up the day after the funeral and decided to live differently. I started that very day cleaning up old paraffin heaters for my neighbours and relatives. I worked all day at this, polishing and shining them until they gleamed, and they paid me for the work. Duck and I started a car washing business the Saturday after the funeral in that cold, cold February and washed six cars that first Saturday, and then up to twelve then fifteen cars every Saturday morning and into the afternoon. The minister was our first customer. I started a paper round with Duck, and helped the milkman deliver milk in the morning. I saved every penny I earned. I wrote my first piece for publication a few weeks later. It was published in *The Hornet* in the 'This Week's Grouse' slot. I found it after all these decades and I now have it in front of me. It reads: 'We often read about postmen being bitten by dogs when they are delivering their letters, but do you ever hear any sympathy for paper boys? We face the same hazards as postmen, but stories have not been written about paper boys escaping the local dogs, but they have been written about postmen. I am sure other paper boys have the same view.' I was confident in the last sentence because Duck and I had been attacked by the same Alsatian in Silverstream Road; it was held in place by a rusty clanking chain round its neck. I tried to stroke the dog and it went for me. I got a postal order for ten shillings for the letter. But embarrassingly it did take me a few hours of hesitation to open the brown manila envelope from *The Hornet* in Dundee. And that's because the envelope had been franked with a 'Dr Barnardo's Homes . . . 100 Years of Childcare.' Now that I knew that I was an orphan, I thought that I was being taken into a boys' home and that the letter had been addressed to me (rather than my mother) by mistake.

I was frantic for some sense of security and some control over my life. I studied and worked harder, I saved harder – as if this might bring me some security. I filled chocolate boxes with sixpences and they sat all around the front room. I was very good at marbles played out there on the street, I was the best in the neighbourhood even though I had a very unorthodox style (I threw the marbles rather than shooting with them, you had to go back an extra paving stone if you were a thrower), but I would win all the marbles off the other boys and then sell them back to them. My mother always said that there was a queue at the front door from the boys needing to buy some marbles to play with. My brother was astounded when he came home as to where all this money came from. He was usually broke.

Years after my father's death, men would start to come around to our house, 'just good friends, somebody to go out for a drink with', my mother said, and she would play Engelbert Humperdinck over and over again, when I was upstairs, having to cough loudly before coming down to go outside to the back yard and the toilet. 'Please release me, let me go.' That song still makes me feel queasy to this day, a genuine physical queasiness that makes me heave uncontrollably.

One of her friends, Andy, gave me a new set of encyclopedias on their own wooden stand; another, Ernie gave me a new card table to do my homework on. It wasn't my birthday or Christmas. My brother said that they were trying to buy my affections. Some were not so kind. Ginger came around one night, annoyed that I was in the house. 'Not doing homework again, Geoffrey? A boy your age should be out enjoying himself. Not stuck in the house every night.'

He seemed to resent my education. 'He thinks that he is something, that boy of yours. Well I think that he's no better than anybody else. Here's one for you – where does electricity come from?' I was now fifteen, I knew all about the basic components of matter and the flow of electrons. So, I explained carefully and in detail exactly what electricity was and how it flowed. Ginger just sat there on the settee staring at me. He'd been drinking. 'Baaaalicks,' he said eventually. 'You're just talking baaaalicks. My brother's an electrician and he doesn't know where electricity comes from. So, what you've just told me is a complete load of old shite. You've just made it up to try to get one over on me, to make yourself look big.'

'Sorry to speak so plainly, Eileen. But that son of yours makes things up, to make himself seem better than the rest of us. He's a wee snob, all right.'

'Now, be fair, Ginger. He's not a real stuck up wee snob.'

'I'm sorry, Eileen, he is. Definitely. That's the way he's going.'

'He's just got an education. Okay, he might get things wrong occasionally. You'd better check those books, Geoffrey. After all, if Ginger's brother doesn't know what electricity is, and he has to work with it all day, how the hell could your teachers know? Answer me that one.'

Ginger said that he'd had enough and that he was going to the Pigeon Club for a drink. My mother put the TV back on, perhaps annoyed that she hadn't been invited. The TV still wasn't working properly, it never worked, she always blamed the aerial for some reason, so there was much tense twisting of the little aerial to get a better picture.

'If you ever,' she paused, 'ever, became a wee snob . . . if I ever caught you looking down your nose at me . . .'

That always seemed to be her greatest fear. Not me having an accident, or falling below a bus, or getting glassed, or even shot, but me becoming a wee snob, always with that diminutive in front of it, turning my back on her and my background.

Then one night, my mother without any warning asked me how I'd feel living in South Africa. 'Yeah, alright,' I replied, without any hesitation or thought. I just didn't want an argument. My brother, it seems, was less happy with the idea. It was never mentioned again anyway. The new life in South Africa was presumably just some drink-fueled fantasy.

So why Engelbert, and why every night? Perhaps, it was addressed to my father, perhaps he had to release her, to let her get on with life. The nights spent in the cold and the wet beneath the cars in the road couldn't have helped with his health, he had rheumatic fever when he was a boy and that gives you a bad ticker, my mother always said. 'I'm a widow woman now,' my mother continually pointed out, 'with two wee sons, and your brother's always away off youth-hostelling or away climbing. I've only got you and you're no company, up those stairs night after night, leaving me alone in front of the telly . . . and there's nothing on. You're no use at all.'

Psychology became part of my life in the sixth form and I studied psychology as part of general study. I read a couple of books by Hans Eysenck: *Uses and Abuses of Psychology* and *Sense and Nonsense in Psychology* (Eysenck 1960, 1961) and it was his work that really sparked my interest. I liked the idea of precision when it came to studying people, counting, quantification, objectivity. It appealed to an aspect of my personality, that slight fixation with numbers and neatness and certainty. It sat alongside maths, physics and chemistry A level. But I continued with Russian, even though it didn't fit with the timetable, so I had only one formal lesson a week, with little time for Russian conversation. Russian history particularly interested me, the individual and the state and how change occurs – political and economic change, of course. But also personal change, in the midst of all of these other things: the revolution and forced collectivisation, industrialisation, communism . . . the collective farms, 'kolkhozes' (say it over and over: 'kollektivnoye khozaystvo'), five-year plans, terms and concepts that I had never heard before in Legmore Street, dominated by Unionism and the status quo, a system designed to prevent change, to stop change from ever being considered. But I was really interested in change, and change in people, the effects of political upheaval and systemic change on *personal* hopes, fears, aspirations, relationships and goals. How do these things connect? That's what I didn't understand, as a naive schoolboy, and perhaps still don't. And where are the seeds of political change? Are they external to the individual or internal? Does it have to start with a feeling or a thought, a perception, veridical or not, does there have to be an emotional tinge to the whole thing? And why was some change impossible to imagine?

My mother appeared so seemingly contented in that mill up in Ligoniel, going on about Mr Ewart, the owner with the eye patch, looking glamorous, like Douglas Fairbanks Junior, coming to visit once a year, and the smarmy foremen, and the smoke breaks, but only if you were allowed and only if you could get that smarmy foreman to agree. And there was the camaraderie amongst the girls and the inevitable gossip about who was 'a real wee millie' and who wasn't when some of them were out on a Saturday night at the Plaza ballroom in town. Why did she not want to see change there? She was a clever and astute woman who had been dealt few good hands in life; in another place at another time, she could have thought radically about her life and situation, but she never once did.

Psychology, I thought, might hold the key to the questions I was interested in. Are we fixed for all time or tabula rasa to be written on by experience and, if so, what critical experiences, and at what age? I was part of a group, a gang, a sub-culture, voicing sometimes many of the same values as the group – when I was with them, but simultaneously an Academy boy, with a different position, intellectually and emotionally, on almost everything. Was this discomfort I sometimes felt going to be part of the process of change within me, or irrelevant to it? Was I ever going to really change inside? And is change primarily about moving towards something or away from something? And what are the dominant emotions of change – fear, sadness, longing, or, I can hardly even say it, disgust?

And does that disgust, that most unvoiced of emotions, have to be about your surroundings, about the behaviour of those you love, your friends? And would that driver of change be part of becoming a wee snob. Is that what my mother was always going on about? If you're not somehow disgusted with your surroundings will you be stuck there forever? Do you need an emotional push to move on, and what would that emotion be – if not disgust? And where exactly might I end up? This taxed me quite a lot.

But would psychology help me understand these sorts of questions? Could all that counting and categorising and statistics give me the insights I craved? I was also reading Russian literature in Russian and this (in particular Dostoevsky) was giving me some alternative insight into the human psyche – not a monolithic personality in the case of the main character, the narrator, the insignificant civil servant in Dostoevsky's *Notes from Underground*, but some sort of 'inner plurality' in constant motion. Of course, it need hardly be pointed out that the change from a boy who didn't read novels at all to a boy who read Russian novels in the Russian language within a few short years was a significant change (only brought on by a very good school – perhaps the best of schools even). I knew that *I* had not found the principle of harmony, it was a very conscious feeling, but never discussed – who would I discuss it with? Who was in the same boat as me? I am sure there were some but I didn't know them. So it was reassuring, comforting even, to see it articulated by others, even fictional characters. This is Pevear's introduction to *Notes from Underground*.

'What the principle of this harmony is, the underground man cannot say: he has never found it. But he knows he has not found it: he knows, because his inner disharmony, his dividedness, which is the source of his suffering, is also the source of consciousness' (Pevear 2004: xix).

Dostoevsky puts it somewhat differently. The man from underground says 'I am a sick man . . . I am a wicked man', anticipating all criticism, trying to bind his concept of self together from all sides, with that pause in the middle reflecting the instability, in Pevear's word, 'the perpetual "dialectic" of isolated consciousness' (2004: ix).

I saw aspects of my own character here, unarticulated, a little diffuse because language had not been allowed to lay the feelings and thoughts out in any sort of linear and systematic way. I know how to harbour resentments, like the narrator, this little isolated and insignificant civil servant, bullied by the swaggering army officers ('I was standing beside the billiard table, blocking the way unwittingly, and he wanted to pass; he took me by the shoulders and silently – with no warning or explanation – moved me from where I stood to another place, and then passed by as if without noticing. I could even have forgiven a beating, but I simply could not forgive his moving me and in the end just not noticing me', Dostoevsky 1864/1993: 47) – resentments that won't go away – only I know how long they last, just like he does. I know how to make myself feel better through the tiny injustices open to me, tiny injustices (indeed so tiny that others might not even see them as injustices at all) that I myself can inflict on others that remind me of who I am and who I am not. It's not a pleasant set of thoughts. But we all have them.

'There, in its loathsome, stinking underground, our offended, beaten-down, and derided mouse at one immerses itself in cold, venomous, and above all, ever-lasting spite' (in Dostoevsky words). The mouse buried within, hiding in there, roaring quietly, spitefully.

But always longing for some unity, some single concept of self, *any* concept of self, no matter what it is.

'Oh, if I were doing nothing only out of laziness. Lord, how I'd respect myself then. Respect myself precisely because I'd at least be capable of having laziness in me; there would be in me at least one, as it were, positive quality, which I myself could be sure of. Question: who is he? Answer: a lazybones. Now it would be agreeable to hear that about myself. It means I'm properly defined; it means there's something to say about me. "Lazybones!" – now, that is a title and a mission, it's a career, sirs. No joking, it really is' (Dostoevsky 1864/1993: 19).

I read this, of course, with the help of a dictionary word by word, line by line, as if the truth about people, about me, was being revealed slowly in a tablet of stone from the past. It must have been like reading Tyndale's Bible in the early sixteenth century, with the truth at last unfolding slowly and painfully in front of you. The fact that it was so painstakingly slow to translate probably meant that it all seemed so much more profound, a sort of cognitive dissonance in action – you've gone to all this trouble, it must be important. But there were truths embedded in those pages undoubtedly, dissonance or no dissonance, emerging painfully and hesitatingly through the filter of that dictionary.

'In every man's memories there are such things as he will reveal not to everyone, but perhaps only to friends. There are also such as he will reveal not even to friends, but only to himself, and that in secret. Then, finally, there are such as a man is afraid to reveal even to himself, and every decent man will have accumulated quite a few things of this sort. That is, one might even say: the more decent a man is, the more of them he will have' (Dostoevsky 1864/1993: 37).

That was the underground man talking about layers of the psyche, buried deep (in the days before Freud and his 'discovery' of the unconscious), and I hoped that any psychology might help me understand this process of burial, submergence and slow retrieval. And, of course, the beauty of Dostoevsky was that he allowed us to see, sometimes through incidental actions, sometimes through random associations in thought itself, some of the things that a man might not like to reveal even to himself, and thus to recognise those very things within me. Those things that we all have in common – the harbouring of resentments, the anger that won't dissipate with time, the frustrated fury finding other ways to the surface to wreak its terrible revenge – those human things that bind us all together but are never discussed.

There is always going to be that moment with education when you start understanding the world a little better. A little better – a little differently from those around you, I mean, and that pushes you even further away. I would sit on the bus on the way home from school wearing my school cap (the school rules clearly stated that the cap should be worn at all times travelling to and from the school) then I would remove it aggressively as I got closer to home, muttering very quietly, inaudibly even: 'I am a sick man . . . pause . . . I am a wicked man', to see if anyone would notice, to see if anyone might understand the reference or the sentiment. Sometimes, the pause in the middle would be longer, sometimes hardly any pause at all, as if I was giving up on the process of resolution itself, and that search for a harmonious self-identity that had so tormented Dostoevsky, but not, it seems, Hans Eysenck. I was already starting to worry about the promises and procedures of psychology. How was psychology going to uncover these deeper layers, in and from the underground? Does it only concern itself with what people say to everyone, or say to their friends? But what about the things they would never say? What about the things they keep buried?

This disharmony, I must add, has never gone away. I confess that I feel this clash between cultures in how I talk to this day. I say ridiculous things for effect, as if I was back at the corner trying to cheer the group up, usually all delivered in a heavily accented manner, and sometimes very funny, at least that's how they seem to me, as if I was playing a role in a play, without any control over my part, and sometimes close family look at me a little puzzled. It's like a verbal habit, you couldn't call it a tic, it's more like an unconscious routine developed on the corner, a response to boredom and threat, functioning for the group and its collective mood, and now inescapably part of me.

Russian did not fit into my busy school timetable, so I did my translation work up in the back bedroom or on the card table in our front room, the new one given to me by Ernie, looking down Barginnis Street to the turn-of-the-road and my pals out enjoying themselves. I say enjoying themselves, but to be honest this is a relative term, they always looked bored, there was nothing to do at the corner, except go for a wander up the glen, or climb over the metal fences at the back of the park to swim in the mill dam and then get chased, raid apple orchards over the Ballysillan Road and toss away the apples after just taking one bite, 'they're sour as fuck', or as night fell break into shops like the butchers or the chemists.

But, of course, there was always the craic, and teasing each other endlessly in those prolonged routines of insults and counter-insults that lasted not just a night, but weeks and months on end. Those social scientists who have tried to comprehend 'street corner society' would do well to start with these verbal routines, rule-governed and orderly in their own way. Perhaps not quite as orderly as the verbal duelling, the 'sounding', of the gangs in Harlem studied by the sociolinguist William Labov (1972a), where every insult ('Your momma drink pee') has a prescribed set of permissible responses ('Your father eat shit'), matching in form and content and not too personal, never too personal, but nevertheless with room for elaboration and invention ('Your father eat dog yummies'). But there were rules in the ritual insults at the turn-of-the-road, 'I bet your ma's been in a chapel' – 'Only for a fucking pish in the Holy Water.' 'Has your ma ever gone out with a Taig?' – 'Yeah, your fucking da!' over and over again, and dozens of songs and rhymes 'If your name is Timothy or Pat/You'll never get up the Shankill with a Fenian name like that', and endless dirty jokes. I'd memorise the dirty jokes and run through them at nights before going to sleep, immediately after my prayers. I would know the number of jokes, fourteen or fifteen or whatever it was that I'd committed to memory at any particular time, and I'd torment myself if I couldn't remember every single one, word perfectly. The insult routines had very fine nonverbal accompaniments, designed to keep the whole thing on track, without it crossing over into unambiguous aggression. The subtlety of these nonverbal behaviours accompanying ritual insults on street corners have never really been captured in the academic literature.

Life was especially boring on a Sunday, we would go to church and Sunday school, but there was nothing else open, no shops, no cinemas, nothing, even the swings were chained up in the park on a Saturday night and through all day Sunday, so that we would respect the Lord's Day. But then the gang would disappear, and I would wonder what they had found to do and what adventures they might be having, when they were no longer visible, imagined adventures with me stuck behind that card table. But I loved the sound of Russian, I didn't mind saying the words out loud. French sounded odd with my strong Belfast accent.

There were lots of conjugations to learn in Russian which I liked, which tested my memory. It was a way of showing off. With my father gone, there was no one to ask me my homework any longer. And that had always been the verb between the two of us – 'to ask'. 'Daddy, will you ask me my homework?' And he'd wipe the oil of his hands, no matter how busy he was, and leave the engine in the kitchen and take a seat in the front room in his overalls. I knew that my father knew no Latin or French or physics, but it was our little game. I'd preface each conjugation with a few words, then launch straight into 'amo, amas, amat, amamus, amatis, amant'. Now I ran through everything silently in my head, but sometimes the words leaked quietly out as I voiced them. There was no one to talk to about any of it. Nobody knew what any of it meant or pretended to understand. My mother, sitting on the other side of the room, accused me of talking to myself.

'That's not healthy,' she would say. 'Go down to the corner and get a pint of milk for the breakfast in the morning.' 'I can't, I'm working,' I said. 'I have to translate the first six pages of Turgenev's "Pervaya Lyubov" for school tomorrow.' 'You're not working, you're definitely not working, I've been watching you, you're just sitting there gazing all around you. And you've been talking to yourself again, do you know that? You need to get control of that. That could be a real problem as you get older.'

She went back to watching the TV and leaned over to turn it up. 'John Kyle talks to himself,' she added. 'You know that don't you? And not a bit of wonder with all the torment you boys give him. Why do you call him "Squeak"? That poor man can't help it. Do you want the boys from the street calling after you when you get older? There's the boy who talks to himself and nobody knows what the hell he's saying.'

The voice in my head was getting louder. I couldn't help that. 'Ya govoryoo pa rooskee.' It was getting louder and louder, until I was almost shouting it. 'Ya govoryoo pa rooskee.' I was shouting it defiantly. 'Ya govoryoo pa rooskee!' in her direction now, right towards her face.

She was looking alarmed. Just the two of us in that small, damp house. 'Why don't you go and shout that at your friends and see how they react. You used to be such a lovely boy, I don't know what's happened to you. I think it's all that bloody homework. It can't be good for you. What the hell are you saying. Are you speaking in a foreign language or are you just talking shite?'

I had calmed down. 'I am just saying that that I am speaking Russian,' I said quietly.

'How do you say in Russian that "I'm just speaking shite"?' That might be more useful,' she said and went upstairs crying to bed.

Special occasions

New Year's Eve was always special, ever since I was a boy, ever since my daddy was alive. My father, dark like Clark Gable my mother said, but still more like David Niven in his looks ('everybody thought that David Niven was walking down the street in his dirty overalls,' she would say without any trace of irony), knocking on the neighbours' doors in that little grey street on the stroke of midnight, carrying a wee bit of coal, with his wee son beside him. 'First footing', they called it, common in Scotland, but still found amongst the Protestants of Ulster, sons of the Plantation with Scottish names like Beattie. A drink in every house for the first footer; people who had nothing in those little damp, mill houses of North Belfast, sharing what little they had.

However, that all seemed a long time ago.

I picked up the little bit of silver foil from the Formica table in the back-room and opened it up, checking again. Maybe they dissolve if they get too hot. I counted the little pink tabs, laying them out in a neat line with regular gaps between them. I knew there would be a row if I lost one, maybe worse than a row. They had all trusted Rob with their money and he'd scored the tabs, round the back of the City Hall, after standing there for hours with the pelting rain full in our face. This was my first time with him and it showed. I was very nervous. Rob was an old hand at this; he was always doing deals of one sort or another. He had a lot of front which helped in these situations.

He insisted that I go with him that night into town, 'for the company' was how he put it. There was always a lot left unsaid, and an implicit threat in these requests. Rob said that he had to pop into town to see an old friend, 'I want you to come along . . . *just for the company.*' It was a Sunday night, the night when everything was closed in Belfast, including the pubs, and with chained swings in the parks lest the children enjoy themselves too much on the Lord's Day. I had been to church twice that day, I was a junior church-warden at the time, and now I was having to go to town with Rob, but just for the company.

Rob was very good at getting people to do what he wanted by being very vague about what it was that you were actually going to do. You agreed with the smaller things he asked you to do, until eventually you could see the whole picture opening up in front of you, before it dawned on you, and then it was too late, far too late. There was no backing out. He didn't explain what we were going to do that night in the town centre in advance. The 'friend' was a business acquaintance, the transaction was over in seconds. I stood as far away as he could, without drawing attention to myself, chewing on the cord of my duffle coat, and with a little bit of heavy encouragement, and implicit threat, I slipped them into the left pocket of his duffle coat, my lucky pocket, the one without a hole. That was Rob's idea, of course. He said that I looked more innocent than him. I couldn't argue with him. 'Stick them in your pocket,' Rob said. I didn't even nod back; I just did it. It was as direct as that. This, I suppose, was an order of sorts.

There was a lot of security on the streets in Belfast at that time. The Troubles had sealed off the town centre, bombs more or less every night. The buses might be off the road. We might have to take our chance and walk home. We might get pulled. The police or the army would be looking for weapons, of course, not little bits of silver foil. I was rehearsing what I might say. 'Love hearts', that's all that I could think of. Crushed love hearts. My heart was pumping furiously. Rob joked away, but then again he was clean. I was the one carrying. 'I hope you've got your story right,' Rob said. 'You're an Academy boy, you'll be alright. You look plausible.' That was also one of my mother's words, 'plausible'. 'You'd better get our story right,' and Rob laughed at my discomfort.

My 'reward' was this – a free tab, fatter than the rest for going with him and for 'looking after' the gear in my bedroom. Rob said that his mother searched his and that I had to hide them for him in below the school books on Russian and physics, the silver foil peeking out to remind me where they were. It would be my first time. I told him that I didn't want to drop any acid.

Rob replied that I had no choice. 'We're all in this together,' he said.

So I did my research in the library. I read Aldous Huxley's *The Doors of Perception*. It seemed to reassure me, excite me even. But then I panicked, there was almost a warning in it.

This is what Huxley wrote:

> From what I had read . . . I was convinced in advance that the drug would admit me, at least for a few hours, into the kind of inner world described by Blake and AE. But what I had expected did not happen. I had expected to lie with my eyes shut, looking at visions of many-coloured geometries, of animated architectures, rich with gems and fabulously lovely, of landscapes with heroic figures, of symbolic dramas trembling perpetually on the verge of the ultimate revelation. But I had not reckoned, it was evident, with the idiosyncrasies of my mental make-up, the facts of my temperament, training and habits.
>
> (1956/2004: 5)

Huxley had not bargained for 'the idiosyncrasies of . . . [his] mental make-up', his 'temperament, training and habits'. Huxley, it seems, was a poor visualiser in everyday life, with very impaired vision because of an eye infection picked up when he was young, his hallucinogenic experience therefore was not one of fantastical images but one of seeing the mundane in new ways. 'Those folds in the trousers – what a labyrinth of endlessly significant complexity!' (1956/2004: 16).

I realised there and then that on this trip, this one virgin trip of ours, we might well not all be in this together, as Rob liked to think, at least in terms of our probable psychological reactions to the drug. I worried about the temperament and habits of some of my friends, as well as the context in which we would be taking the drug, hardly the context of the relaxed mystical explorations of Huxley. This would never be the ideal situation to explore the doors of perception, to go beyond our practical, everyday perceptions which are devoted, at the best of times according to Huxley, to our survival, to reach the *Mind at Large*. We were going to drop acid in a war zone, where 'survival' in a much more tangible and immediate sense was central. This was not 'survival' in the sense that human beings are all essentially Darwinian creatures that have evolved to survive, this was survival in the sense that tonight if you hear a loud noise, jump into the shadows at the side of the road and hope that they don't see you. I thought that this psychedelic experience might not be the best of ideas.

So here I was, not able to back out, examining them carefully on the table in the backroom. I could hear my mother cleaning upstairs, the brush digging in frustration at the corner of my bedroom. I put the silver foil in my pocket and hurried up. It was no place for prying eyes. School books everywhere, posters on every wall, pictures torn out of magazines drooping down from the ceiling, images of a different world, Rod Stewart, David Bowie, Free, and the drawers full of different things that I was 'looking after' for Rob, with little choice on my part – stuff stolen from the chemists, bottles of pills waiting to be deciphered, 'work out what's the good stuff', a loose bike chain, some long-playing records lifted from God knows where. You couldn't open the drawers they were so full.

'Look at this mess,' my mother would say. 'You make this house look like a right hole.'

'It's a hole anyway,' I said, 'without my help.'

The night before, however, was bad. My mother left my bedroom door open, which she always did when she sensed trouble. 'That blast was very close; I'd say the Crumlin. What do you think?'

'I'm trying to sleep,' I shouted back. 'That's what I think. It's bad enough living here without a running commentary every bloody night.'

'I'm only trying to make conversation,' she said. 'You never talk to me anymore; it wasn't like this when your father was alive.' Then the sobbing started. I lay there thinking about my dad, until I, too, felt like crying, but privately, then another blast snapped me out of it. Probably the Crumlin, I thought.

Moke called about seven the next night. My mother answered the door, hovering around, pretending to tidy. 'You two off out tonight to bring in the New Year? I wish I was going.'

'Just a few beers,' said Moke, and I pushed past her onto the street, touching my lucky pocket, mumbling a goodbye.

'Rob's aunt is out for the New Year,' said Moke. 'We've got the house to ourselves. What did you get? Purple Haze?'

'They're more pink than purple,' I said, 'but genuine.'

'They'd better be,' said Moke threateningly.

'Rob actually scored them,' I replied. 'He made the call. I'm just looking after them for him.'

He knew that would shut him up.

The gang were all there already; Jack Bruce from Cream was singing 'Born under a Bad Sign.' One lad had brought five cans of Harp lager with him, having obviously drunk one already on the way. 'No beer,' said Rob. 'I've heard it stops it working.' I handed the silver foil to him. I knew that Rob would be the master of ceremonies. I knew that Rob would be in charge; Rob liked the theatre of it all.

Rob uncurled the silver foil and handed them out slowly, and with some little flourishes of the hands. 'Can I wash mine down with Harp?' said the boy with the lager.

'Just swallow it,' said Rob, 'without the lager. Use your own spit.' 'Here's yours,' he said to me. 'Take it.' I did as I was told.

And there we all sat for the next hour, in another small, dark, damp room, the only sort of room that we'd ever known, but this one lit with a candle, all cross-legged, all waiting silently for something to happen.

It was Duck who first noticed the flickering after-image when somebody moved. 'Jesus,' he said, laughing hysterically, as much in relief as anything else. Then, by a process of magic contagion, the euphoria worked through the little group, all hunched up in our duffle coats and pants with heavy, wet, flared bottoms. Time slowed, the flame of the candle danced with the music, finding the beat within minutes, and lit the grinning faces, pulsating red then green. Belfast was finally at peace. Rob started swaying gently with a slight sardonic grin on his face, and we all watched him attentively.

'What did I tell you?' he said. 'I said that I would get the good gear. We could all move to London and become big dealers, except for your man over there. He's going to go off to university and leave us all behind. Free trips all round for the rest of us.' And they all laughed hysterically at this. I felt mellow, melting into the cushions, now soft and luxuriant. The room had been transformed. We were in a cave, with a flickering light, messages from the changing shadows appeared on the walls. I sat trying to interpret them out loud. I thought that some of them were in Latin. I read the Latin inscriptions out slowly to the group. 'Look at your man trying to show off,' said Rob. 'Fucking Academy boy.'

The night stretched out into this long, luxuriant night of pleasure. All the cushions, cheap and stained, were now made of soft yielding velvet. I looked round at my friends, some giggling, and some tracking their hands in space, some following the colours up and down the walls. But then suddenly, and without any warning at all, the door swung open. A tall figure in a long coat stood there aghast. Everybody giggled at the joke, somebody was dressing up, nobody stirred, but my heart was racing with the unexpected nature of this sudden spectacle. Then the lights went on and somebody shouted that it really was his aunt back early. All I remember was trying to get onto my feet and the pushing and shoving as the rest tried to get up as well. We stumbled down the stairs and onto the street. She was shouting after us. I half ran one way, my heart pumping louder than I had ever heard it, the others disappeared into the dark. The rain stopped, and I paused to get my breath, the puddles were now emerald green. I had never seen anything so beautiful; I can remember them to this day. I stamped in one and the splashes, like radiant sparks caught by the streetlights, hung in the air. I stood there in the empty street, jumping into puddles, staring at magical patterns of light, giggling like a child.

A sapphire black taxi glided up beside me. Somebody was obviously lost. Maybe they would like to trip out, that was my one thought. I wanted to be kind. After all, I had still one tab left to share. I treaded carefully over the ground, rolling now like the deck of a ship. There were two other men in the taxi with red balloon faces that might pop. I leaned towards them, unsteady on my feet, trying to hear what they wanted, trying not to giggle. One man reached out and grabbed me forcefully by the collar.

'Thanks mate,' he said. 'I thought I might fall.'

'What's going on?' the man said. He looked at me carefully.

'Your man's taken something,' he said to the others. 'There are terrorists roaming the streets of Belfast, and this little fucker decides to wander through this magic wonderland of North Belfast.' They were all laughing and I was still giggling. Helpless. I got slowly and carefully into the taxi. That was the beauty of the Troubles – when you have enemies, you automatically, it seems, have friends or allies that are prepared to look after you.

Nobody said a word on the drive but I watched every street light changing colour and glowing towards the heavens like searchlights. And there was Rob waiting for me. He was watching his hands make shuddering afterimages in the air.

Rob had arrived a few months earlier from somewhere on the Shankill and taken over our little gang, or tried to. I met him for the first time with two of his friends at a pop concert at Dunmore greyhound stadium. I remember how trendy he looked, compared to the rest of us. There was just something about him. My friend Bill and I were with two girls that we didn't know well. Rob didn't know them, but maybe vaguely recognised them, but perhaps was jealous that we were with someone. So, after a few minutes' innocuous chat, he pulled a hatchet out of his denim jacket and swiped it at Bill's head. Bill ducked and then stumbled and fell off this balcony, and just lay there moaning. Rob just walked off as if nothing had happened. The next night he turned up at my house (I had never given him my address) and he spent an hour chatting to my mother while I was out running. I have to this day no idea how he got my address. 'What a lovely boy,' my mother said, when I got back from my run, the sweat dripping off me. 'He's got a lot to say for himself, unlike you. You just stand there sweating and not saying anything.'

He used to threaten me by saying that he would tell my mother that I always put two bars of the electric fire on when she went out.

Rob was unpredictable. One night at the corner he turned on one of his old, long-term friends and in some 'play fighting' dragged him around the street for about twenty minutes. The lad was in a head lock and dragged backwards along the grimy street. One of his shoes came off, I'll always remember that, I wondered if I should pick it up. It just went on for so long that it made the whole thing really humiliating to even watch. But it was his unpredictability and his knowledge that facilitated his ascent in our little gang. At that time in Belfast unpredictability could be a serious advantage. Life was becoming much more violent on the streets, and if people were wary of you this gave you some advantage. You never knew what they might do. He had a dangerous authority about him. You didn't challenge his statements or plans. And he knew how to get things; he could be a great facilitator.

He told me that he wanted me to go shopping with him. He could tell that I needed some new gear. So we started in Burtons in Royal Avenue and made our way around a number of shops. Shops where I would look longingly through the windows. Rob shoplifted a pair of Wrangler jeans and a leather jacket. To celebrate we went to the Wimpey for lunch. I told that him that I had no money. Rob said that you don't need money. We had a double cheeseburger each and two cokes right in the middle of the restaurant. When we finished Rob asked for the bill, and then told me to go with him to the toilet. Rob had stolen a waitress' pad of bills and he simply wrote a bill out for two coffees. 'You hand it over at the checkout,' Rob said. It was a test of sorts. Of course, I did what I was told. Rob just stood glowering at the lady behind the checkout and threw a few coins onto her little table. She said that she had seen us eating. Rob denied it. 'I wouldn't eat the crap in here if you paid me,' he replied. Incredibly, she let us go without paying for the meal. The Wimpey became our regular Saturday treat – we never paid.

To bring the two sides together in the Troubles, the local church had decided to organise a disco for the local Protestants and Catholics. I could sense that this was going to be trouble, especially because two of the local senior churchwardens were going to act as security. They were both very nice, my mother always said, young Christian men, well out of their depth for this sort of thing, I thought. Rob seemed to feel that he had something to prove to them all, and within ten minutes of the disco starting, he chose some random Catholic boy to knock out with one punch. He just walked up to him and punched him. The force made him fall on top of the lad. Craigy said that the lad wouldn't have gone down in the first place if Rob hadn't fallen on him. The churchwardens ran around switching on all the lights and the disco finished very early.

But my most vivid memory of that awful night was some Catholic lad that he trapped down by the bottom gate of St Mark's Church. The lad was terrified. Rob punched him and his lip started to bleed. He had gone white as a sheet. Craigy insisted that Rob should let him go.

Nobody seemed to want to go home that night. But I could sense that there was going to be serious trouble. You sometimes need this sixth sense on the street. We walked down the road in a large group, my heart beating fast because I knew there was something I wanted to do. I wanted to ask Carol out, but I was beaten to it by my friend Jim. He did it in a sort of joking way, and she wasn't sure that he was being serious, but I was politer, and she said 'Yes'. I drifted off home happy.

'Home early tonight,' my mother said. 'How was the disco?'

I heard the next morning that later that night Jim had got stabbed in the knee and had to hijack a bus to take him to hospital with the knife still stuck in his knee. Everyone remembers that. It was a joke for years about the corner. Was that important to how life unfolded? He went on to join a Protestant paramilitary organisation, the Ulster Volunteer Force. He got eight life sentences for his part in six murders and two attempted murders.

I've no proof as to whether his stabbing and any humiliation that followed it (because he was stabbed in the knee which is strangely a very funny image) played any role in his future path but I've always suspected that it did. Perhaps that's why I was destined to become the type of psychologist who believes that personal experience (and your memory of it distorted with time and perhaps through unconscious purpose) has a major role to play in making us who we are, and that even political action (and what could be more political than the Troubles in Northern Ireland) seemingly borne out of higher level constructs, ideology, religion, social class, group allegiance, and perceptions of deprivation and injustice can sometimes be traced back to small, almost incidental moments that make a difference in one's life, like ending up with a knee cap with a knife hanging out of it and the resultant humiliation in front of the whole street. And the resentment, of course, like Dostoevsky's non-hero, the resentment that you can't shake off and stays with you.

But that was all in the future. All I knew after that night of the disco in the church hall was that life was getting darker. It was my friend Bill who said that if he had the chance, he would go across the water to university. We had gone for a walk up to the television aerial on Divis. 'Don't stay here, it's going to get a lot worse,' he said. I hadn't seriously contemplated it before then, but I respected Bill's opinion. And my emotions about the place and my bonds to it were being shaken. That sacred spot, which I clung onto in my memory and in my imagination, that place for my father and I, the White Brae, our Sunday walk down by the wee shop, was where three unarmed and off-duty soldiers from the 1st Battalion of the Royal Highland Fusiliers were murdered. It was a honey trap operation – they'd all been drinking in Mooney's in Cornmarket and invited to go to a party. One was seventeen, one was eighteen, and one twenty-three. The two youngest were brothers. They were apparently shot while relieving themselves, two were shot in the back of the head, one in the chest.

A twelve-year-old boy found the bodies. He said, 'We were just standing there frightened and not knowing what to do. Two men came along and one of them touched the head of a man who was lying over another. His head fell back, and the man said, "They are stone dead."' The coroner later commented: 'You may think that this was not only murder, but one of the vilest crimes ever heard of in living memory.'

This was the happy, familiar place where the memory of my father was rooted, and now it was a horrible, dark place of depravity and murder, and misguided intention and action. And I was starting to see some of that misguided action very close to home, and left contemplating how it might feel in the cold light of day. The youngest soldiers were my age. I was being given a chance at a life. I applied to universities across the water and kept my fingers crossed for my A level results that summer as I worked on a building site in Chippenham.

My results turned out to be amongst the top two or three from my school. I got grade As in maths, physics, and chemistry (in the days when A grades were extremely uncommon), but not in Russian, which was the subject I had to study in my spare time. That was the one result I dwelt on and dreamt about. The only one.

Chapter 2

Abandoning and abandonment

Figure 2.1 Copyright Bill Kirk/Belfast Archive Project

> Such [linguistic] principles . . . are a priori for the species – they provide the framework for the interpretation of experience and the construction of specific forms of knowledge on the basis of experience – but are not necessary or even natural properties of all imaginable systems that might serve the functions of human language. It is for this reason that these principles are of interest for the study of the nature of the human mind.
>
> Noam Chomsky (1972: 42) Problems of Knowledge and Freedom

The work and the arguments of the linguist Noam Chomsky shook psychology to its very foundations. His attack on the principal paradigm of the day, 'behaviorism', led to its terminal decline. Chomsky stressed the creativity of human language, the way that we effortlessly produce sentences that we have never heard before and we do this using a set of rules or linguistic principles. He argued that the study of these principles might well tell us something profound about the human mind and how it operates. It was an exciting time to study psychology, particularly in one of the best-known behaviourist departments. It was especially exciting if you didn't mind confrontations. The skirmishes had now moved from the streets of Belfast to the seminar rooms at the university, and I was enthralled. When I dared to critique Chomsky a number of years later, the hand-written letter that arrived from MIT made me gulp. Chomsky was more than prepared to stand his ground and I was now in the firing line.

When the vultures come

So what is my earliest memory from childhood? Psychologists sometimes ask you that – in films at least, when they're trying to get a glimpse into your soul. Try to imagine this then. When I was in my cradle (it's a dark, confined space with a strange sort of lighting, I can't remember where in the house exactly), a bird, a vulture actually, came down to me, and opened my mouth with its tail. It struck me several times on my lips with this long tail of his. Bizarre, but that's why I remember it so vividly. It's just not what people expect – a bird in the house, a vulture, its tail against my lips. Some just say accusingly that it's not a memory at all, no infant or child could have dreamt that and where did the vulture come from anyway? In Belfast of all places? Really? Indeed, some people have suggested that this is some sort of fantasy transposed back into the past. They even say that all early childhood memories originate in this way – they only arise much later and are an expression of present wishes and desires, perhaps unconsciously held, which are then transposed back, rather than being any sort of genuine fragment of the past. But what could it possibly mean? Is it somehow connected with the innocence of suckling where we take our mother's nipple in our mouth? But it's a vulture using its tail to open my lips – what's the significance of that?

I'm reminded that in the hieroglyphics of the ancient Egyptians, the mother is represented by a picture of a vulture, and that a Mother Goddess had a vulture's head. It was also believed in antiquity that vultures were impregnated by the wind. Fathers were not necessary for propagation and the birth of the young in the case of vultures. I am, therefore, in this odd, disquieting memory of mine, the baby in the cradle, the vulture-child with no father. My father is not dead or absent, I never had a father – a father was never really necessary for me. I have thus no male figure to identify with, no role model. I've only got a mother; I've only ever had a mother.

But there's something else that might be highly relevant here – the Mother Goddess with the vulture's head in Egyptian hieroglyphics had a body in the shape of a phallus. So, if you understand the symbolism, and know a little about the hieroglyphics of Ancient Egypt (well documented in my childhood encyclopedias, of course), that might suggest that it was a phallus that was striking my lips with its tail.

So, what does all this mean? You might well conclude that this wasn't my earliest memory at all but an erotic fantasy of mine as a child – homosexual in content and form, percolating through these encyclopedias of mine somehow, the encyclopedias that I took to bed every night. Where else would this vulture stuff come from? I'm mother-fixated, they say, the father role model rejected. It's highly symbolic, indicative of an emerging (homo)sexuality and requiring all of my early learning and scholarship to allow the 'memory' to be couched in symbolic images with several layers of meaning and psychological distance. It was troubling, worrying, revealing, either way it told me too much about myself. If it were true, that is.

But this isn't my earliest memory, this is Leonardo da Vinci's earliest 'memory' as analysed by Freud in his famous psychobiography of the great artist (Freud 1910/2001), trying to understand da Vinci's character and his 'pathological' sexuality – his homosexuality, that is. I read this book as I prepared for university and felt a little confused.

My earliest memory is different to this, it's me falling into some nettles at the top of our street, crying, and being abandoned, left alone to cry, but maybe only for a short time, I can't tell. That's the point about some memories, time isn't accurately encoded in them, a moment can become like hours, hours like a moment. My dreams, as I recall them, usually involve me falling, flailing to the ground. Falling and abandonment seem everywhere in these early experiences of mine – real, imagined or dreamt. There are no vultures, no tails tapping on my lips, no hidden hieroglyphic messages, nothing requiring great scholarship and erudition to describe, let alone to experience.

Freud draws upon his great interest in antiquity to analyse Leonardo's story, true or fantastic, digging through layers of semiotic coding to reveal the fundamental essence, but as I read this as an eighteen-year-old I thought how might this ever be relevant to me and my most private experiences, where I didn't have the learning and scholarship or depth, to either remember, or more importantly fantasise in, such disguised and concealed ways, or have the parallel learning and scholarship to even begin to interpret it, like the learned Dr Freud. My encyclopedias never went that far.

Not to mention having to deal with the anxiety that I might have got it all wrong in the first place, and somehow got the wrong end of the stick. Psychology, or at least certain types of psychology, seemed to have been borne of bravado. Freud never changed his view of the origins of Leonardo's homosexuality even when it was pointed out that Freud may have mistranslated 'nibio' in Leonardo's account as 'vulture'. 'Nibio', it turns out, is better translated as 'kite' rather than 'vulture', which would seem to leave a lot of the semiotic untangling somewhat misplaced. The whole theoretical interpretation was founded on the bird with the tail in the memory (or dream or fantasy) being a vulture. Without that, we have no Egyptian hieroglyphics, no interpretation of the bird as mother, no impregnation of the bird without a father, no phallus-shaped head, no penis tapping at the mouth, no forced oral sex, no invited oral sex, no nothing. It was a kite all along.

But Freud stuck to his guns even when his guns were seemingly pointing in the wrong direction. I would never have that confidence, the hubris to do all this. This could never be for me. And when we move from exotic recollections of vultures tapping on a baby's lips with their tail to an infant falling into a pile of nettles at the top of the street, where does that leave the interpretative process, the scholarship, the discipline, the sorts of individuals who might benefit from psychoanalytic therapy or speculation?

I suppose that I wanted a psychology that spoke to me and might tell me something about recurrent dreams of falling and early memories that were all about pain and abandonment, real or imagined. My school sent me to a clinical psychologist for advice about careers (rather than for treatment) and he recommended a specific psychology department in Birmingham University. We didn't discuss vultures' tails, just useful and important psychology that can help, practical psychology. 'Behaviorism,' he said. 'That's what they do over there; it can be very useful.' I was on my way.

My mother asked me how it had gone when she got home from the mill. 'Good,' I said, 'he suggested Birmingham University, they're big on "Behaviorism" apparently.'

'That would be good,' she replied, 'you could do with learning about your behaviour and how to behave yourself better.' We didn't discuss it much after that.

But even after months of planning, I still dreaded leaving. Carol's father gave me a lift to the boat. Carol's big grey eyes were tear-stained already on the way down the Shankill Road. My mother wanted to come along.

'Perhaps we could have a wee drink on the way back,' she said to Carol's dad, Cecil – a man who was fond of a drink himself, but only on certain occasions – the weekend, the golf club, out after work, out at lunch time with the guys from the factory, not on a week night on the way back from the docks having dispatched this boy growing his hair long, with odd views and probably odder desires, onto the Liverpool boat.

I carried a suitcase in one hand and a record player in the other. I was wearing a new suede jacket in that early 1970s style which I had bought in Petticoat Lane Market in London. I can still remember the day that I bought it and that smell in the air – that heady mix of suede, incense, and maybe something else, that aromatic, faint smell, exotic-looking women with long flowing hair, long dresses that skimmed the surface of the street as if they were floating on the surface of a lake. Wild images of abandonment, free love, new knowledge, drugs . . . who knows. Carol and I had hitchhiked to London and got dropped off in Church Street in Kensington. An impossibly handsome man walked past with long blond hair and his tight jeans tucked into a pair of knee-length pink suede boots. That was my first image of London, I thought that all of London must be like this.

We went to a free concert in Hyde Park to watch Humble Pie. We drank a bottle of red wine and I talked openly for the first time ever about my father, and my love for him. I cried in front of her, something that I had never done before with anybody. I had exposed my vulnerability for the very first time. We slept in Green Park for the weekend, she had to sneak into the men's toilets because they were the only ones open; we went around the bins of Soho restaurants looking for discarded food. It was still a magical weekend until I went to the toilet and realised that the man standing next to me was wanking furiously and staring down at me. I put mine away and walked out mid-flow.

'Fucking wanker,' I said as I walked out. He smiled back at me. That surprised me.

Carol's father was perhaps right to be worried about my aspirations although perhaps he didn't know enough about me or my character or my discipline.

We stood at the dockside, Carol's large grey eyes running with tears. I had never cried *in public* before (crying in front of Carol that one time was a very intimate act rather than a public act) and I wasn't about to start here and now, but my shoulders did heave slightly – an inaudible and virtually imperceptible twitch of sorrow, which Cecil noticed immediately. That slight heave of weakness. That slight signal of a lack of manliness. What were his last words to me? It is hard to recall exactly, but it was something like 'Pull yourself together for God's sake.' I can certainly remember the sentiment after all these years – the gist, the message, the point. Perhaps he was worried that the next time he saw me, if he ever did, that I would have transmogrified into something else, something even more frightening to his established ways. The Academy had kept me in check, but my Academy haircut was growing out already and I was starting to look less like the regimented grammar school boy – disciplined and governed by a host of external forces. It was time to find myself and discover my calling, but what was that to be? I read *Oz* and *It* and dreamt of the new freedoms ahead, hedonism, tuning in, and at least pretending to drop out, but I had only had one girlfriend who I was leaving behind on the dockside with my mother looking at her watch to make sure that she could still get to a bar in time.

'I never get out, Cecil,' she was saying, 'and all these bombs are making it worse. There are no buses running anyway. But I never got out even before the bombs. I need a wee chum to go out with, but they have all got their husbands. I've got nobody – only our Geoffrey and he's running away to leave me. He swore that he wouldn't go off to university and here he is, as happy as Larry, with that bloody record player under his arm. You want to hear what he plays on it. The words are absolutely bloody disgusting: "When I get you in a corner, I'm going to show you what it's for." You know what they're talking about in that song, don't you, Cecil?'

'I can guess, Eileen,' and Cecil flashed a look at Carol and then at me which said it all.

'Exactly,' said my mother, 'you couldn't trust young people these days, not like our day. We'd have had the arse scalped off us for that kind of carry on.'

Cecil's steely blue eyes looked straight into mine. 'You had better behave yourself,' he said, 'I'll have my eye out for you.'

I walked alone out towards the boat and looked back longingly. I climbed aboard, waved and went inside, looking for a chair for the night crossing. I had never been to Birmingham before. My mother had been once for a wedding, sometime after the war, with my father.

'Your father said that he had never seen so many hard-looking tickets in his whole life. He wouldn't want any of them.'

That was about all I knew about Birmingham – that it was very large, that it was full of hard-looking tickets and that it had a good psychology department, at least according to the one source that I had consulted. What type of psychology I didn't know. Nor did I know that in fact there were different schools of contemporary psychology (as opposed to historical psychology like Freudian psychoanalysis), and that the psychology department that you chose to study in could have a very significant influence on what you might learn and, therefore, on your ultimate destiny.

The boat journey was rough, and I slept very little. I felt slightly nauseous. I rang Carol from Liverpool. She told me that my mother and her had indeed gone for a drink on the way back to some bar on the Shankill. She heard, for the first time, my mother's little bar room jest, 'I lean [as in 'Eileen'] on the bar, you buy the drinks.' I'm not sure that Cecil would have been very amused by this. They bumped into my Uncle Jim, my dad's brother, in the bar. I always think of my Uncle Jim a very emotional man. But this judgement is based on just a single event. When my father died, my mother invited him round to our house to go through my father's clothes to see what he might want and what might fit him. I remember him going upstairs into the front bedroom and looking into the big wardrobe. He touched the lapel on my father's good suit and burst out crying and went back downstairs without saying a word. His face down, buried in his hands. He hovered at the front door before finally saying: 'I'm sorry Eileen, I can't take anything of Billy's.' I noticed that he smelt of drink. I did my usual trick of trying to control my emotions and pretended to watch TV. His crying set my mother off, so I turned the TV up. My mother ran upstairs shouting 'Billy'. Tears stung my eyes, but I wiped them furiously, little rivulets of tears getting halfway down my cheek and leaving no mark with my guarded attention. 'I'm going out,' I shouted upstairs and went down to the corner. A few of the lads were down there hanging about outside the chippy.

'How's about ye, Beats?' my friend Colin said. 'How's your mother?'

'Very upset,' I said as nonchalantly as I could.

'She's bound to be,' said Colin, 'my mother is still upset, and my father died three months ago. Have I just seen your Uncle Jim? He's just gone into Paddy's for a few jars – to calm his nerves I bet, and I'm sure he's going to get full.'

That night of the Liverpool boat he got full again. He was driving a bin lorry at the time and according to Carol he couldn't remember where he'd parked it. I don't think that Carol's father would have been very amused at a man losing his bin lorry because of the drink.

I fell asleep on the train to Birmingham and woke up at New Street station. I got a taxi to my hall of residence and walked into my new home. I picked the bed by the window and fell asleep. A few hours later I was woken up by an English accent – an accent that I'd never heard before, the West Country, Devon. It was my roommate, Mervyn. I had been to England before to stay with my Aunt Agnes and Uncle Terence in Chippenham during the summer holidays, working in various labouring jobs and building sites, but I had never seen the likes of this – a farmer's son with a thick syrupy accent, with an honest and open face. He was a geology student and I told him that I was going to study psychology. His only comment was that there would be lots of girls on the course; geology, he said, however, would unfortunately be full of men. He was very envious. That night he introduced me to his friends from geology and we had a formal dinner with the guest speaker, Joe Grimond, the leader of the Liberal party. One of his friends was called Nick – his father was a judge and he came from the Channel Islands.

This was a little different from my own social background. He offered me Pernod in his room. 'It smells like aniseed balls,' I said. I had never drunk Pernod before and after a number of glasses I walked unsteadily to the meal. I don't remember much about the meal itself, but I have a vague memory of picking up a bread roll. I don't know what happened next, but according to Mervyn and Nick I threw the bread roll at Joe Grimond while he was speaking, and he had to duck to avoid it. After that, I think I passed out. But I heard somebody ask who the 'oik' was.

My next recollection is being woken up in the morning by a tutor who asked me angrily and repeatedly where my bedclothes were. I had no idea. The window was open, so I suggested that perhaps they were on the lawn outside. He asked me if I was joking. I noticed that my suede coat, my pride and joy, that jacket which had taken two trips to London to find, was lying curled up in the corner of the room. It appeared to be covered in vomit. This coat was the symbol of my new beginning, and now it was ruined. My tutor explained slowly that I had disgraced myself and that if I hadn't just got such good A levels then they would be kicking me out of the hall immediately.

My punishment, however, was much worse than this. It was my realisation that you don't change just like that – I had acted just like one of the turn-of-the-road gang after a few free drinks, causing some sort of commotion, as we liked to call it – just for the craic. I felt a deep shame and embarrassment.

But the craic had now gone, and I lay there wondering when I was going to be shown around the university psychology department and what they might make of me and how I might behave there. Behaviourism was very much on my mind, as was my own behaviour.

Beyond freedom and dignity

The psychology department smelt of sawdust soaked in acrid rat urine. It hit you as soon as you went into the building. Psychology shared a building with Mechanical Engineering ('Mech Eng' in my new uni argot) and the whole ground floor was dominated by a large glass box full of, well, rats. It was an operant conditioning lab devoted to that most influential theory of human behaviour, at that time. The theory was that human behaviour was a series of responses governed by the stimuli that preceded it and the stimuli that followed it. The theory was as simple as that. Those stimuli that followed behaviour either reinforced the behaviour and made it increase in frequency (positive reinforcement), or made it decrease in frequency (negative reinforcement). If you want to understand why people act in particular ways, all you have to do is analyse and understand these behavioural contingencies. Those who believed in this form of psychology were called behaviourists or

Skinnerians after B.F. Skinner – the most radical and influential exponent of the theory. They whispered his name – it felt, at times, like a cult.

Our behaviourism lecturer was the most charismatic teacher that I had met up to that point in my life. He was called Derek. He had a warm, friendly smile and seemed to lecture without any notes. Early on he told us the long story about the Gardens of Versailles and the automata whose every movement was influenced and directed by the movements of the public moving through the gardens. There was a series of trigger points. His point was to show that even real-looking movements, something close to human movement to naive observers, could just be automatic responses requiring no consciousness, no cognition and no planning; just automatic responses to certain stimuli in the environment.

This theory held that in order to develop a science of psychology you don't need to study all of that inner stuff that goes on inside the mind – too messy, too hidden, too subjective – you just need to study the input and the output. It was a form of psychology that conceptualised people as 'black boxes'. There might be something going on inside the black box, but there was no way of seeing what it is, no reliable way that is, it would all be far too subjective.

I thought at the time that this may be true of some behaviours that we might execute without much thought, but surely not all behaviours and in one tutorial I plucked up enough courage to say this. 'No,' said my lecturer, 'all behaviour, even language itself. It's just a set of learned responses, learned through association.' The theory influenced all branches of psychology. The Birmingham Psychology Department had a very strong clinical sub-division and in that sub-division they were now 'treating' homosexuality using this theory. They were using aversive conditioning to 'cure' homosexuality like it was a disease by associating positive reinforcement with looking at pictures of women and punishment when looking at pictures of men. So, people would be strapped into a chair and they would be shown images of nude females and then images of naked men would pop up. You could look at these but after variable delays (so you were never sure when) you would be punished with an electric shock – a 'mild' electric shock as stressed by our lecturer, 'at least not too bad'.

But one of our radical social psychologists said this did nothing to 'cure' homosexuality, it just made them impotent and they could no longer get aroused with their object of desire. 'Ask these so-called clinicians what *cure* means in this context,' he suggested conspiratorially. I wanted to also ask them what 'homosexuality' meant in this context. David Bowie had just released Honky Dory. It was the first time I had ever seen a man in make-up and a dress. We went to see him at the town hall, it was a small audience, we were transfixed by this image of gender fluidity, although that is a much more modern term, they called them 'gender benders' then, with the emphasis on 'benders'. My friends Rosalind and Sharon suggested that my friend Nick and I should dress as women and enter a beauty contest at the university. It was part feminist critique, 'it's outrageous that they're still holding beauty contests in this day and age', part high jinks, part the two of us dressing up for the first time in full make-up and drag. Rosalind and Sharon insisted on doing the make-up. It was a bit over the top, and we both felt very uncomfortable when we sat there in the chair in the dressing room and saw what they had in mind for us. We needed some dope to help us relax. Nick had long, wavy blonde hair and I had long dark hair in ringlets down to my shoulder. We were giggling uncontrollably. All I remember about the evening is Shaking Stevens, the guest artist that night, coming into the changing room and seeing Nick and I get ready, and leaving immediately, saying that he wouldn't get changed with us two in the room. I was wondering if suspect feminine dressing, or dressing up, even in special circumstances, might be enough to see me strapped into those therapeutic electrodes.

But maybe you just need one person to push you to dig a little deeper. I was charmed by Derek, the Skinnerian in the department, and B.F Skinner, at least, offered something radical. I needed something radical, something to change my world. His focus was on behaviour and just that – he wanted to 'follow the path taken by physics and biology by turning directly to the relation between behaviour and the environment and neglecting supposed mediating states of mind' (1974: 20). In other words, for his 'scientific analysis of behaviour' he wanted to exclude all consideration of states of mind, feelings, plans, intentions, character or personality. How radical his views actually were jumped off the pages when I first got a copy of *Beyond Freedom and Dignity* from the university library.

In the first chapter, he started writing about things that I felt that I knew something about, but they came with a warning. His argument was that mental constructs about feelings, thoughts and intentions are mere inventions to explain behaviour. Thus, he argued 'the possessed man does not feel the possessing *demon* and may even deny that one exists. The juvenile delinquent does not feel his *disturbed personality*. The intelligent man does not feel his *intelligence* or the introvert his *introversion*' (1974: 21).

But the problem was that I wasn't quite sure that I agreed with any of it – I *felt* that I was intelligent and (on occasion) somewhat introverted. According to some, I was a juvenile delinquent and felt 'different' in many social and educational contexts, and (according to my mother at least) I was at times a man possessed (and certainly when faced with the challenges of Tolstoy on a card table in Legmore Street with all the chatter going on in the background). These did not feel like mere inventions, but were they critical to my actual behaviour? Well, I suspected that they were in a way. I felt possessed and angry before I threw my Russian vocabulary book around the room to make my inner state obvious to my mother and any bystanders. We felt like delinquents because that's how others were treating us and therefore occasionally we had to act up to play the role, to show what we were capable of, to do what was expected of us. My own personal feeling (that word again) was that these other feelings might well be instrumental in initiating the action, or inhibiting the action. Skinner was saying that I could do what I like, but I wouldn't be contributing to any 'scientific analysis of behaviour' if I wanted to contemplate these feelings.

Skinner's approach was to put all of the emphasis on the environment. All behaviour was learned or conditioned, but not conditioned in the way that Pavlov had talked about it – he had developed a form of stimulus-response psychology in which all behaviour was regarded as reactions to various stimuli (so-called 'classical conditioning'). Skinner argued that there is another form of conditioning where what happens next is crucial, that is, after the behaviour is emitted,

> it is now clear that we must take into account what the environment does to an organism not only before but after it responds. Behaviour is shaped and maintained by its consequences. Once this factor is recognised we could formulate the interaction between organism and environment in a much more comprehensive way.
>
> (1974: 214)

Skinner argued that once we do this we can formulate a science of psychology in terms of 'operant behaviour' (behaviour which operated upon the environment to produce consequences) then (in terms of its practical import) we can (and must) change the environment and the consequences to change behaviour.

His radical view was summed up in one short phrase – we shouldn't be giving credit to someone for their own good behaviour or blaming them for their bad behaviour, rather, 'A scientific analysis shifts the credit as well as the blame to the environment' (1974: 27).

At one level, I liked this perspective because I felt that I had spent a life being seen as somehow blameworthy when no one understood the context or contexts in which my behaviour was operating. Skinner was saying that we need to change the focus away from the individual to the environment, away from personal causation to environmental contingencies.

But, if the truth be told, I was both alarmed and overwhelmed by how difficult this process might be – this search for contingencies of positive and negative reinforcement, which increase the frequency of the act or decrease the frequency of the act, seemed incredibly complicated and confused. So how do you identify positive or negative reinforcement? Can you do this a priori or can you only do this when you see what's actually happened to the behaviour – was it repeated or not? In other words, could something be an aversive stimulus for one person and a form of positive reinforcement for another? Was the whole thing not therefore completely tautological? Positive reinforcement leads to an increase in the behaviour. How do you know that it's positive reinforcement – because it is associated with an increase in behaviour. And what about individual differences – differences in character and personality, differences in thoughts and feelings, differences in plans and intention, which were to be excluded from this new science. Why did my friends find shouting at Squeak so rewarding? Why didn't I? Why was it positive reinforcement for them and not for me? Don't forget you're not allowed to look inside the black box. Why did Rob find dragging his friend along the street by his neck in front of us all so rewarding? Why didn't we find this ritual humiliation a source of positive reinforcement?

Another great focus of Skinner's theory was his entrenched argument that we should move away from punishment as the principal mechanism of environmental control to positive reinforcement. He says that we are locked in a world where punishment, or the threat of punishment, is the preferred mode of controlling behaviour: 'a teacher threatens corporate punishment or failure until his students pay attention; by paying attention the students escape from the threat of punishment (and reinforce the teacher for threatening it)' (1974: 33). Skinner argues that the great (and perennial) pursuit of freedom by human beings is to attack those who arrange aversive conditions and to weaken or destroy their power.

As a group back there on the street my friends rallied against anyone who arranged aversive conditions for them, whenever possible. But Skinner also wrote 'the aggressive behaviour is not necessarily directed towards the actual source of stimulation; it may be "displaced" towards any convenient person or object. Vandalism and riots are often forms of undirected or misdirected aggression' (1974: 34). Again, this seemed to make some sense (why did we fight working-class Catholics? Why did we fight each other?) and yet the devil was well and truly in the detail, and the detail, particularly the details of actual behaviour in real situations, was completely absent from his account.

Had Skinner made close observations of displaced aggression? Had he studied vandalism and the behaviour of gangs? Had he studied how failing pupils fight back against the system and act out towards their teachers – the masters (literally they assumed) of so much aversive conditioning? I saw no evidence of this, no evidence of any detailed studies of actual behaviour on any of these topics, and this was from the so-called master of 'behaviourism'.

The intellectual dilemma – the sheer impossibility of unravelling behaviour in everyday life in terms of identifying relevant contingencies – was revealed most starkly in Skinner's chapter: 'The Design of a Culture'. In the context of writing about the design and redesign of cultural practices, he writes about the moral panic in the US at the time about the nation's youth, he dismisses the familiar academic and media analyses (framed as a 'spiritual crisis', 'alienation', 'generalised despair' etc.), instead asserting the 'troublesome *behaviour* [in question] is not actually described and nothing that can be done to change it is mentioned' (1974: 144). But his solution was not to go into the field to actually describe the troublesome *behaviour* in question, nor was he inclined to offer any detailed descriptions of what the behaviour might be like, but instead to build and establish a controlled environment – a Skinner box for rats or pigeons to be put under the microscope as their environmental contingencies (always involving food) were manipulated in various ways in terms of what he calls 'schedules of reinforcement'. That was his solution.

He says without any sense of irony or intellectual modesty:

> a culture is very much like the experimental space used in the analysis of behaviour. Both are sets of contingencies of reinforcement. A child is born into a culture as an organism is placed in an experimental space. Designing a culture is like designing an experiment; contingencies are arranged and effects noted. In an experiment we are interested in what happens, in designing a culture with whether it will work.
>
> (1974: 151)

I sat staring at my white rat in the Skinner box in that department in Birmingham with that smell of rancid rat pish in the air. It made my eyes water. There was nothing in that box in front of me except a lever to press to get some food, and lots and lots of rat droppings. It had been there for a while, my rat was a very slow learner, and perhaps a very nervous rat, but according to Skinner, I should only blame myself for this, I was the master of the external contingencies – I was responsible for the slowness of the learning, that is, not its evident nervousness (although perhaps that too). My reward must not have been delivered fast enough or consistent enough. I thought of my childhood gang and the multiplicity of contingencies from every level up in that great aversive edifice in which we found ourselves, your pal who could turn on you, your parent who got angry in grief, your neighbour chucking bricks over the wall because she'd nobody else to take it out on, your teacher stroking your hair and then getting the cane out to make your thumbs swell, the other gangs, the police, the state, the system, from within, from without.

I wanted to shake Skinner so hard that his glasses would fall off and land right in that box in front of me. He would have called it 'displaced aggression', no doubt, I probably would have called it something else. But I was always worried that I was just not getting it, that there was a depth here that I was missing. Derek just kept smiling at us all and pointing us towards these Skinner boxes as if the truth lay there somewhere in that box in front of us. I didn't have the confidence, of course, to question it fully, so I learned how variable-ratio reinforcement schedules predict the way that gamblers keep on putting money in slot machines when they are not winning, and how superstitious behaviour arises (it accidentally precedes reinforcements) and how you just need to reinforce visual attention to children in class to make them committed pupils. Single little threads to hold onto in order to prove the usefulness of my calling.

But I didn't really believe it.

Empty lives

But I was being drawn into psychology more and more (despite Skinner); elsewhere it seemed to be posing deep questions about the world around us (although still not as deep and important as Dostoevsky, it seemed) and allowing me to see common, everyday things in new ways. What is linguistic knowledge and where does it come from? Do parents teach their children to talk? Are we born with innate knowledge? How important is experience to how we think? Does our language affect how we think about the world? Names came flooding in – Chomsky, Fodor, Whorf – all with a certain glamour about them. Chomsky, in particular, was in direct opposition to Skinner and I liked that. They both couldn't be right.

I was particularly taken with the work of Benjamin Lee Whorf in those first few months, a linguist with potentially profound ideas about human experience and human psychology (I realised early on that psychology had only vague and sometimes very thin boundaries with neighbouring disciplines – most of the influential figures were linguists or, perhaps more accurately, linguistic philosophers). Whorf argued that all higher levels of thinking are dependent on language and that the structure of the language one habitually uses influences how you understand and experience the world around you. I remember one telling sentence by Stuart Chase in a foreword to one of Whorf's books: 'The picture of the universe shifts from tongue to tongue.' I loved that sentence.

Whorf studied the Hopi Indian of Arizona and their language and speculated about how this language with its particular syntax and grammatical categories might connect to their everyday behaviour in comparison to our more familiar languages (which he called 'SAE' or 'Standard Average European – language like English, French and German). In SAE we have a three-tense system for describing time – past, present and future. We use nouns to describe aspects of time – summer, winter, January, February, morning, noon and night, just as we use nouns to describe other objects out there in the world. There is no difference in how we use these particular nouns – they have the same properties as other nouns and, Whorf argued, this affects our perception of time. Our thinking about time becomes 'objectified'. We say 'tomorrow is another day', 'I'll start my work on Tuesday', 'Friday is always a good day'. But Whorf wrote: 'Without objectification, it would be a subjective experience of real time i.e. the consciousness of "becoming later and later" – simply a cyclic phase similar to an earlier phase in that ever-later-becoming duration' (1967: 142). Tomorrow is never another day – it's just the present getting later.

Hopi has a different way of describing time – they don't use nouns to describe things like 'summer' and 'winter' but something akin to an adverb, such that 'Nothing is suggested about time except the perpetual "getting later" of it' (1967: 143). The consequence of this, according to Whorf, is that there is a 'coordination' between their language system and their everyday behaviour. 'A characteristic of Hopi behavior is the emphasis on preparation. This includes announcing and getting ready for events well beforehand, elaborate precautions to insure persistence of desired conditions, and stress on good will as the preparer of right results' (1967: 148). When time is a series of objects, lying next to one another in a row, you can always leave preparation off to the next day, or the day after that, because after all tomorrow is a new day, the first day of the rest of your life and all such clichés.

I suppose that it was one of those small shocks that make you question life around you, to see things differently, to wake up. I felt that I was waking up out of a long slumber.

And I loved Whorf's own story of how he got into this area of research. I loved the *personal* narrative. He worked for a fire insurance company and had to investigate the circumstance surrounding how fires start. He realised early on that it was not necessarily the physical situation per se that was critical in causing a fire but the *meaning* of that situation for the individuals involved. One important aspect of this meaning is the linguistic description they (and we) apply to the situation. We behave very cautiously near petrol drums, for example, but very differently around 'empty petrol drums'. Once we label them as 'empty', we behave much more carelessly around them – we smoke next to them, we toss cigarette butts into them, we cause these fires inadvertently because we apply a certain linguistic label to the situation. 'Empty' as a term, Whorf argued, is inherently ambiguous. It can mean (1) 'null and void, negative, inert' or it can mean (2) 'more or less empty – but with stray rubbish, gas etc. still inside'. In Whorf's words: 'The situation is named in one pattern (2) and the name is then "acted out" or "lived up to" in another (1), this being a general formula for the linguistic conditioning of behavior into hazardous forms' (1967: 135).

I liked the idea that one's personal story could feed into psychology and the fact that Whorf's early experience working in insurance helped him develop his ideas and sent him off on his anthropological mission to Arizona and the Indian tribes that resided there.

There was a little common room on the first floor of the Psychology building and I loved the coffee machine that dispensed milky coffee into a plastic cup, and we'd sit discussing Whorf and Chomsky and what influences how we think. We never had coffee at home in Belfast – it was too expensive my mother always said. Our biggest treat was to drive out to the airport on a Sunday night in our wee car to watch the planes take off and have a milky coffee. To this day that is what I associate milky coffee with – sitting watching planes and my mother saying: 'Billy, wouldn't it be great to get into one of them planes and fly somewhere else, somewhere away from here.' Now I drank a milky coffee out of a plastic cup every morning and afternoon, basking in my new sophistication as I discussed Skinner's view of the human condition and thought about Whorf and how my language might affect my perception of my world.

Carol sent me food parcels every week, usually with at least one chocolate cake, but occasionally I got the odd letter from my friends from the turn-of-the-road. But they had little to say and I was always surprised by how illiterate the letters were, if I'm honest. They couldn't spell. I wasn't used to them writing, I was used to them talking. They were funny and coherent, in their talk, but the letters weren't. My mother kept me updated on the comings and goings – our local pub 'Paddy's' was burned to the ground, and the shooting got worse. Someone shot through the window of the Rocks' house, two doors up. 'They opened up with a sub-machine gun through the front window,' my mother told me. Some IRA man from Ligoniel had shot someone at the corner and it was said that he had escaped through the Rocks' house and over the yard wall (presumably using the foot in the toilet door technique that I had practised). Some Protestant gunman had shot through their front window as a reprisal. Nobody was killed, thankfully.

My mother liked to tell me what my friends were getting up to: 'Your pals are all walking around in balaclavas, like the fella in the big picture.' My new university friends were nice Jewish, middle-class girls like Rosalind and Sharon from Prestwich in Manchester. They were very conscientious and very concerned to do well. We would sit in the library together in the afternoons and they would be surprised at how quickly I would finish my assignments. One of them gave me a 'woolly pully' because I didn't have any jumpers, just vests bought from Kensington Market. They told me that I needed to study harder – this wasn't school. My brother had always said that I was the biggest swot that he had ever met, that's why I did well but, of course, this is all comparative. Now I reappraised this view of myself. I seemed to be working fewer hours than everyone else but somehow more effectively. I was the top student.

'It's getting worse around here. You're alright,' my mother would say. 'You're out of it. They're trying to drive the Protestants and the Catholics apart,' she said. 'There are little ghettos springing up all over the place. All of our Catholic neighbours are leaving. It's terrible, you don't know what it's like. And some of your pals are in the middle of it.'

'Which ones?' I'd ask.

'How would I know; they've all got their masks on. But some of them are very polite to me. They say: "How's it going Mrs Beattie? How's your Geoffrey? Is he still living across the water?"'

'Surely you could tell who it was by the way they speak?'

'No, you can't,' she said, annoyed at the question, 'it's harder than you think. I think that they disguise their voices and those balaclavas interfere with their speech anyway. They've started marching up and down the road, you want to see them all. Some of the officers are English, they've got lovely voices, very serious. But you can tell the ones that were in the CLB with you, they're the ones that can do all the marching correctly. They do their right-turns and their about-turns properly. Some of them just do it arse about face.'

I'd ask her about specific individuals, but it was hard to get a straight answer.

'Sure, nobody goes out anymore. There are road blocks everywhere with these guys in masks manning them. But some of them give me a big wave when they see me, and I give them a wee wave back. I just play along. You wouldn't know who you were waving at.'

There was a pause. 'You're alright, you're out of it. You always told me you wouldn't go, but as soon as you did your A levels, you were off. Just like that. Your brother's off climbing and working in Scotland, and I'm all on my own.' She was starting to sob. I stayed silent, waiting for her to regain her composure.

'So how are your studies?' she asked eventually.

'Great,' I said.

'So, what have you been learning so far?' she asked.

'Well, I've learned that we are a lot like rats, at least in terms of our behaviour, or our operant behaviour as we call it.' I had Derek's voice in my head.

'Really?' she said, 'and who exactly is "we" here?'

'Everybody,' I said. 'The whole world.'

'Me included?'

'Well not you personally, but everybody.' I said it slowly as if talking to a non-behaviourist or a child.

'Do you mean everybody else apart from me?' You could hear the anger rising in her voice. There was another pause.

'Jesus, I've never heard so much shite in my life. Some people are like dogs, I'll give you that – all bark and no bite. Shout at them and they run away with their tails between their legs. Some of the jokers in the paramilitaries are like that. But rats – never like rats. Have you ever seen a rat close up? I know you and your pals used to throw bricks at rats down Harmony Hill just to get them to run in different directions all over the place. But have you seen them close up? In my street there's lots of rats now. I have to live with those bloody things day in, day out. They're sly, cunning little creatures. To be honest a few of them do remind me of your mates, one or two of your mates were sly little shites. But you're not all like that – you've got many faults but you're not sly, mainly because you're a terrible liar, and you're definitely not like that. You tell your lecturer from me to try a new approach. Tell him that you are a Belfast man and a good wee Ulster Prod. You may have your faults, we all do, but one of them is not being a rat.'

I tried a different approach. 'Have you heard of the Garden of Versailles?'

'No, I bloody well haven't,' she said 'but I have heard of the Hanging Gardens of Babylon. It's one of the Seven Wonders of the World. You used to get me to ask you these bloody lists every night from your encyclopaedias just in case you forgot them. The Hanging Bloody Gardens of Babylon – I don't even know where bloody Babylon is. So, what's in the Garden of Versailles?'

'Automata,' I said, trying to sound profound.

'What the hell are automata?'

'It's like an automatic person that just reacts. They've no mental life or consciousness – just behaviour and stimuli and responses that govern a reaction. They're just like people in a way. If you do something and you get what we call a "reinforcement", like a pleasure, you do it again and again.'

'Just like people, you say? What sort of people? Who's like that? We've all got behaviour and a "reinforcement", but we've also got something else. We all know what's right and wrong, that's why we go to church. Otherwise we would just do what the hell we liked. I know some women who are like these "automata" – good things, we used to call them in the mill. They would go with anybody. They might be, what do you call them, automata. Just out for the wee reward, the wee bit of pleasure. But most of us think of God and the Bible and what we should do and that's why we don't just do what the hell we like. Tell your lecturer that we're not rats and we're not the other things – good things – easy women, good things, just governed by what comes next. Do you understand me?' There was a long pause. 'Do you still go to church?' she asked.

'Not really,' I said 'I've been too busy.'

'You're too busy for church? Keep on the way you're going, and you'll end up as one of those automata things – out for number one. Just out for what's around the corner.'

'But I want to do well,' I said.

'You will do well; you've always done well. Ever since your Aunt Agnes gave you sixpence for every exam you passed, and you kept passing every exam, you had these chocolate boxes all over our front room full of sixpences. Your brother used to come home from his climbing and wonder why there were boxes full of money spilling out all over the place. He asked where you got it. He asked whether you were going shoplifting all the time. You'd do anything for those sixpences.'

'But is that not just rewards and stimuli and responses?'

'Of course it isn't,' she said. 'You wanted to study, it was something in you. The sixpences just helped to bring it out. Don't just go along with all of this stuff they're telling you over there. Remember who you are, Son – you're nobody's mug. I never had to make you study in your back room. You've got something; you've always been a bit different. But you have some absolutely fatal weaknesses. You're always trying to please people – to tell them what they want to hear, even when they're talking shite. If they're talking shite just tell them that they're talking shite, but do it in a polite, English sort of way. There must be a word for it. Let me know when you know that word because I'd like to use it as well. Too many people talk shite. Just tell them that in their own language. Then they'll understand.'

New horizons

I do have real trouble remembering any sad or depressing moments from my time as an undergraduate, at least while I was at the university. My home, however, back in Belfast was being bombed mercilessly. And that Christmas of my first year, I got a job over the Christmas vacation as a postman. It was an interesting time to be a postman in Belfast, because it was the time of the letter bomb, and householders would step away from the door when you pushed a letter or package through. You could hear them scrambling to get away behind the locked door. I would be shouting 'sorry' at them, as I pushed the letter through and onto their mat. One postman, I recall, had his arm blown off when he picked up his mail for the day.

I had long hair which fell in ringlets down to my shoulders, tight jackets with furry colours (fake fur, of course), vests and loon pants with suede stars sewn onto them by Carol. I would heave the postbag over my shoulder. My appearance and that bag made me the subject of some interest to any passing army patrol. They would pull up beside me.

'Are you a fucking girl or an excuse for a boy?' they'd say. 'What's in the bag?'

'Post,' I'd reply.

'Don't try and be cute with us. What sort of post?'

'Letters and stuff.'

'Letter bombs?'

'Well, your guess is as good as mine.'

'Up against the fucking armoured car, we're going to search you.' I always thought that they called the armoured car 'pigs' for good reason.

I met up with Duck that Christmas for a drink. I went to see him in a local drinking club near the turn-of-the road. It had security on the door, some man I didn't know, and perhaps not even local. There was a metal cage to walk through. There were a lot of people walking through the metal cage to get into the smoky, bare room behind it. Our local pub Paddy's had been burned to the ground, and this now was the only alternative. My hair was now in ringlets down to my shoulders, a bit like Marc Bolan's I thought, I was wearing a pair of green boots from Kensington Market, and a woman's fur coat that made me itch.

The security man looked shocked at my appearance, and clearly didn't know me or recognise me. 'Members only,' he said. I explained who I was meeting there – he knew Duck alright.

'Step back, and let the regulars through,' he said. He nudged me with a little force against the motley brick wall to allow others to get past, and glanced at me suspiciously every now and again.

'No drugs allowed,' he said, 'you know that, don't you?'

I had only been away for a few months, but such was the speed of change that it all felt a little strange. So I stood there in the cold until Duck arrived. He was obviously a regular and he'd already had a drink. He was greeted warmly by the security man.

'Jesus,' he said turning to me, 'what's happened to you?'

We sat there in the gloom of the bar and he spent an hour or so telling me how bad things were getting and how I was well out of it, and how they were getting 'organised'. We laughed about old times and he asked me what I was learning across the water – I said 'psychology'.

'We need some of that around here,' he said. 'It's all going fucking crackers.'

We talked about all the good old days of our youth and all the old characters – Charlie Chuck, Roseanne, Squeak.

'Oh yeah, he's still about,' said Duck, 'and his shoes still fucking squeak. They're probably the same shoes!' We both laughed so loudly that serious men from the next table looked at us disapprovingly. Men probably from the organisation, the local paramilitary organisation, that is.

'You don't want to mess with those boys,' said Duck. 'They're at the centre of things, if you know what I mean. They're the big men around the corner now. They're the new Mr Bigs.'

I reminded him of that night all those years ago when I'd been caught by the policeman and brought home for tormenting old Squeak. And Duck started to laugh and then stopped himself, as if remembering something.

'You didn't even shout at him,' said Duck, 'it was the rest of us. You just ran the wrong way. Did you get a hiding from your da for it?'

I told him that my father never hit me, ever.

'Fuck me,' Duck replied, 'how did he get you to do all that homework then? He must have been bribing you.'

I asked him what happened in Squeak's old abandoned lorry, when someone had relieved themselves one night, and he laughed again.

'That was me,' he said. 'You might have guessed it. Do you want to know the truth? I thought it was empty. I wouldn't do that in a place that was being used – in somebody's home.'

And I have to confess that at that precise moment Benjamin Lee Whorf popped right into my mind, from nowhere. It was just that word 'empty', like some magical stimulus it reminded me of something. So this is what education does to you, I thought. It takes you out of one social context and in an instant it lifts you up and lays you down in another, without any volition or control on your part.

I sat there in that heavy fugue of cigarette smoke in that grimy drinking club, thinking of our little pristine common room in the university and our discussions about linguistic relativity and whether words and language affect how you think, or vice versa, and wishing (if I'm totally honest) that I was back there. But I was still staring at Duck, nodding away at his every word, encouraging him to tell his story, but with a secondary dialogue going on in my mind.

'I didn't think he was still sleeping in it at the time,' said Duck, 'there were some old filthy sheets lying about, but I thought it was abandoned – even by him. I was a wee bit nervous when I was in the lorry because I thought he might come back and catch me in it, so I had to go. So I did a big shite right in the middle of it. I didn't do it to upset him. I'd no choice. I didn't want to dirty myself on the way home.'

I laughed in the way that you do, when you don't really mean it. But he took it as sincere.

'The good old days,' he said, 'all the craic, great days.'

Of course, I was sitting there wondering whether Duck really *thought* that the cab was 'empty' merely because of how he he'd described it, or whether it was just something, just a term, to justify his actions. In other words, I was wondering whether language, and the use of that term, wasn't the cause of the behaviour, as Whorf had maintained, but a consequence of his behaviour, a social consequence, part of that great social act of justification. And this in turn made me wonder about Whorf's other work and whether those people who had caused those fires back in New York City by tossing their cigarettes into empty petrol cans were really fooled by that term 'empty', and its potential inherent ambiguity, or whether they too were justifying their careless and consequential actions only after the event (I've written a lot about this issue and the nature of justifications since then from ordinary people trying to deal with trauma, see Lee and Beattie 1998; Beattie 2018a, to violent doormen, see Jordan and Beattie 2003, and even trophy hunters, see Beattie 2019). Duck could now see that I was a little distracted.

'There's always something going on in that auld head of yours,' he said, 'I hope it's not about how you can avoid getting the next round of drinks in.'

I also wondered about where my personal narrative might leave me when it came to psychology. I suspected that there might never be any possibility that I would ever be able to write about the things that I had observed in my life in psychological monographs and papers. The world might not yet be ready for Duck and Squeak and disputes about linguistic relativity and the meaning of the word 'empty' in abandoned lorries, with a pile of shite sitting in a bed, waiting for its occupant to come home from a night imbibing buttermilk. But this was the life I knew – indeed the only life that I knew.

Duck and I stayed in the drinking club until closing time, and I walked home to the sound of distant gunfire, distant because it wasn't at the turn-of-the-road, it was perhaps a mile away, maybe less. It was loud.

My mother was waiting up for me when I got home, upset that she hadn't been invited out, even to that wee club with bare walls and the unfriendly man on the door.

But soon it was time for me to leave again with more tears. And my mother alone in that house, in that street, in the Troubles. I had to get back to my studies.

When I was younger I used to pray to God every night to help me with my exams so that I could do some good in the world. I'd never internalised any of my success, it was always down to God. But now I started to take credit for my work as the A pluses came rolling in and Rosalind and Sharon and all the other nice Jewish girls looked on in amazement. People wanted to work with me on projects and I became very popular. I got 100 per cent for my first year statistics exam – apparently the mark had never been awarded before – and First Class marks in all my exams, including my subsidiary subject – physics. The Head of the Department of Physics, who coincidentally was from Northern Ireland, but not, of course, from my specific part of the province, asked to meet me to try to persuade me to drop psychology and study physics instead. I was second in physics (to a student from Hong Kong) out of a very large cohort of students, including the single honours students. 'You'll never be satisfied with psychology,' he said. I got a faculty prize from the Faculty of Science and Engineering at the University of Birmingham at the end of my first year – I was told that it had never been awarded to a first year psychology student before. I loved the work and my new life but started to dread the calls home when I rang my mother every night. I was worried about what I might hear about the violence on the streets and how she was getting on. Her loneliness was heart-wrenching, I had to harden myself.

That summer, I stayed with my Aunt Agnes and Uncle Terence in Chippenham and worked on various building sites. Carol worked in a laundry and my mother came over to visit. Towards the end of the summer my brother Bill invited Carol and I to visit him in Chamonix where he would be climbing with his girlfriend Kathy. We were thrilled. This would be our first taste of a different sort of life, the glamorous world of Chamonix.

We'd never been abroad before, so we hitchhiked to Dover and spent the night sleeping in a culvert by the side of the road in Calais before setting off to Paris. I was used to sleeping rough, my friends and I would hitchhike to Newcastle in County Down at the Easter holidays and sleep rough for a few days and eat cold creamed rice out of tins, and drink Mundies wine at nights; Carol wasn't used to any of this, however. We had sleeping bags but no tent on our trip to France, and she was terrified of spiders so she asked me to do a sweep of the culvert before she'd go to bed. The hitchhiking in France was bad and it took us many days to get to Chamonix. We arrived in the middle of the night. It was very cold, much colder than either of us had anticipated, a hard frost on the ground. My spontaneous idea was to go to the youth hostel and knock them up to see if we could stay there for one night. Then we could meet up with my bother the next day and stay with him to fully experience this other glamorous world of jet-setting men and girls with the deepest imaginable tans, which we had only seen in magazines and in my imagination in Bill's stories: sitting round fancy continental tables in their show-off climbing gear, sipping Chartreuse and eating fondues, and thinking of tomorrow's great adventures on the snow-capped hills of the Alps lit delicately and exquisitely by the setting sun. (I had only ever climbed with Bill in the Mourne Mountains just by Newcastle in Northern Ireland, which could be quite beautiful, if it wasn't raining too hard, but they were far from glamorous.)

After some time of incessant but polite knocking, the warden came to the door. Carol glanced at me, I'll always remember that look of fear and uncertainty, as the door creaked open. The warden peering out from behind the door looked slightly startled. 'Pas possible!' he exclaimed. We looked incredibly dishevelled, my ringlets were down past my shoulders, my hair was slightly matted from sleeping in drains all the way from Calais to the Alps, like two orphans possibly begging for food in the middle of the night, and quite lost. He opened the door wider and stood there in his stripy pyjamas, open-mouthed as Carol tried to explain in her halting French (but still better than my socially conditioned, anxiety-ridden attempt at any French) what we were doing there. He shrugged ostentatiously, accompanied by a loud and long blowing sound right into our faces. It felt wet, almost as if he was deliberately spitting on us. He announced that the youth hostel was full, and said 'pas possible!' for a second time but even louder, not so much as an exclamation of surprise this time, more as a determined and unambiguous sign of rejection. He was telling us to go away immediately. We hesitated only because we had nowhere to go. Carol had slept in drains for me, I wasn't going to ask her to freeze to death as well.

The warden, embarrassed by our immobility, asked to see our youth hostelling cards. Carol tried to explain again in her halting French that we weren't actually members of any youth hostel association even in our own country. His look of surprise was exaggerated and theatrical as if he didn't want us to miss the fact that he had never come across anything in his life quite like this before, and it was followed immediately by a look of quite real and spontaneous disdain. He shooed us away in that Gallic and very French style and slammed the door shut. We just stood there for a few minutes and Carol started crying again (but tried to hide it). We had nowhere to go; it was freezing.

But suddenly I had a plan, I tried the other doors of the youth hostel until I found one that hadn't been locked properly and we sneaked in. After quite a few minutes groping along in the dark, we found what must have been the ski store and we decided to bed down there for the night, so we unfurled our sleeping bags. However, I like to brush my teeth every night so I announced that I needed to find a bathroom. Carol decided to come with me, she didn't want to be left on her own. The next minute we were caught by the warden. I can still visualise that light of his torch turning a corner in the corridor, like some ominous searchlight from a Second World War film; I can still feel my heart racing.

'C'est pas vrai!' he shouted and made an exasperated gesture that was unmistakable in any language.

He pushed us along the corridor and told us to get our belongings. Carol was crying. He opened the side door of the hostel (which we had accidentally left ajar) and a blast of icy cold wind blew in. He hesitated and said that we could stay for one night only but that 'the girl' would have to go to the girls' wing. He led her to another building while I stood in the dark waiting for him to come back. He shone his torch up and down me, he could see that I was quite dirty because we'd been standing by the side of the road for many days hitchhiking (and sleeping in drains), and he very kindly asked me whether I would like a shower. He led me with his torch to the shower room and then shone his torch into where the showers were. I went in and got undressed. The warm water felt heavenly as I washed my hair. When I got out of the shower he was just standing there holding my towel, which shocked me a little. He asked whether he could dry me. He made a hands-apart rubbing gesture, just in case I couldn't understand his French. I declined as forcefully as I could without angering him. 'Non, merci,' I said politely and with an attempt at a smile. He stood in front of me, watching me dry myself. I thought that it might be because he was French.

He said that he would let me sleep for nothing in his room, he said it in French and then in English, he was obviously in a hurry, but I said that I couldn't sleep without Carol. He said that he would fetch 'the girl', oddly he never called her by her name – I always thought that Whorf might have something to say about this as well. Carol and I got into my sleeping bag on his floor. He poured something into three small glasses, and offered us each a drink. 'Schnapps,' he said. I knocked mine back, Carol told me afterwards that she had trouble swallowing and couldn't drink it. It took her ages. I fell straight to sleep. I have, after all, always been a good sleeper. Carol wasn't quite so lucky, and she said that for several hours the warden would come and shine his torch on me while she pretended to sleep. I didn't ask which parts of me the torch might be illuminating.

The next morning we went to the British campsite to find my brother only to discover that he had moved on to somewhere else in the Alps where the climbing might be better. The other British climbers had no idea where he had gone to. So we were stranded in Chamonix with no money, and no way of getting home (Bill had assured me that we didn't need money and that he'd look after us), and we had to go back to the youth hostel to face the warden. We explained the situation and he just smiled. He was in complete control now. He agreed to let us stay for nothing as long as I slept in his room. We argued for a long time, eventually he made a loud 'huuufff', and gave in. Although the youth hostel was 'full', he gave us a dormitory room to ourselves, but said that he would come to check each night that we were staying safe. Every night we'd put a chair against the handle so that he couldn't get in. You could hear him trying the handle and swearing under his breath. This was not the first taste of the glamorous jet-set lifestyle that we'd hoped for.

We survived in Chamonix by me shoplifting food from the local super-market which we shared out with fellow hostellers. I found a way of climbing into a posh open-air swimming pool during the day so we developed a golden tan over the four or five weeks we were there. My mother would have been very proud of my tan. We were well-fed and a golden brown. Sometimes, it seems, you do learn useful things when you come from the gutter. You learn how to survive for a start.

The warden thought we would never leave, and we only did when Carol was caught trying to pinch a chocolate yoghurt. That was her one and only attempt at theft and she just looked so guilty that the checkout lady asked to look in her bag. She then asked to look in my bag. I can still hear her voice, 'Voilà!' as she pulled out a packet of saucisson. 'Voilà!' as she pulled out a packet of cheese. 'Voilà!' as she pulled out a whole roasted chicken. 'Voilà!' as she pulled out a pair of roller skates. I had been getting slightly carried away. The skates weren't for me, but for a fellow youth hosteller who said that he was desperate to do some roller skating. They confiscated my passport.

We walked to the fountain in the centre of Chamonix; Carol was very upset. To cheer her up, I bought her a crepe with chocolate sauce (bought with my very last francs). We were just about to start eating them when the gendarmes went past in their blue van and waved my passport at me. They asked us to get in the back. They took us to the gendarmerie and started filling in some paperwork. Perhaps it was Carol's big grey, tear-stained eyes, which were always beautiful even when they were filled with tears, per-haps even more so, but they stopped mid-sentence, and one said in broken English that we needed to leave Chamonix and indeed leave France imme-diately. That was the deal. They ripped their form up. They gave us a lift to the hostel and waited for us. We packed quickly and the warden waved us off. He looked very sorry that I was going but I suspect that he was slightly relieved as well. It had, after all, been a very long stay – we'd been there for well over a month. I think that he was getting a bit anxious pretending that the hostel was full. The gendarmes took us to the border. I think that it's called being deported.

Carol had loved most of the trip but found some parts very stressful, whereas I thought that it was a bit of an adventure, and when she dropped a bottle that she was carrying as she was getting off the ferry at Dover, she burst out crying and told me that she never wanted to see me again. But I knew that she didn't really mean it.

Bill just laughed when I told him the story, when he finally returned from his own adventures. I never even bothered to ask him where he'd been. I also explained that on that first morning there, I'd reconnoitred Chamonix to find places to sleep rough if the warden had kicked us out. It was a hollow with a stream meandering through it, peaceful, hidden, perfect I thought, but Carol was horrified; it was full of spiders. I told Bill that I knew that somebody else had stayed there because there was an empty can of Heinz baked beans sitting just by the river, as if someone from the UK had opened it and eaten the beans cold before moving on. Bill told me that it was him on his first day there.

We had independently found the same heavenly spot to live temporarily. That's brothers for you. There's this bond that cannot be broken.

Plato's legacy

I was flourishing in my new-found freedom away across the water, after the vacation ended, and my discipline kept me focussed. Carol joined me at the start of my second year (despite what she had said) and we lived incredibly happily in an overcrowded student house in York Road in Edgbaston, just off the Hagley Road. Everyone was in couples, so we had twelve students to one bathroom. Many of them were art students and you would hear them sawing at night as they turned the ramshackle furniture in their rooms into ramshackle furniture without legs – 'interesting objects', they said, maybe even works of art. There were always queues for the toilet, which meant that we were always late leaving for the two- or three-mile walk to the university. I wore platform shoes or, worse, platform sandals made out of bright shiny PVC and I would stalk into university in the mornings, at some speed. It's very hard to walk in platform soles at a fast pace but even harder to turn without going over on your ankle. I would look for turning circles on the pavement or keep heading in the wrong direction.

I was enjoying my studies greatly, I never talked about my background, and I was encouraged enormously by several of my lecturers, who took a real interest in me. One in particular was Ros Bradbury who clearly saw something in me in a way that I hadn't experienced before. She was interested in the psychology of language and for that reason I gravitated towards that area more and more as a potential area for my dissertation. The more I read, the more I became interested in language as the real intellectual battleground for psychology, particularly the work of the linguist Noam Chomsky and his theories of deep and surface structure. This work offered me something that behaviourism didn't.

Chomsky first came to the attention of psychologists when he published a highly critical review of a book on language by Skinner (*Verbal Behavior*

1957). It was a devastating critique. Skinner put all of the emphasis on experience and learning (an 'empiricist') as the basis for all human knowledge although his book, *Verbal Behavior*, was very short on actual examples of observed language behaviour in context. His examples were made-up examples to illustrate various theoretical points. Chomsky was a 'rationalist', believing that much of human knowledge was innate, and in the case of language defining for the species.

Skinner had argued that utterances should be viewed as learned responses to specific situations. For Skinner there was no essential difference between the general laws of learning and the laws that operate when learning language, as we've seen. In reply, Chomsky (1959) claimed – and no one has seriously disputed since – that the majority of utterances we produce are ones we have never spoken in precisely that form before, and that the majority of utterances we hear and comprehend without difficulty are ones we have never heard before. Think about the sentence 'The psychology student, fronting as a postman, shook his bag to make sure there were no bombs in it, but only a soggy jammy dodger fell out.' Almost certainly novel (but I should check), completely comprehensible, and interestingly true. I still don't know where the jammy dodger came from.

Chomsky (1957, 1965) lay great emphasis on the *creativity* of language and creativity, he argued, can only be explained if we credit speakers not with a repertoire of learned responses (as Skinner did) but with a repertoire of linguistic *rules* used to generate or interpret sentences. The body of rules constitute the *grammar* of the language – their job is to assemble or describe grammatical sentences, as judged by speakers, and only grammatical sentences. Because the rules generate rather than simply describe sentences, this type of grammar is known as a *generative* grammar. He also insisted that the grammar must explain why speakers feel some sentences to be 'related' and others 'unrelated'. So, the following four sentences are all rather different in form, yet speakers accept them as closely related:

1   The postman with long hair shook the bag.
2   Did the postman with long hair shake the bag?
3   The bag was shaken by the postman with long hair.
4   Was the bag shaken by the postman with long hair?

In contrast, two sentences may be identical in form yet feel very different, for example:

5   The postman with long hair is difficult to wash.
6   The postman with long hair is reluctant to wash.

In 5, the postman is on the receiving end of the wash whereas in 6 he's the one doing the washing (I was thinking of the youth hostel again).

Chomsky's solution to this dilemma is to propose that every sentence must be given two grammatical descriptions. The *surface structure* of a sentence is its description as produced but underlying this is a separate *deep structure*. Sentences 1 to 4 concerning the postman and the bag have different surface structures but the same deep structure, and that, Chomsky argues, is why they are felt to be closely related. In contrast, sentences 5 and 6 about the postman's attitude to washing have the same surface structure but different deep structures and are therefore felt to be distantly related. Sentences like 'Striking miners can be dangerous' are ambiguous because they permit two or more different deep structures. In this case, three different deep structures – 'Miners who are on strike can be dangerous', 'It can be dangerous to strike miners' or 'Miners who are striking (in appearance) can be dangerous'.

Chomsky developed a theory of *Transformational Grammar* to get from the deep structure to a speakable sentence – different transformational rules would generate each of the sentences 1 to 4 from the same underlying deep structure. Chomsky's goal was

> to characterise in the most neutral possible terms the knowledge of the language that provides the basis for actual language use by a speaker-hearer. . . . No doubt, a reasonable model of language use will incorporate, as a basic component, the generative grammar that expresses the speaker-hearer's knowledge of the language.
>
> (1965: 9)

This theory inspired psychologists to try to find evidence of the psychological reality of transformational grammar in terms of how individuals go about producing and understanding sentences and gave rise to the discipline of *psycholinguistics*. There were many exciting things about this work. It highlighted that behaviourism with all of its self-imposed constraints could not get close to understanding or explaining that most human of everyday activities, the use of language. Language was not just about what was on the surface, there was a deep structure and rules. It was not just a set of associative links.

But there was more than that, much more, that appealed – there was this thread linking him to Plato and the concept of innate ideas. Chomsky argued that although children make certain kinds of errors in the course of language learning (like the overgeneralisation of the past tense – e.g. 'taked'), there are some errors that they simply don't make. Consider the sentence 'The dog in the corner is hungry' (Chomsky 1972). From this we can form the question 'Is the dog in the corner hungry?' The question is how do we do this? One way, called a *structure-independent* operation by Chomsky, is to identify the left-most occurrence of the verb ('is') and move it to the front of the sentence. Very simple and it works (in this instance). Another way would be to use what's called a *structure-dependent* operation, meaning an operation that doesn't just consider the sequence of elements that make up the sentence but also their structural relationships and specifically the fact that 'the dog in the corner' is the subject noun phrase of the sentence. Using this operation, we have to identify the subject noun phrase of the sentence and then move the occurrence of 'is' following this noun phrase to the beginning of the sentence. Either type of operation would work in this first case.

But consider forming a question from the sentence, 'the dog that is in the corner is hungry'. If we apply the structure-independent rule we would end up with 'is the dog that in the corner is hungry?' which is clearly not grammatically correct. Instead, we have to use the structure-dependent rule, first locating the subject noun phrase ('the dog that is in the corner'), and then move the occurrence of 'is' following that to the front of the sentence, forming: 'is the dog that is in the corner – hungry?'

Chomsky maintained that children make many mistakes in learning language but they *never* make the mistake of applying the structure-independent rule in forming questions despite its evident simplicity and the 'slim evidence of experience' for the child to learn one rule rather than the other. He argued that these types of operations are examples of formal linguistic universals or principles of universal grammar – a sort of innate knowledge of language that we all share and are not dependent on our upbringing and our earliest verbal interactions. In his book *Problems of Knowledge and Freedom*, he wrote:

> Such principles . . . are a priori for the species – they provide the framework for the interpretation of experience and the construction of specific forms of knowledge on the basis of experience – but are not necessary or even natural properties of all imaginable systems that might serve the functions of human language. It is for this reason that these principles are of interest for the study of the nature of the human mind.
>
> (Chomsky 1972: 42)

Competence in language, knowledge of language, binds us all together. We are all born, regardless of class or position, with these innate principles, with this innate knowledge, hard-wired in our brain. It didn't matter whether you were from Eton or from the gutter in Belfast (or not as the case might be). I felt that my life was changing; I was being drawn into the world of ideas. I felt energised and free.

Of course, it is one thing to propose a deep structure grammar for language and another to show how this operates in terms of everyday processing – in terms of the production and comprehension of language in everyday talk. This might not be straightforward. With some excitement, one night I tried to run the theory past my mother on the telephone.

'What have you been learning, son?' she began.

'Let me tell you by asking you a question. . . . How do we form questions in English?' I'd say.

'It's easy, we just do it.'

'Okay. Give me the question from "the dog in the corner is hungry".'

'Is the dog in the corner hungry?'

'Great! How did you do that?'

'I just asked the wee question like you told me.'

'Okaaaay. Now give me the question from "the dog that is in the corner is hungry".'

'Is that wee dog over there hungry?'

'Well, that's not quite correct, is it?'

'What's wrong with it?'

'You didn't use the right words.'

'I did use the right words for *that* question. If it's sitting in the corner all on its own, it's going to be a *wee* dog that's feeling a bit sorry for itself.'

'What I mean is – you have to form the question without using any other words, and only use the words in the original sentence – *all* the words in the original sentence.'

'Like a wee puzzle, you mean?'

'Ah, not really. I'm trying to expose your innate knowledge. Have you heard of Plato? Chomsky? Er, I thought not. There are things that we know without having been taught them. Just try again.'

'I can't remember the original sentence.'

'"The dog that is in the corner is hungry" – just form the bloody question,' I sounded impatient, irritated, like a wee patronising snob. These ideas were changing how I thought, I wanted her to understand.

'The dog's probably not bloody hungry now,' she replied and hung up.

Carol asked me what was wrong, as I hurled 'Reflections' across the room. This momentary loss of control meant that the book lost several pages and never fully recovered.

But my mother's confusion did highlight an important, indeed critical point, about the argument and its validity. Why do we assume that in order to form the appropriate question that we have to start with the simple active affirmative declarative sentence? It's critical to the theory of transformational grammar but is it true? This is a proposition that I accepted readily to join the Chomskian club, to be part of that new discipline of psycholinguistics. You have to accept certain statements as fact, but perhaps the antecedents of questions have a different origin. After I calmed down that night, I started reflecting on this.

But I must say that I loved the intellectual battle between Chomsky and Skinner, between Chomskians and Skinnerians, it was like a fight between two gangs, each with its own charismatic leader. It reminded me of past times. And I knew which gang I wanted to join.

There were lots of studies which looked at the comprehension of language and the effects of so-called transformational complexity on that, but far fewer looking at linguistic production. With language comprehension, it's easy to determine the input to the brain for the task – the sentence that you're presenting to the experimental participant. But what's the input when it comes to production? – the input, the thought that gives rise to the speech itself is so, well, mysterious. How does what William James called 'The intention of saying a thing' (James 1890) become transmuted into a specific plan for the actual linguistic output? But one psycholinguist called Frieda Goldman-Eisler had written a brilliant little book called *Psycholinguistics: Experiments in Spontaneous Speech*, published in 1968, in which she analysed where speakers pause when they are talking and demonstrated that these pauses (brief periods of silence which she called 'unfilled' pauses) are connected to the planning of speech – many (but not necessarily all) seem to have a cognitive function. Some, for example, occur at grammatical boundaries to mark out clauses and sentences and may be functioning to segment the speech for the listener. Perhaps a close examination of these pauses could hold a clue as to how language is planned and assembled and provide some insight into the psychological reality of transformational grammar (or not, as the case might be). This was a topic that would occupy the next ten years of my life, as I attempted to watch the human mind in action and uncover the deep and mysterious relationship between thinking and language.

I kept my excitement and my decision to myself, as I planned my dissertation. Whenever I rang my mother, I noticed that her pauses were getting longer and more frequent. Sometimes, there was just silence at the end of the phone.

Another problem with the working class

I came up with a very simple idea for my undergraduate dissertation. Frieda Goldman-Eisler had ingeniously shown that the location of unfilled pauses in speech of durations above 200 milliseconds could be used as an indicator of ongoing cognitive activity. These brief periods of silence were longer and more frequent when speaker performed a more cognitively demanding task like the interpretation of the point of a cartoon (fairly sophisticated cartoons taken from the New Yorker) rather than a description of the pictures in the cartoon, and pauses are reduced in frequency and duration when speakers repeat a message or plan it in advance. In addition, they seemed to show some regularity with respect to both syntactic and semantic units in speech. They could potentially tell us something about how linguistic utterances were generated in real time. They could tell us whether transformational complexity from Chomsky's theory had any psychological reality from a *production* perspective. They could tell us whether syntactic clauses were the primary unit of linguistic production, again following on from Chomsky's theory, or whether meaning and semantics (and semantic units) dominate the production process, at least in terms of the occurrence of these pauses for cognitive planning.

But, of course, there's a problem in all of this. How do we all know that *all* pauses have a cognitive function? Are some surplus to requirement? We have to pause to mark out syntactic boundaries for listeners – for example at the ends of sentences. But is there any cognitive activity going on during those pauses? Clauses, after all, are critically important structural units from the perspective of linguistic theory. And what happens if people just pause for no good reason at all, just for a mental break or just because they're bored? Goldman-Eisler herself had not really dealt with this issue. Indeed, when she had written that 'pauses are an index of cognitive activities' (Goldman-Eisler 1967: 122), she seemed to be implying that this is true of all pauses.

My simple idea was to use an operant conditioning paradigm to either 'reward' or 'punish' silent pauses, to try to make them increase or decrease in frequency to see what happens to the speech itself. Is the temporal structure of speech (the pattern of silence and phonation) flexible? Can speakers produce the same coherent speech with fewer pauses in the 'punishment' condition? You can see that I was attempting to introduce something from Skinner – the basic operant conditioning paradigm of following certain behaviours (in this case unfilled pauses of a certain duration) with positive or negative reinforcement. I may not have subscribed to the whole Skinnerian theory and this grand attempt to reduce the human condition (including freedom and dignity) to principles of operant conditioning, but I did see some merit in using operant conditioning as a tool to explore the hidden mechanisms of the human mind.

The experimental procedure itself was very simple. The experimental participants had to tell nine stories over nine trials from a beginning that was provided. A voice-operated switch operated a light when the participant paused for 600 milliseconds, the light remained on until a further speech sound was emitted. In one condition (the 'reward' condition) the participants were told that 'A green light will come on when you are doing particularly well. The green light means "good". The more frequently this light comes on, the better is your telling of the story. . . . It is important to note that every aspect of your story-telling will be assessed. The actual content and how you tell the story are both taken into account in your assessment.' In the second condition (the 'punishment' condition), the experimental participants were told that 'A green light will come on when your performance is judged to be poor. The green light means "poor". . . . The more frequently this light comes on, the poorer is your telling of the story.'

In other words, the positive or negative reinforcement was the *apparent* evaluation of the stories, and the reinforcers occurred at certain critical points. They were not dependent on the content of the speech at all, merely on the basis of silent pauses of a certain duration. The subjects in the study presumably assumed that some sort of real-time computer analysis was evaluating aspects of the content of the stories and feeding the evaluation to the light switch. The content of the speech was assessed and all words transcribed and counted, and all unfilled pauses (periods of silence) and filled hesitations like filled pauses ('ums' and 'ahs'), repetitions (repeated words or syllables), false starts (where a speaker starts a construction, abruptly stops and starts again), and parenthetic remarks (common words and phrases with little apparent content – like 'you know', 'I mean', 'sort of') analysed and counted, and marked on the transcripts.

So what did I find? In the reward condition, unfilled pauses greater than 600 milliseconds in length (the critical value for the light to come on) increased in frequency by about 25 per cent by the final conditioning trial; in the punishment condition, they decreased by 35 per cent by the final 'punishment' trial. In other words, the pause structure of spontaneous speech can be significantly modified through reinforcement and punishment of unfilled pauses of a pre-selected duration using visual stimuli defined in particular ways. And very interestingly, these changes occurred in the apparent absence of participants' awareness of the actual experimental contingencies. The participants did sometimes notice that the light (the reward or punishment) came on when they weren't talking but they seemed to assume that the light was responding to something that they had said before the pause. In other words, behaviour can be modified without conscious awareness of the mechanisms of change even in this simple situation.

The punishment condition was, of course, of particular interest. If all pauses are used for the cognitive planning of the speech, then how can speakers continue to produce coherent speech of similar quality with fewer of these 600 millisecond pauses (an average of 35 per cent less)? The answer seems to be that speakers used filled hesitations, like repetition, false starts, filled pauses ('ums' and 'ahs') and parenthetic remarks (like 'you know'), to compensate. Filled hesitation (but particularly repetition) significantly increased in the punishment condition in the critical trials.

This simple study did tell us something about unfilled pauses in speech and their flexibility and function. If you imagine that the manipulation, a light signalling good or bad, is analogous (in some respects) to what happens in everyday talk when listeners actively signal their response to what we're saying through various visual and vocal back-channels (head nods and 'yeahs', brief flashes of interest or boredom), then it suggests that context and particularly social and evaluative context can affect these pauses. It also tells us that we might need a broader definition of hesitation pauses to include the filled varieties if we want to build models of linguistic production using hesitations. These filled pauses and repetitions started to fill the silent pauses to ward off the negative and punishing green light.

I became excited by this work as an undergraduate and aware of the connection between the social situation (and the importance of social contingencies) and the cognitive aspects of the generation of spontaneous speech. In other words, the connection between the social situation (and all of its constraints) and thinking. Ros Bradbury had real faith in me and my abilities. She left me to it. I never discussed my social background with her, I never talked about the Troubles, or mentioned my friends who were now popping up on the front pages of newspapers. I had a strong Belfast accent but she may have thought that was just how every person from Belfast sounded, and that it wasn't some sort of a stigmata.

Carol and I invited her for dinner in our room and that was our first dinner party, at an old battered oak table in front of the gas fire with a poster for Lou Reed's 'Transformer' on that wall and that indelible image of the male model with the cap and the huge erection in his blue jeans, with 'Vicious' playing in the background. The swelling was rumoured to be a banana, and perhaps a nod to Andy Warhol, the manager of the Velvet Underground, but it was a very odd shape for any banana that I had ever seen. I had smashed a mirror (by accident) some months previously, and the fragments were stuck in a haphazard fashion above the fireplace, so that when you looked at yourself in them it gave you a disjointed and fractured image, a sort of twenty-first-century schizoid man theme. Maybe more than a nod to Captain Beefheart ('Mirror man, mirror me; Mirror than, mirror me; Mirror man, mirror than, Mirror land, farther than' – I think they were the words). It looked ridiculous. I apologised about the state of our student house, but there was no embarrassment in my apology, not even about the smashed mirror and the Captain. These after all were student digs, reflective of a temporary state, they were meant to be dingy. Legmore Street always seemed to be a reflection of us, our family; that's what I saw in people's faces.

Ros was a good conversationalist, and when Carol went downstairs to make the coffee, she told me that I reminded her of her husband who had been an anthropologist and who had died a few years earlier. I never asked her to elaborate because I was slightly embarrassed, but I think that she liked my passion when I talked about my work, I think that was it. She commented that she had taught in Africa while her husband was doing fieldwork out there and that the biggest problem that she'd found with these new students of hers was that they wanted to accept everything that they read in academic books and papers as gospel, without ever questioning it, and completely uncritically. She seemed to be implying that this would never be my problem. It was a subtle enough message.

She suggested that I should apply to do research for a Ph.D. and I applied (with her encouragement) to Oxford, Cambridge, UCL and Sussex, which were considered the best psychology departments in the country. Her husband had studied at Oxford (I believe); Ros had a friend who was a Dean at Sussex. So I applied tentatively with details of my undergraduate dissertation and was shocked to be invited for interview at all four. Indeed, I was offered places at each of them, and chose Cambridge because my potential supervisor Brian Butterworth worked in this area, and had carried out his Ph.D. under the supervision of Frieda Goldman-Eisler at UCL. We hit it off immediately. He turned up in a leather jacket: I had had my hair cut and bought a suit and wore a tie. I spent the first few minutes of the interview explaining that I never wore ties in real life, not since I left the Academy. I talked about my dissertation and how I would extend it. He liked my interest in the detail of experiments, in the numbers, I think that he recognised that it would complement his own academic skills. I could have worked with Ann Treisman at Oxford, the future wife of the Nobel Laureate Daniel Kahneman, who was charming and clearly very clever, and again very interested in my empirical work as an undergraduate, but I always felt that I made exactly the right decision.

I then had to apply to a college at Cambridge and I chose Trinity. It is, of course, the greatest and most prestigious college at either Oxford or Cambridge. More Nobel prizes than France (such a Trinity cliché), six British Prime Ministers (all Tory or Whig), several kings and future kings of England, Edward VII, George VI, Prince Charles, great scientists, artists, philosophers, mathematicians, historians – Sir Isaac Newton, Lord Rutherford, Niels Bohr, Lord Tennyson, Lord Byron, Sir Francis Bacon, Bertrand Russell, Wittgenstein, Charles Babbage, G.H. Hardy, Lord Macaulay, G.M. Trevelyan, E.H. Carr (and, of course, a whole host of Soviet spies, including Kim Philby, Guy Burgess and Anthony Blunt art historian and Surveyor of the Queen's Pictures, although his extra-curricular activities weren't known at the time). It was like choosing Belfast Royal Academy all over again. All of the colleges at Cambridge were so far beyond my expectation and experience, I thought to myself why not aim for the best, and then disappointment would be easier to deal with. I waited to hear and worked towards finals on my undergraduate dissertation and on an extended assay on a critical appraisal of artificial intelligence as an approach to language understanding. And I read more widely.

I discovered that I wasn't alone in being interested in pauses in speech and what they might tell us about the planning of language. One of my other lecturers suggested that I might like to look at an important book called *Class, Codes and Control* (first published in 1971, reprinted 1974) by the sociologist Basil Bernstein, which he explained was now dominating education faculties and the training of teachers in this country. The quotes on the cover were daunting enough, almost intimidating. Josephine Klein wrote in the *British Journal of Educational Studies* that 'His honesty is such that it illuminates incidentally several aspects of what it is to be a genius.' Olive Banks in *New Society* wrote that 'Bernstein is probably the most creative mind in British sociology today'.

I could see from the introduction that Bernstein proposed that working-class and middle-class people used distinctly different linguistic *codes*, either the elaborated code of the middle class or the restricted code of the working class. This is what Bernstein had to say about the elaborated code:

> This speech mode facilitates the verbal elaboration of subjective intent, sensitivity to the implications of separateness and difference, and points to the possibilities inherent in a complex conceptual hierarchy for the organisation of experience. It is further suggested that this is not the case for members of the lower working-class. The latter are *limited* to a form of language use, which although allowing for a vast range of possibilities, provides a speech form which discourages the speaker from verbally elaborating subjective intent and progressively orients the user to descriptive, rather than abstract, concepts.
>
> (1974: 62)

The speech mode of the middle class which facilitates the verbal elaboration of subjective intent is termed *elaborated code*; the speech mode of the working class, which discourages the speaker from verbally elaborating subjective intent is termed a *restricted code*. Consider the following (invented) examples from Hawkins (1969):

> Three boys are playing football and one kicks the ball – and it goes through the window – the ball breaks the window – and the boys are looking at it – and a man comes out and shouts at them – because they've broken the window – so they run away – and then that lady looks out of her window – and she tells the boys off.

This is, according to Hawkins, typical of the way five-year-old middle-class children tell stories when presented with four pictures showing in turn three boys playing with a football next to a house; the football going through a window, a man gesturing wildly, and the children running away while a woman looks out of the window. Hawkins claims, however, that working-class children of the same age typically provide a very different verbal description with respect to these picture cards, for example

> They're playing football and he kicks it and it goes through there – it breaks the window and they're looking at it – and he comes out and shouts at them – because they've broken it – so they run away – and then she looks out and she tells them off.
>
> (1969: 127)

Bernstein says that the first story is *universalistic* in meaning – 'meanings are freed from the context and so are understandable by all' (1974: 179). He says that the second story is *particularistic* in meaning – 'meanings are closely tied to the context and would be fully understood by others only if they had access to the context which originally generated the speech' (1974: 179).

One important measure that Bernstein's associates have used to measure how context bound the speech is, is the number (or ratio) of what are called exophoric and endophoric references. Exophoric references are deictics (such as 'it' and 'they') which refer back to something beyond verbal context. 'They' in the example above from Hawkins as in 'They're playing football' is an exophoric reference. In the examples Hawkins provided, the child began the description with an exophoric reference; this reference of course would not be clear to anyone who did not have the pictures in front of them. Endophoric reference, on the other hand, refers back to something already identified in the verbal context, for example 'it' in the sentence: 'Three boys are playing football and one kicks the ball and it goes through the window.' According to Bernstein, one important aspect of the particularistic meanings of the restricted code is the heavy usage of exophoric as opposed to endophoric pronouns. Exophoric pronouns tie the message to nonverbal context; endophoric pronouns do not.

Bernstein (1974) outlined the typical characteristics of a restricted code. It's got a lexicon drawn from a narrow range. Meaning is condensed (because, according to Bernstein, 'The speech is played out against a background of communal, self-consciously held interests which removes the need to verbalise subjective intent and make it explicit' (1974: 77)). There is reduced verbal planning and therefore more fluent utterances (following Goldman-Eisler 1968). There's an increased reliance on the nonverbal accompaniments of language. These, according to Bernstein, 'will be a major source for indicating changes in meaning'. Utterances are more 'impersonal' – 'in that the speech is not specially prepared to fit a particular referent' and the content of the speech 'is likely to be concrete, descriptive and narrative rather than analytical and abstract'. The major function of the restricted code, according to Bernstein, 'is to reinforce the *form* of the social relationship (a warm inclusive relationship) by restricting the verbal signalling of individuated responses' (1974: 78).

This theory was sweeping through sociology and education. These were grand claims and what I was learning from psychology is that you always need to look at the evidence carefully, and this, I suppose, was now my calling, maybe my first calling. I enjoyed looking at the details of experiments and the numbers.

I noted that Bernstein originally tested his hypothesis of class-related linguistic differences by investigating the speech of two social groups differing considerably in class background: one group of post-office messenger boys and one group of boys at a private boarding school. Bernstein tape-recorded different groups discussing the topic of the abolition of capital punishment and found that all his major predictions were confirmed. His principal finding was: 'The working-class subjects used a longer mean phrase length, spent less time pausing and used shorter word length. Holding non-verbal intelligence constant, social-class differences were found in the same direction' (1974: 92). Since Bernstein hypothesised that 'Fluency and hesitation would seem to discriminate between two kinds of speech and differentiate levels of verbal planning' (1974: 89), these observations would at first sight seem to support Bernstein's theory of verbal planning differences in the two codes.

Bernstein subsequently analysed the differences between the speech of the groups at the word or lexical level and in terms of simple grammatical features. Bernstein found that the middle-class groups used a higher proportion of the following features: subordinations, complex verbal stems, passives, total adjectives uncommon adjectives, uncommon adverbs, uncommon conjunctions and egocentric sequences. The working-class groups on the other hand used a higher proportion of personal pronouns.

But how sound was Bernstein's basic methodology (and don't forget – this was supposed to be the work of a genius, according to the critics)? I noticed immediately that Bernstein's middle-class and working-class subjects were treated differently. This difference may have been critical in generating his findings. This is Bernstein's explanation as to why they were treated differently:

> It was thought that the working-class group would find the test situation threatening and that this would interfere with the speech, and consequently all working-class groups had two practice discussions (one a week) before the test discussion. This was not the case for the middle-class groups as such trials were impracticable.
>
> (1974: 84)

In other words, one group were practised in the task, one group were not.

I knew from the research of Frieda Goldman-Eisler that this could indeed be crucial. In 1961, she had demonstrated that practice reduces pausing in speech and, it should be noted, Bernstein found that the practised group spent less time pausing than the non-practised group. Any attempt to draw inferences about levels of verbal planning on the basis of amount of pausing, given this procedural inequality, then is not justified.

But there is one other important difference between the two groups: some of the working-class subjects knew each other, the middle-class almost certainly did not (p. 84). Since Bernstein had suggested that in the restricted code meanings are condensed because 'the speech is played out against a background of communal, self-consciously held interests', it seems especially unfortunate to use acquaintances or friends in the working-class (restricted code) group. Friends may indeed have communal interests and many condense their meanings (see Vygotsky 1965). The problem here is that Bernstein has confounded class and relationship of subjects, a confusion which may indeed be critical. In other words, Bernstein's original empirical investigation was very poorly executed and controlled. His principal discovery concerning pause differences between the two groups is, because of this poor methodology, theoretically uninterpretable. His discovery of statistical differences in the use of certain lexical and grammatical features is perhaps less suspect but also less interesting. 'Trivial' grammatical features are unfortunately not what Bernstein's grand theory was about.

Subsequent attempts to test the theory also failed to produce conclusive results. Take the notion that the elaborated code is characterised by a higher level of verbal planning, with the critical operational measure, according to Bernstein, being amount of pausing. Hawkins (1973) analysed the speech of young (6½- to 7-year-old) working- and middle-class boys and girls as they made up a bedtime story for a teddy bear. Hawkins focussed upon the speech of forty-eight subjects and analysed all unfilled pauses longer than 300 milliseconds. The prediction of course was that the working-class subjects should be most fluent in terms of speech rate per minute. But this was not what he found. He found that the working-class girls were the most fluent while the working-class boys were the least fluent. The middle-class boys and girls fell somewhere in between. The working-class boys paused longest and the working-class girls for the shortest amount of time overall. The results were not in line with the prediction. But worse was to come. When the forty-eight stories were submitted to experienced teachers to be graded, the stories of the working-class girls were judged to be best (despite the fact that this group paused for the least amount of time and yet amount of pausing was meant to reflect amount of verbal planning). This led Hawkins to the inevitable conclusion: 'Perhaps we need to question, then, our original assumption that greater fluency inevitably means less planning and hence inferior quality.' In other words, not only did Hawkins not produce confirmatory evidence for Bernstein's hypothesis linking codes and verbal planning, his empirical evidence in fact leads one to doubt the very validity of the operational measure Bernstein proposed.

But perhaps it was naive in the first place to assume that different social classes could be compared in terms of pause rates in order to draw conclusions about levels of verbal planning; naive for a very important reason – it ignores social context and its influence on pausing in speech. Goldman-Eisler (1968) demonstrated that some delay in output of speech was necessary for novel encoding but that is very different from saying that all delays in output (all unfilled pauses in speech), regardless of context, are connected with verbal planning (the subject of my dissertation). We may pause for other reasons, for example, to segment speech for the listener to facilitate decoding, to ensure that they are getting the message. Therefore, it seems that even in conversation not all pauses in speech are used for cognitive planning.

In monologues the situation gets much worse because there is not the same pressure to keep up a steady flow of speech. In conversation, if you remain silent for too long someone may interrupt, in monologues there is no one to interrupt. Hawkins had his subjects tell stories to teddy bears, they presumably never interrupted – they had special privileges (rarely found in natural contexts). They could get bored with the task and then resume after a pause. I noticed immediately that the longest silent pause recorded in the Hawkins study was 67.1 seconds. This contrasts with the kinds of pauses studied by Goldman-Eisler (1968) of just over 200 milliseconds. In samples of discussions involving adults she found no pauses exceeding three seconds. Whatever Hawkins' subjects were doing during that one minute plus pause, it was probably not verbal planning of the clauses and sentences that followed. Of course, it is interesting and pertinent that Bernstein himself had originally analysed speech taken from discussions and he had obtained (in his view) confirmatory evidence for his theory, although as I have said, because of the methodological pitfalls of the study, even these results are not readily interpretable.

The important point is that Bernstein should have recognised that social context, as well as the cognitive operations involved in language, will exert a powerful influence on the temporal structure of language. This, however, was not done. Bernstein's claims do not evidently generalise across social context and he never specified in which contexts differences should obtain. Contexts have been almost randomly sampled. The ensuing results seem almost equally random.

Bernstein's theory was a powerful one linking cognition and social processes. It sought to explain the underachievement of working-class children in schools. One of its major problems however is its failure to recognise that speech is a medium adapted for use in the context of natural conversation. In certain types of conversation, pressures to keep the floor may mean that temporal structure becomes well used for cognitive operations and that pauses in speech may be a useful index of verbal planning. In other contexts, the flexibility of speech asserts itself. It may change its whole shape and the temporal structure may reflect a good deal more than the operations connected with the encoding of speech. Hawkins found this to his cost.

Do working-class and middle-class people speak differently? The answer seems to be of course they do. Certain phonological, lexical and even grammatical features do seem to be affected by social class, but these features appear to be part of a continuum rather than arranged neatly into discrete codes, as Bernstein had suggested. Do working-class and middle-class people have differential access to different speech codes which either facilitate or discourage the 'verbal elaboration of subjective intent'? This is the heart of Bernstein's theory. But the evidence is impossibly weak – it is sometimes contradictory and often theoretically uninterpretable. Bernstein did observe some class-related speech differences but they do not support his general claims. Perhaps the last word here should be left to the sociolinguist William Labov. He is referring specifically to the work of Bernstein:

> There is little connection between the general statements made and the quantitative data offered on the use of language. It is said that middle-class speakers show more verbal planning, more abstract arguments, more objective viewpoints, show more logical connections, and so on. But one does not uncover the logical complexity of a body of speech by counting the number of subordinate clauses. The cognitive style of a speaker has no fixed relation to the number of unusual adjectives or conjunctions that he uses. . . . The relation of argument and discourse to language is much more abstract than this, and such superficial indices can be quite deceptive.
>
> (1972b: 258)

Unfortunately, the deceptiveness fooled many and I was angry at that. I realised that academic research matters. Generations of trainee teachers were being taught that the problem of the working class in terms of their under-achievement in schools was their limited language, their *mode* of speech, fixed rigidly in place by the nature of their social groups (like IQ, another unwavering stigmata, but a function of early environment). Unfilled pause in speech, according to Goldman-Eisler, are indicators of thinking and planning as we generate linguistic utterances, so what Bernstein was effectively saying was that the working class don't think properly when they talk. Their lack of success in education wasn't anything to do with perception or bias, either explicit or implicit – nor was it being told that they were from the gutter and that there's no point in aspiring. It wasn't lack of encouragement, nor lack of a quiet place to study, nor social isolation, nor trying to maintain discrepant roles, nor having few role models, nor unclear goals, nor trying to work at a card table in the front room with neighbours chatting away next to you, nor worrying about what the gang have been getting up to and when the police might be calling round. It was the fact that they don't use an elaborated code – the 'evidence' being that they don't pause enough when they talk – and the evidence didn't even support that – the working-class girls, in the Hawkins study, were the most fluent (they paused least but produced the best stories) while the working-class boys were the least fluent (paused most but produced the worst stories).

Bernstein had tried to explain the underachievement of working-class kids like myself by saying that they (we) were 'limited' to a form of speaking that was not conducive to abstract representation and intelligible communication. It was a form of speaking used to reinforce social bonds but not so good at anything else. I disagreed profoundly with this, I was upset by the shoddiness of the research and the ridiculous generalisations from his very narrow data base. A sample of essentially *twenty-two* subjects to develop a *general* theory of linguistic codes (Bernstein 1974: 85), with weak one-tailed statistical tests (1974: 86), inconsistencies in the data, statistical symbols used incorrectly (even the 'less than' sign – 1974: 84). The work, at times, was shoddy in the extreme.

But the research wasn't just shoddy, there were two fundamental and critical design faults – the fact that the working-class participants knew each other and the fact that they were allowed to rehearse the task. There are undoubtedly the most important influences on the crucial linguistic and psychological variables that he was investigating (forms of reference and pauses in speech). This was experimenter bias of the worst order, and dangerous experimenter bias at that because it would allow the conclusion that the working class really cannot help their academic underachievement because they don't have access to that special code, that special code of the middle class, that secret code.

I saw it as just another put down, *you know*, I really did. But that's just how I talk, you know, I can't fucking help it.

And, perhaps, I needed to remind Bernstein that filled hesitations can substitute for unfilled pause when the 'social' contingencies are changed. Parenthetic remarks like 'you know' may well be effective alternate devices (just like repetitions) for finding time to plan utterances. If you recognise this point, then you need a broader definition of hesitations linked to verbal planning and, therefore, new measures of pausing, phrase length and speech rate (the basic measures that Bernstein built his sandcastle on).

I could have referred him to a new study that went into press a year later in the *Journal of Psycholinguistic Research*, by two researchers from the University of Birmingham, which had demonstrated just that. The study had attracted excellent reviews. I was now about to be a published researcher (Beattie 1979a, Beattie and Bradbury 1979).

Chapter 3

Getting ahead of myself

Figure 3.1 Copyright Hugh Mckeown/Belfast Archive Project

> When an individual intentionally or unintentionally conducts himself in a way that others consider situationally improper, and shows thereby that he is either alienated from, or an alien to, the gathering, what other information can this provide them about his current condition – apart from what his impropriety tells them about his likely fate?
>
> Erving Goffman (1963: 217) Behavior in Public Places

Nobody has ever written about everyday social life quite like Erving Goffman. He was a talent like no other. I was fortunate enough to watch him in action with those who feel that human social life is easily understood in terms of simple categories of behaviour that can be applied objectively and cleanly irrespective of context or *social* situation. However, it wasn't just what he said that I remember so vividly about that day in London but the 'situationally improper' way that he did it, constantly interrupting, asking an inappropriate question, challenging convention and dogma, leaving us all to wonder about what these infractions could tell us about this alienated individual apart from his 'likely fate'. It was both masterful and perturbing, like every one of his brilliant books.

Byron's room

I was told that both the dissertation and the extended essay got the highest marks ever awarded in psychology at the University of Birmingham. I got the top First (there were two that year, some years there were none) and a Faculty of Science and Engineering prize. I was also accepted by Trinity College Cambridge, home of kings, prime ministers, great scientists, artists and philosophers and now, it seems, me. But first I had to work through the summer, serving petrol at a service station on the M6 near Birmingham. I did the night shift. But it was a good summer, the work was very easy compared to the building sites and it was all very good-humoured. It was the year of the Birmingham pub bombs and Belfast accents were not popular in that part of the country. Back in Belfast, many of my friends from the corner had now joined the various Protestant paramilitary organisations, the UDA and the UVF, to wage war on the IRA, to terrorise the terrorist, is how they put it. Most of my fellow workers at the service station found it a little hard to believe that I had just got a First and was now going on to study at Cambridge. They called me the Blarney Boy, full of tall tales. But they got the name on my wage slips right, on the building sites it had just said 'Paddy'.

I arrived in Cambridge in early October in a pair of platform soles that I bought second-hand in the Bullring market in Birmingham. They were brown with a Ziggy Stardust stripe somewhere down the side. They had been worn extensively when I bought them, and someone handily had hammered a nail through the inside of the shoe to keep the platform heel in place. Not surprisingly it was very uncomfortable, and it made my heel bleed every time I wore them. Platform soles were no longer fashionable, but I had got used to my new position in the world. My guess is that they had never been fashionable in Cambridge. Every now and then the heel would snap off wrenching may ankle.

It was time to say goodbye to Carol again – and again it was a difficult parting. I rang my mother to tell her I was going.

'If you ever become a wee snob I'll disown you. This place is up in flames and you're going off to sit on a boat in the middle of a bloody river.'

'A punt,' I suggested.

I think she misheard. 'You're not far wrong there, I know a lot of people might describe you as a little c***.'

I arrived at my graduate digs in Burrell's Field and unpacked. I said hello to my new housemates – a mixture of mathematicians and scientists, most English, one Canadian, one American and one Czech. Every single one seemed to notice that I was stalking around the house in a pair of platform soles but were far too polite to comment on it. That night we were invited to our college tutor's rooms for a welcome meeting. He seemed affable enough. He was very short, with ruffled dark hair and a distinctive speech style. We stood in groups drinking chilled white wine served with a variety of canapés including smoked salmon. I had never had smoked salmon before. I looked out at the beauty of Neville's Court and thought of Lord Byron living opposite, and Newton, and Wittgenstein, and Russell. Wittgenstein and Russell were now especially important given my new interest in language and linguistic philosophy, but I found them very difficult coming, as I did, from the background of empirical psychology which likes testable empirical ideas. I drank the chilled white wine thirstily for I was indeed thirsty and drinking – that is the physical act – saved me from having to talk for a few moments. For the past few weeks I had noticed that the slight stammer that occasionally afflicted me seemed to be getting slightly worse. It was highly unpredictable. My mother said that it was just an 'affectation'.

'I've heard that the posh English people do it just to make themselves look more interesting. You want to be more like them. You only ever stammered when you were lying, that's why I can tell. You've never been a good liar.'

To save myself from conversation I probably drank too much. There is clearly a social rule about the speed and frequency of drinking and the amount of talk that you're supposed to do. I didn't get the balance right. The University of Birmingham was a very good university, but it sounded a little bit dull in the present company, and as for Belfast and Legmore Street, and the boys in the balaclavas, that was definitely out of the question. So, I listened instead.

'Of course, I was an undergraduate at Trinity. . . . Great to be back!'

'I'm over from Harvard,' an American accent chirped.

'I got a First at Oxford predictably enough, but I heard that it's good to move between the two universities' (as if there were only two universities, but perhaps here there were).

My stammer fuelled by drink was now so bad that they probably couldn't tell which part of Ireland I was from or indeed whether Brummie accents were different to how they had ever imagined them. I had been directly asked about my alma mater, but I'm not sure they understood the response. I walked back to my college over the bridge past the university library and to Burrell's Field. I thought of Carol and felt quite alone. I set my alarm clock to get me up in good time for my morning meeting with my tutor but slept in predictably enough with a sore head and then stalked in my platform heels back to Neville's Court. I was perhaps twenty or thirty minutes late. I knocked on his door and opened it. He sat behind a large desk, looked up with a mixture of impatience and displeasure, and simply made a hand gesture and waved me away.

'You've missed your appointment,' he said. There was nothing about arranging another meeting or seeing the secretary or coming back next week – just a cursory dismissive hand movement and his comment. It was my fault, of course. I walked out through Great Court and went for a coffee on Trinity Street and felt as alone as I ever had.

That night my new housemates and I all met in the kitchen. We were all entitled to dine in college every evening, but they liked to cook for each other and I said that I'd like to join that group.

'Do you cook?' they asked cheerily. It wasn't really a question about cooking, of course, that could have been answered with either a 'yes' or a 'no', but a polite invitation to discuss those dishes that I liked to rustle up. My cooking back home in Belfast consisted of me putting the potatoes on at five o'clock on the dot for my mother so that when she got back from the mill she could have the dinner ready for six o'clock. I didn't peel the potatoes or anything like that, I just 'put them on' – in other words I lit the gas ring. As a university student Carol cooked for me every night – stuffed peppers, curry, ratatouille, many dishes that my mother had never heard of nor tasted, and neither, of course, had I. As a family back in Belfast, we ate out once a year on Boxing Day at the International Hotel. When Carol and I started going out she said that she would like to cook a meal for me and had asked me what my favourite dish was. There was no hesitation, there was one dish that I preferred over all others – 'potatoes, raw egg and raw onions.'

'What?' Carol said.

'Potatoes, raw egg and raw onions,' I replied, 'that's what it's called.'

Carol looked puzzled. 'I'm not sure that's an actual dish, how do you make it?'

'Well,' I explained 'you boil the potatoes and mash them up on a plate, making sure that it's all nicely spread out all over the plate, and then you peel a raw onion, a whole raw opinion, and cut it up onto the potato and then you break two eggs being careful not to get any shells onto the potatoes and mash the whole thing up.'

'It's lovely,' I said, 'all yellow and mushy.'

Carol looked aghast. 'Did your mother make that dinner up?'

'I think it's a traditional Belfast dish,' I said.

'Well, I'm from Belfast and I've never heard of it.'

'My mother always said that raw onions are very good for your skin.'

'But what about the raw eggs? Are they healthy?' she enquired. 'Aren't they supposed to give you salmonella or something?'

'Raw eggs are good for you – body builders eat them.' But she clearly wasn't convinced by any of the merits of this dish.

Carol never cooked this for me and that night she made stuffed peppers instead. 'Stuffed what?' my mother said when I told her 'It's unbelievable what they stuff these days. I've never heard of that.'

But that night in Burrell's Field I was clearly on trial. Exotic smells filled the kitchen. I stood in the corner by the one remaining electric ring cooking potato omelette with some notes that Carol had made for me hidden to the side. I peeled the potatoes badly, I cracked the eggs. The Czech student cooking away next to me kept looking at what I was doing. Impressed, I thought, at my speed and efficiency and my ability to crack eggs without getting any of the shell onto the plate, or at least not much of it. I took the meal up to my room to eat, I was really looking forward to it – the first time that I had ever cooked for myself. I cut into the omelette, but it was very hard – too hard to eat. I went down to the public phone and rang Carol.

'You did cook the potatoes first, didn't you?' she asked.

I told her that I thought that the eggs sizzling in the pan cooked the potatoes. I could hear her laughing from all of those miles away, from way across the water. I took my plate back to the kitchen and tipped the omelette into the bin and went back to my room and ate a whole packet of chocolate digestive biscuits.

The next night they were all there in the kitchen cooking and laughing. I waited until they had finished and then asked if I could join the group; my stammer was full blown. 'Unfortunately, no Geoffrey,' they said, 'we've seen your cooking, and we're not at all sure that you would fit into our group. We have specialists in Thai, Chinese, Indian, Eastern European, your speciality seems to be raw potatoes.'

And they all laughed again at this odd product of this backward culture from just across the water, where only women belonged in the kitchen – those sexist barbarians, in this great age of women's lib, who seemed to believe that men belonged in the shipyard, or on the building site or out there on the street, in the wind and the rain, lying on some sheets of sodden newspaper sticking to the grey tarmac below some second-hand broken-down wreck of a car, all heading for the early grave.

I went back to my room on my own and opened a second packet of chocolate digestive biscuits and stared out through the sash windows of Burrell's Field, past the painting of the Death of Chatterton by the Pre-Raphaelite painter Henry Wallis, which I'd bought on my first day in Cambridge – the poster of the painting that is. This was my one Cambridge affectation. The image of the Romantic hero, the seventeen-year-old English early Romantic poet Thomas Chatterton dead on his bed, from suicide, his precocious talent, rejected and despised, killing himself with arsenic. The windows in the painting were a little like Burrell's Field. I had noticed that straight away but that was where the similarity ended, and the rejection, of course. But his was a noble sort of rejection based on the ignorance of his talent and envy about its unforgivably precocious nature, replaced in mine by something blameworthy within the rejected, ignorant, boorish and sexist outmoded cultural beliefs that somehow had constrained the learning and experiences, and seemingly permeated into the soul, of this excuse for a Cambridge man.

I missed Carol very much.

I walked over and smeared the chocolate from my fingers all over the dead pale face of the Young Chatterton and felt alone and isolated, both person-ally and culturally, and felt like howling with tears, indeed I felt like howling so loud that it would stop their noisy, disturbing communal laughter.

My personal and social identity lay bare on the floor in a small untidy pile of wrappers, whose purple branded colours, I noticed, matched the colours of the Young Chatterton's pantaloons. I stared at these colours back and forth, comparing and contrasting. What sort of pre-cognition was this? How did I know to buy that exact poster for this very night? I heard my mother's voice: 'Pull yourself together for God's sake', and I finally managed to smile at my own stupidity. This, I thought, cannot be the time to give up, or even howl.

I opened Wittgenstein's *Tractatus Logico-Philosophicus* (Wittgenstein 1922) and tried again to read it, to understand its deeper significance, if there was any, to get beyond the first page.

That's the problem with psychology, I thought to myself, it can narrow your vision rather than expand your mind.

The low temperature building

It's never easy starting a Ph.D. because it really is a world of possibilities, almost infinite possibilities when you think about it, you just need to know where to start. I hesitated before starting because I was doubting how much I really knew, if anything. Brian had three new Ph.D. students starting that October, all interested in language – the philosophy of language, language development and me interested in pauses in speech. He asked which one of us would like to go first and make a seminar presentation to a new research group that he was setting up. I volunteered to give a talk based on my extended essay, a critique of artificial intelligence as applied to language. After all, it had been awarded the highest mark ever awarded to an essay in psychology at the University of Birmingham. I was told that it too was publishable, just like my dissertation. I shone with confidence as I volunteered.

So I went away to write the talk in that lone room looking out past the young Chatterton to the garden of Burrell's Field. Suddenly, doubts started to appear in my mind. Sometimes you can write a sentence with great confi-dence but when you have to say it out loud and potentially be questioned on it, it's a different matter. There were a couple of arguments that I had used in the essay that I now wasn't so convinced of – indeed I wasn't entirely sure that I fully grasped the complexity of some of the underlying arguments. But I pushed these negative thoughts to the back of my mind. Surely nobody would ever ask about this?

Our postgraduate offices and Brian's office were in the Low Temperature Building, on the top floor, just opposite the famous Psychological Laboratory on the Downing Site at the University of Cambridge. The seminar was to be held in the seminar room in the main building. I sat there with my talk on my lap, hand-written on acetates, waiting for the audience, who I assumed would be fellow postgraduate students, to arrive. Brian sat beside me, commenting on each individual as they entered the room – 'There's Professor John Morton, you've probably heard of his logogen model – I've got great problems with his model – he knows my objections, of course, we argue about it constantly. There's Dr Bernard Comrie, very smart, he's a linguist who works on linguistic universals, . . . there's Professor Brian Josephson he's a bit of a character, he was awarded the Nobel Prize in Physics last year for some experimental work that he did when he was a twenty-two year old Ph.D. student here at Cambridge. You don't need to worry about him though. He's just an enthusiastic amateur when it comes to psychology, even when it comes to artificial intelligence, although that is a bit closer to physics and he does know a thing or two about that,' and Brian laughed politely and quietly at his own joke. . . . The list went on and on. I think that I had started to shake. The other two Ph.D. students sat grinning at me from the front row.

Brian introduced me, all I remember hearing was 'Birmingham'. That's all. Birmingham. My attention had narrowed significantly. I tried to speak. The first word that came out was 'ah', which, of course, isn't a word. It's a filled pause, a hesitation filled with noise, the very thing I study. There was a tremble in my voice. I'm sure that the front row was grinning more now. Belfast accents have a sing-song quality at the best of times, with a rising intonation at the ends of sentences, as if we are asking questions all the time, or unsure of what we're saying. I proceeded for about ten minutes, bombarding them with statements that sounded like questions, filled pauses, repetitions, and I'd now started saying 'you know' every other sentence. Then a hand went up from the back of the room, a room that I noticed had suddenly got much warmer. It was on that precise part of the talk which I had recognised beforehand was my weakest point, the area where my knowledge was shakiest, where I had the thinnest slither of understanding. It was the question that I dreaded, it would expose me fully. It was partly the way the question was phrased. The speaker began 'Surely you're not saying . . .'

I hardly listened after that opening. He was clearly implying that only a fool would say what I had just enunciated. I couldn't remember whether he was a psychologist or a linguist, a world expert or an enthusiastic amateur, a Nobel Laureate or a technician that had just wandered in, all the names and descriptions of those in the room were now muddled in my head, I was so tense that I could hardly remember anything, and I was thinking that maybe Wittgenstein himself had popped along. The truth is that at that precise moment in time (very embarrassingly), I couldn't remember whether Wittgenstein was alive or dead, all I remember being told a few days earlier was that he liked to call into the Arts Theatre in Cambridge in the afternoons and eat a pork pie, and that to me sounded awfully contemporary. Perhaps it was the ghost of Wittgenstein that was now in the room there to expose my philosophical muddle. I couldn't see the face of the person who had asked the question, perhaps nobody had asked it, perhaps I had imagined it, perhaps it was my conscience talking, calling me out, calling me a fraud.

Somebody jumped in and then another. 'No, of course, he's not saying that. Only a fool . . .' I wanted to put my fingers in my ears. They were arguing over what I was intending to say, over what I meant. Some attributed great learning and understanding to me, some thought that it was just a fine ironic touch, some thought that I was just being provocative, 'and he's succeeded', one erudite and very refined voice from the back suddenly shouted.

But this was just the start. They then started arguing about the substance, the theory, the underlying epistemological assumptions, about grammar, typology, implicature, linguistic universals, Boolean logic, fuzzy logic, neurons, signal detection theory, neural networks, mathematics, physics. Everybody had their say, except me that is, sitting there with nothing to say, shaking, and trying to control the more obvious bodily movements.

After an hour or so (although that is only an estimate) Brian took control again. 'All very interesting,' he said, 'but I'm sure that Geoffrey's got a lot more to say on this. I think that we should let him continue.' And again all eyes were fixed on me.

My filled pause was even longer this time. It came out like 'aaaaaaaah', as if I had been stabbed in the neck, and I heard myself saying 'I think most of the points that I was going to make have been covered,' and I left it at that. The group then started chatting amongst themselves, the front row still grinned, and Brian seemed to turn his back on me to chat to somebody else. I sat staring straight ahead with my hands clasped tightly, the sweat from my hands was making the non-permanent ink on the acetates run. They looked like the streaks on a woman's face after she's been crying on a night out, the mascara running everywhere.

They all went to the pub afterwards, I went home. No, I didn't go home, I went back to my room in Burrell's Field, my mind was blank. I stared blankly out of the window, too terrified to start up even an internal dialogue.

I went to that seminar group every week for a year and didn't once dare open my mouth again. I know that for a fact because a record was kept of all of the questions and answers in the seminar each week and my name was completely absent. Brian pointed this out to me.

Eventually, Brian called me into his office and explained that if I didn't speak, he would stop inviting me to the group. So I plucked up the courage at one talk and asked several questions. When I saw the transcript the following week, there was just a question mark where my name should have been. Nobody knew who I was any longer. I'd become anonymous. I also noted that when I was asking those questions, I had developed a very distinct stammer which was now there most of the time.

Of course, I had shown in my dissertation that you can produce filled hesitation in normally fluent speakers by changing the social contingencies (and 'punishing' unfilled pauses through apparent negative evaluation), and I needed those social contingencies to change. I thought that there was only one way to do this – I needed to learn properly. I went to classes in linguistics, and talks in the evening in Trinity on philosophy and literature, I went to seminars at the Chaucer Club in the Applied Psychology Unit. I had been lulled into a false sense of security by what I now recognised as my modest-enough academic achievements so far. I realised that I had a long way to go. I needed more background knowledge and confidence, to hold my own. I had to develop an inner critic for my ideas and realised that I couldn't leave this criticism to others in a social or academic situation. I needed to challenge myself in advance, and if it looked a little odd, me just sitting there, in silence, gesturing away, arguing with myself, back and forward, to and fro, Punch and Judy, then so be it. I might look a little out of place in the Copper Kettle on King's Parade, just sitting there, over a coffee, talking to myself, with an internal dialogue that sometimes leaked out into an embarrassed social space of foreign language students and tourists, but that was the price I was going to have to pay.

So this is Cambridge, I thought to myself.

Finding my feet

I sometimes think that this is when I started studying for real. It was no longer enough just to acquire enough knowledge for an A grade or a First, it was about understanding the depth inherent in all ideas (even ideas that sounded banal on the surface), and developing that critical (and sometimes controlling) voice in my head. However, Ph.D. students can get lost in their reading and thinking and one of Brian's new research students dropped out at the end of his first year because he was spending too much time just thinking and not enough time doing actual research. This left a very serious student from Dublin, John, who was interested in linguistic development and myself both working with Brian and, of course, vying for his attention. John and I were very competitive, we both played squash together and we would take turns at giving each other a black eye on the court, with our racket rather than our fists. It always got a little heated. Always just an accident, of course, but the regularity was striking.

John would make jokes about me not being properly Irish since I was a Protestant from the North, whereas he was a proper Southern Irish Catholic.

He said to me a few times: 'You're not really anything, are you? You're neither an Irishman or an Englishman.' He never saw this as overly provocative, he just wanted a discussion about identity, I think. But perhaps that's just me trying to be kind. At Cambridge, you could often get away with saying very hurtful things and then pretend that they had a deeper significance. A significance that the recipient of the message, the victim, just couldn't see.

In Belfast I had played badminton to a very good standard up in St Mark's Church, we had made it to the Belfast junior badminton finals one year, and at Cambridge, I started playing again. It came back very quickly. This gave me a good social base. I played for Trinity first team and was then selected to play for the university (the Cockerels) against Oxford. I was badminton captain at Trinity going into my second year and I was awarded college field colours. I won the College Singles tournament each year (and the doubles trophy with my partner). I never mentioned my social background in Belfast. My badminton partner happened to bring this up one day. He said that he had another friend from Northern Ireland and he never mentioned his family background either. 'His father is a High Court judge and it would be too risky if people found out, given the security situation over there,' he said. 'I bet that it's something similar with you.' I just nodded. 'Something like that,' I said.

I appreciated that sense of history in Trinity, dining in the Great Hall, under the portrait of Henry VIII, the founder of the College, by Holbein (the original painting was destroyed by fire in 1698, the one hanging in Trinity was by Hans Eworth dating from 1567). Trinity was founded by combining Michaelhouse and King's Hall established by Edward II in 1317. Trinity's flag has the royal standard of Edward II. History, and Royal history, was written through the very fabric of the place.

The enjoyment came in moments, just feelings, but perfect feelings of contentment, still moments when you just breathed in the dusty air and glanced around the room, over the clatter of plates and the cut-glass chat. It was always a slightly disembodied feeling, as if I was looking down at myself, in the midst of noise and motion, in a slight translucent bubble that breathed against the noise. Just sitting there in my academic gown, time stretching out, imagining what my dad would have thought of this.

'I couldn't have seen *this* happening,' he would have said. 'My wee man, my wee soldier, does surprise me sometimes.'

Prince Charles was back dining on High Table tonight. I'd seen him arrive in his helicopter that afternoon just to the side of Burrell's Field and there he was trooping in with the Fellows, in a light-grey suit with a great tan. The Fellows were much paler. My mother would have appreciated that tan. She'd be asking him whether he used coconut oil from the tin like us. She'd want to know what his secret was.

He had graduated from the college a number of years previously and we had the same college tutor. My tutor liked to drop his name into conversations on occasions. I watched Prince Charles chatting, animated, the fellows animated in response. Polite, refined conversation, still maybe my biggest hurdle, especially about anything to do with culture, and classical music in particular (I can feel myself freezing as I even write this down).

It was while doing my badminton training that I had my 'idea' for my doctorate. One small idea that drove my Ph.D. forward and acted as the key to my future. If I call it an 'idea' it makes it sound very important, like something of significance, but it wasn't that kind of idea, it was an everyday observation, a random thought, an occurrence. Indeed, it is so mundane that it's difficult even to say it – whatever mental processes underpin and generate spontaneous speech must have to be so quick and so flexible that they can operate in everyday conversation where responses to previous turns at talk often occur without any perceptible pause, they may even overlap with the previous turn. That was the 'big' idea.

So why might this be of any significance to anybody? Well, proponents of the new discipline of psycholinguistics, this combination of psychology and linguistics which tested the psychological reality of linguistic theory including transformational grammar, were busy timing subjects in sound-proof rooms covered in egg boxes as they carried out various linguistic transformations on simple active affirmative declarative sentences. They were trying to work out the time it takes to generate a passive sentence, or a negative sentence, or a passive-negative sentence and so on (sentence with various transformations) to test the psychological reality of Chomsky's influential (indeed paradigm changing) theory. Some transformations took several hundred milliseconds in the lab, some even longer. So what was going in conversations where everything seemed to happen so quickly? I decided to study pauses in speech taken from actual social interaction (rather than from isolated sentences recorded in sound-proof rooms) to try to gain some insight into the fundamental nature of psycholinguistic processes, to uncover the relationship between thinking and language in real time. In social interaction, there are constraints on pausing – that could be very valuable.

But what kinds of talk should I study? I wanted to study talk that was as natural as possible but I needed to video-record it. So why not study the talk that happens in our observation room day in day out – tutorials and seminars? That was the obvious choice, and was my second good decision. I was interested in the underlying psychological process in talk and testing the psychological reality of linguistic theory, but at the same time I became highly knowledgeable about what actually happens in university tutorials (rather than what people thought went on in tutorials or remembered about them). Why do students not contribute more to tutorial discussion? This was (and is) a frequent complaint of academic tutors. I found that it was often because tutors interrupted students when they did take the floor, using a particularly powerful form of interruption called an overlap, where the person doing the interruption anticipates a possible end point in the first person's speech and jumps in quickly (Beattie 1981a, 1982a, 1982b, 1983). Overlaps are associated in some contexts (but not all) with dominance in talk. It's not necessarily an intentional and deliberate strategy, it's more part of the unconscious and routine aspects of everyday behaviour. But it is nevertheless a very good device for maintaining the status quo – with the academic tutor staying in control at all times. Needless to say, this got me interested in the organisation of conversations and how everyday conversations reflect and amplify power differentials in other situations.

Of course, once you start studying talk as opposed to monologues into a tape recorder in this more 'natural' context (Beattie 1982c; Sears 1986), you notice immediately that a range of nonverbal behaviours seem to be connected to this process of linguistic generation. So I started studying hand movement and gesture and patterns of speaker eye gaze as they accompanied speech to try to decide between alternative theoretical positions on the cognitive or communicative functions of individual pauses in speech. Many of the co-verbal hand movements are iconic in terms of the nature of their representation, and bear some resemblance to the accompanying speech (Beattie 1983, 2016), be it speech about the physical world, or more abstract speech about ideas and the conceptual world (common, of course, in Cambridge tutorials and seminars). I was confronted by issues to do with iconicity, and behaviours, like eye gaze, affected by the cognitive constraints of the human brain that become meaningful signs (Beattie 1978a, 1979b, 1981b) or cues in interaction, like turn-yielding signals, as a consequence of information processing limitations (Beattie 1977, 1978b, 1979c, 1981c). I was interested in how patterns of speaker eye gaze are influenced by the semantic planning phases of temporal cycles identified through relative hesitancy and what happens to the fluency and coherence of speech when eye gaze at the listener is not averted at these critical junctures. I studied how speech-focussed hand movements coordinate with these planning cycles and how the more complex movements occur at different parts of the temporal cycles compared to the less complex batonic movements (Butterworth and Beattie 1978).

This work helped lead to the development of a new theoretical perspective on human communication. At the time the underlying assumption was that verbal language and nonverbal communication were quite separate channels of communication with quite different functions. Verbal language (speech) communicated semantic information about the world (physical or mental), nonverbal communication was thought to act in primarily social ways to communicate 'interpersonal relations', to communicate emotion, to govern the flow of talk, or they were used for various self-presentational purposes. My research suggested that this was not the case (Beattie 1981d, 1983, 2003, 2016). In psychology these days, most recognise that human communication is indeed multimodal, it operates through several modalities at the same time – speech, paralanguage, tone, bodily movements are all connected when you look closely enough. This was not so widely understood at that time. I had a clear vision of my Ph.D. Whenever Brian was asked what my Ph.D. was about, he usually said 'the whole world is in there'. He meant the whole world of communication – speech, linguistic encoding, movement, gesture, eye faze, turn-taking, the works, basically.

Carol moved to Cambridge at the start of my second year to do a PGCE at Homerton College. We lived in a basement flat owned by the college in Chesterton Road. I had never been so happy. I worked all day in the lab analysing human behaviour in great detail and played sport in the evening for the college; Carol started playing badminton again and singing in a choir. Whenever Carol told me excitedly about some important material from her course – the work of Basil Bernstein on social class and language, I explained patiently why, in my view, it was just plain rubbish. My confidence grew and I now looked forward to the psycholinguistic seminars, and Brian sometimes pointed out that my hand was usually one of the first to go up. I completed a number of studies in my second year and sent each of them off to various journals. One by one they were accepted by leading international journals, without a single paper being rejected. I was now twenty-three and clearly changing for all to see. My accent was getting softer, I seemed to have stopped saying 'you know' to make time for what I wanted to say. I even wrote a theoretical critique of Chomsky's work in *Reflections on Language* (Chomsky 1976; see Beattie 1979d). I sent it to him at MIT and he wrote back almost immediately, arguing with some (indeed many) of the points that I'd made. It was hand-written, single spaced, and ran for over six or seven pages of A4. It is one of my proudest possessions.

My brother and my mother came to stay with us that Christmas and she made Bill and I wear our university ties (Bill, in the meantime, had gone to Lancaster University to do a degree in Environmental Science) and we went to a pub on the Cam on Christmas Eve. We had never been so happy as a family since my father had died. My mother and Bill loved Carol. We went punting on the Cam, I had got a part-time job punting one summer during the conference season, so I was a bit of an expert. When my mother asked me what I was studying now, I just said 'pauses', and left it at that. She thought that I said 'paws-es', and that it might be part of animal psychology. 'You always loved the auld animals,' she said. 'They followed you everywhere back in Legmore Street.' We drank Black Russians until midnight and then Bill set off to drive the 490 miles to Aviemore to take a group out climbing in the morning. That was just him, anything seemed possible. I needed to be reminded of that.

My research was very fine-grain, showing the connections between speech and nonverbal behaviour. These nonverbal behaviours work alongside language in the processes of communication. But it was an abstract knowledge, my transcriptions looked like no conversations that you have ever seen, page after page of them.

The truth is I never really wanted to leave Cambridge at that time but my head of department, Oliver Zangwill, popped in to see me one day and told me that I was an unusual Ph.D. student, ready for a permanent lectureship before my three years were up. 'You've made excellent progress, I see, the publications are coming out nicely. Why not apply and see what happens?' I applied for a number lectureships and got accepted at the University of Sheffield almost immediately. There were two interviewees that day – the other candidate was completing his DPhil at Oxford. I realised that Trinity College, Cambridge, was always going to be an extraordinary signifier, indeed a life-changing signifier. It was a good department in a modern building with a forceful and authoritative head, Kevin Connolly who was a very good psychologist working on the development of motor skills in children. He came to dine in the college with Carol and me after I had been appointed and told me that he had always secretly wanted to be a poet, to read literature, to write creatively about the human condition.

'But,' he explained, 'I went the other way,' as if you *had* to make that choice.

Changes

Things seemed to be going very well. I started in May and had to leave Carol behind again for a few months at least. When I got to Sheffield there were a number of boys from my form in school who were still students at Sheffield (studying architecture – a longer course), whereas I was now a lecturer. They commented on how much I'd changed, even my accent.

I could never have anticipated how momentous the next few months would be. We stayed in a lecturer's house that summer while he was in Malaysia doing research, and then moved into a tutor's flat in a hall of residence. My brother came to visit us but obviously wasn't impressed by the appearance of the other hall tutors. 'Do you really fit in here?' he asked.

I seemed to be moving further and further away from my roots, getting vaguer and vaguer about my past until sometimes I felt that I really had none at all. My focus was on psychology, and temporal rhythms in speech and iconic gesture, and critiquing others and academic debate, my accent changing slowly – but changing year by year. I can remember that Christmas before my brother Bill died, climbing in the Mournes with him in sunny, unseasonable weather. The two of us sat in a small hollow high in the Mournes, our coats off, laughing at the things my mother would say, laughing at the accents, laughing at how Van Morrison pronounces the 'a' sound in 'water' in the song 'And it stoned me', like the wee East Belfast man that he was. But secretly we liked how he said it because he was like us. My brother wearing his ski instructor sweaters and with his Italian sports car, he was just back from Chamonix or Val d'Isere, me with my new Cambridge background. Occasionally the wee Belfast words would slip out, making us both laugh. 'Would you ever move back to Belfast?' he asked, and he never waited for an answer. Our whole lives were in front of us on those bright, clear mountain peaks.

I can see his smiling eyes now, as he leans back. I will always have that smile in front of me, with his head back in that sunlight on a bright, crispy morning. We had sandwiches with us that day; he had got up earlier than me and made them. We had three each, and a pint of milk between us, one drink each until we drained it. He was getting married in April, I was to be the best man, and after that he had one more expedition to get mountaineering out of his system, he explained. He was going to the Himalayas, and the mountain was called Nanda Devi, the Goddess of Joy. I had never heard of it. He told me that my best man's speech had better be a good one. 'I've told my girlfriend that you're a clever wee shite, so don't let me down.' The last time I saw him was at his wedding, when his friends and I were carrying him, lying prone across our shoulders, to his car, like you would shoulder a coffin to the grave.

And then within a matter of months, no more than that, really, just months that can be counted down one by one, he had died and Carol had been dragged by her coat under a train that she had been trying to board at Sheffield station. He died the month after I was awarded my Ph.D. And all the lives of our little group from the turn-of-the-road had changed for good, and that bright future that seemed so clear that day had somehow dulled. That period is just a few vivid moments now. I remember two telegrams arriving simultaneously, one from my Uncle Terence saying 'Serious accident to Bill. Ring home.' I can't remember what the other telegram said, it was from my mother, it was probably vaguer. The face of the telegram deliveryman is just a blank in my memory. I recall the hand reaching out towards me, the movement from the bag, the two telegrams like playing cards spaced out in a hand in front of me, as if I could take my pick. But I had to read both, and one was worse than the other.

Carol and I were living in an old coach house in Sheffield, infested with rats in the loft, which crouched down below a leafy road that led towards the university from the rich suburbs, where the men who had run the British steel industry had once lived such prosperous lives. I remember my heart pounding as I went to the public telephone up on the road to ring home and the question forming in my mind as I half ran and half walked along that road. 'How serious?' I was almost rehearsing it. I can remember my relief that there was nobody in the phone box; it was a Sunday morning, and the streets were deserted. I must have been running towards the end when I got to the telephone box, and I rang my mother's number. As soon as a quiet voice other than my mother's answered the phone, I knew exactly how serious the accident was. If he had been injured my mother would have been there on the other end of the phone, angry with him and angry with me. I had prepared myself to hear her rage. She always hated him climbing; she never saw the point of going out into the country and into high places loaded with all that equipment. That's what she always said when the three of us would be sitting in front of the fire. But this was some other woman's voice and then a long silence filled with my dread, and then my mother's voice drowned in, sobbing. 'He's dead,' she said, 'your brother's dead.' The breaking of the worst news was as straightforward as that, that short vowel sound in the word 'dead'.

Bill was near the summit is all we ever heard, when he fell. We had a service in the house though Bill never returned home, his body lay below a pile of stones on a Himalayan hillside with a few details of his life scratched with a stone or an ice pick on the side of a grey slate-type rock. It read: 'Here lies Ben Beattie' ('Ben' was what his friends called him). A few of his friends who had served their apprenticeships with him and stuck with their trade came to the funeral; some had moved on, one was now a fireman in Belfast with stories of smoke-damaged bargains to be salvaged from shops that had been blown up, one was in insurance. Both were in professions that were now good sound businesses in Belfast. The old house was too small, and the crowd of friends and neighbours congregated on the pavement with some on the stairs.

Bill's wife of a few months was there, and she slept that night with my mother in the front bedroom. Bill would have laughed with embarrassment to hear about that. I would have loved to see his face. 'She's really middle class,' he had told me when they first met, and I liked the way that he had used the word 'really', as if to say he had landed on his feet. 'I've told her about the old house,' he said, 'and she says that she understands that it's not very modern or nice, but I don't think she does.' We both then made that kind of face that you do, like kids when they're dreading something and they want to show it. And now she was here without him to supervise the experience. I laughed myself at the thought of her and my mother in the same room.

He didn't leave much behind. He had a diary that I was allowed to look at before it was taken away from me. 'It'll just upset our Geoffrey too much,' my mother said and then she complained that I never got the clothes back that I had loaned him. She cried for months on end, every time I rang her, just as she had done for my father, although I had to listen to that from the back bedroom. But she always said that the loss of a child is the hardest thing to bear. 'My wee son' is how she referred to him. She never seemed to take in any of the details of his death and still years later she would ask me what country Bill had died in. Or she would ask 'How did he fall?' Or 'How long was it before they found his body?' But she didn't really want an answer.

The next few months were bleak; I got very depressed. Carol tried to console me. I told her that she didn't know what it was like. It was also a very bad winter weather-wise, there was heavy snow, and five months later, Carol had her accident. I saw her the morning it happened in the hospital, before they amputated her left arm, which had been crushed by a train. I can see the shine of her long dark hair on the white pillow. I had slept in after she had got up to go to Leicester for the day. She was working as a prison psychologist and had to administer a psychological test to someone on remand in a prison. My professor's secretary had to come to my house and knocked the door three or four times to wake me up. She told me that Carol had had an accident, but she thought that it wasn't too serious. 'I think that she's fallen off the platform, that's all,' she said. 'Platforms aren't too high,' she said. 'It's not such a big fall. She'll be alright.'

I thought that she meant that Carol had fallen over in her platform soles. My mental image was of Carol tottering over on her platform shoes, big platforms with four-inch black soles with red stars or Ziggy thunderbolts on them, shoes from a few years previously imported into this dream-like sequence.

My professor, Kevin Connolly, was there and waited with me in the hospital waiting room and as the doctor came in to talk to me I recall jumping up and hitting my head on something and wanting my injury to be serious, but it wasn't. The doctor described what had happened at the station: Carol was late for the train to Leicester and tried to board the moving train, she slipped between the train and the platform, her coat caught and she was pulled under the train. He explained how they had to amputate the arm. 'Is there any alternative?' I asked, as if he had forgotten to consider any. He shook his head without looking at me and led me in to see her. Carol was conscious when I got there. She did not smile at me. Then she immediately apologised because she said that she knew what I had been going through with my brother's death. 'I'm sorry,' she said, and she did smile a weak, half-hearted sort of smile. The memory of her apology kills me to this day.

I held her limp, lifeless hand in what I suppose was my pathetic attempt to show that this hand, which was to be removed, was still part of her and of us. I was wearing a white puffer jacket that my mother had bought for me that Christmas and it got smeared up and down the sleeve with her blood. And when they wheeled Carol off to theatre I had to ring my mother and tell her what had happened, and her neighbours went to the chemist's to get her some tablets and she arrived later that day, on Valium and alcohol, after the arm had been amputated and she stared at my sleeve, as if I might not have noticed the blood that was streaked right down it.

Carol never complained about what had happened to her. I always thought that this was amazing, although I never told her this to her face, and I thought that it demonstrated a great side of her Ulster Protestant character, that quiet Ulster Protestant determination just to get on with life, no matter what happens to you, that great ability to cope with adversity. Not a bit of wonder, I thought, that Ulster Prods, or those from Ulster Protestant descent, like Davy Crockett, Sam Houston, Kit Carson, John Colter, 'Stonewall' Jackson and President Andrew Jackson, shaped the history of the United States. I always like to remind myself sometimes that seventeen Presidents of the United States come from Ulster Protestant stock.

How did President Theodore Roosevelt, whose people were from County Antrim, describe the Ulster Prods, called the Scots Irish in American affairs to distinguish them from the Catholic Irish?

> strong and simple, powerful for good and evil, swayed by gusts of stormy passion, the love of freedom rooted in their very heart's core. Their lives were harsh and narrow; they gained their bread by their blood and sweat, in the unending struggle with the wild ruggedness of nature. They suffered terrible injuries at the hands of the red men, and on their foes they waged a terrible warfare in return. They were relentless, revengeful, suspicious, knowing neither ruth nor pity: they were also upright, resolute, and fearless, loyal to their friends, and devoted to their country. In spite of their many failings, they were of all men the best fitted to conquer the wilderness and hold it against all comers.
>
> (Roosevelt 1889/2004: 199)

In the War of Independence, forty per cent of Washington's army were Ulstermen. And what did Washington himself say about these Ulstermen: 'If defeated everywhere else, I will make my last stand for liberty among the Scots Irish of my native Virginia.' Among the signatories of the Declaration of Independence five were Scotch Irish, and the Secretary of the Congress, which adopted the declaration, was an Ulsterman, Charles Thomson from Maghera, County Londonderry. The Declaration was printed by an Ulsterman, a John Dunlap from Strabane.

We might not be proper Irish but we were something.

Carol sometimes got depressed. 'It's only natural,' my mother said, but Carol never complained, and she never attempted to justify any failure to do whatever a busy and active life would require. She was twenty-five when the accident happened. She went on to bring up three children (the first, Zoë, born the year after her accident, and Ben and Sam in the next five years) and drive and cook and sew all with one arm, and open bottles gripped between her thighs, and hold dresses with her teeth as she pushed the needle through, and cut meat for the family held on boards with nails sticking out of them (made by her father), and play competitive badminton with me, serving and hitting the shuttlecock with her one good hand, until one day when some opponent protested that this was surely against all the rules of this most English of games. Somewhere it must be written in the rules, he said, that you couldn't just drop the shuttlecock and hit the shuttlecock with the very same hand. 'It must give you an unfair advantage.' I thought that he was joking, and I am sure that I must have laughed, but he was quite serious about it. He had this sanctimonious expression on his face as if he had caught us cheating. 'But that's the English for you,' my mother said when I told her. 'They're a strange bloody people when it gets down to it.'

Carol only ever complained that she could not greet her children with her arms outstretched in the way that you should, and could not clap her hands when she saw them in concerts or getting prizes or running races, except by slapping her right palm down on her right thigh in a muffled sort of ritual that drew attention to itself with its oddness.

We had moved on all right, but not quite in the way that we thought that day in the sunshine in the mountains above Newcastle. And my mother stayed in Belfast, alone in her grief.

Goffman, the corner boy

I wrote about Carol acquiring an artificial arm for the magazine *New Society*. It was strange that I had written my first ever published piece just after my father's death. Perhaps it's the only way I can articulate difficult, personal things. Carol was young and beautiful, surrounded by old, decaying people, fingering plastic arms and legs. She eventually got fitted with her artificial arm and she would go out self-consciously and awkwardly with this plastic object, the colour of a cheap doll, attached to the stump of her arm just so that people wouldn't stare. Just for their sakes, to allow them to perceive some symmetry in the world. The arm didn't do anything, it just filled the sleeve, it was for other people rather than her. We tried to laugh about the way that the 'Bionic Man' was on television, and that surely the engineering of artificial arms had progressed since the war, but no, there was a 1940s or 50s feel about them, in the plastic, in the strapping, in the way that they talked about them. My article was reprinted in the *Journal of Biomedical Engineering* and in *Action*. I felt huge anger and a sense of injustice on her behalf, it was controlled in the article.

I expressed something in the article about human experience, direct observation, painful and biting, not wrapped up in academic jargon. I had, of course, always felt trapped between worlds (the gang and the world of learning), but now I felt it all over again. I started to think that I was a psychologist trapped between worlds – the world of psychology as I understood it, especially the Cambridge version – the enlightened and elitist version, which I had grown to love, rigorous and academic, conducted in the laboratory for the most part – controlled, somewhat artificial admittedly (but developing an abstract knowledge grounded in the brain and neuroscience with implications for all behaviour) – and the real world, the world out there, the world of direct experience, the world of meaning and pain, the world I had left behind not so long ago. I was being pulled in different directions. The science that I was now pursuing was telling me more and more clearly that thinking in speaking relates most closely to hand movement and iconic gesture, where, as we speak, the hands unconsciously draw images without the benefit of a mental lexicon, but still perfectly meaningful. Unconscious meaning in the hands, spontaneously created and unconsciously expressed, as one psychologist put it. Indeed, I was starting to see these movements accompanying speech as parts of the same basic underlying process of thought in action, as David McNeill, from the University of Chicago had started to argue. One system is linear and sequential, one is wholistic and imagistic, but they are perfectly meshed together in complex and interesting ways. Hand movements make thought visible. But thinking impacts on other nonverbal behaviours as well, behaviours like head movements, head nods and shakes, eye contact, gaze direction, sniffs, yawns, lip licks, posture, fidgets, self-adaptors, foot slides, foot kicks, foot taps, and the list goes on and on. I had become an acute observer of human beings through my work, but it was an abstract knowledge – detailed and logical.

That autumn I was invited to attend a NATO Advanced Study Institute in London where the top internationally-acclaimed academics on interpersonal behaviour – Erving Goffman, Paul Ekman, Robert Rosenthal, Klaus Scherer and so on – acted as faculty to promising young postdocs who were the students. I was obviously considered promising enough to be invited. The postdocs from very good universities from a range of NATO countries would sit at desks like first year students and get lectured at. I had to leave Carol on her own in Sheffield, coping with one arm. Carol urged me to go, six months after her accident. Paul Ekman was to outline his exciting new work on the micro-analyses of facial expression and his work on the detection of lying through micro-expressions. My work on the micro-analysis of pauses and gesture was clearly relevant to the uncovering of deceit and dovetailed nicely with his own work. I was interested in how we read the truth from the body or how we are fooled either deliberately or unintentionally in our everyday lives. I was interested in the broad strategies of deception that people use, and the micro-behaviours that can give the game away. It is about the way that we fool others and the way that we can fool ourselves.

The other students on the course were very friendly and very able. I met a very good black female student from Harvard (whose name I've forgotten) and a linguist from the University of Gothenburg called Jens Allwood. I was introduced to the famous sociologist, and one of my heroes, Erving Goffman, outside a tube station on a wet and crowded London street by Jens. I have just looked Goffman up on Google Scholar and I see that he ranks third of all time on academic citations in sociology just behind Karl Marx and Pierre Bourdieu (Goffman has 315,558 citations). I will always remember this untidy-looking grey raincoat he wore. He was quite small and Jens, who is very tall, towered over him. Goffman smiled at me benevolently and said: 'I've heard great things about you, Geoffrey.' I was astounded – I must have blushed with embarrassment and pride. I said very little to him, I felt intimidated to be in his presence; Jens, however, was not so retiring. Jens, like some Swedes, laughs very loudly and was not in the slightest intimidated by his presence. Jens told me that Goffman liked to go to London casinos to play blackjack; he also told me that he was a card counter, memorising the number of picture cards dealt. Casinos were not keen on card counters. A few years later (before his untimely death) he was the reviewer that recommended publication of what was essentially my Ph.D. as my first book (Beattie 1983) – he described my work as 'extremely interesting' and cited my research in his final book, *Forms of Talk*, published in 1981 (Goffman 1981).

One afternoon in class, Goffman came in late, causing a wave-like, suppressed stir in the crowded room. He chose to sit beside me in the class where Paul Ekman was starting to demonstrate his new Facial Action Coding Scheme (FACS) to show the micro-analysis of the human face in action. I smiled at Goffman, and he smiled warmly back, but I felt very uncomfortable sitting beside the great man, the subject of so much attention from the group.

Ekman started to explained that this was a *workshop* (he put great emphasis on this) and that we were going to learn how to code facial expression. This was not a seminar with discussion (he repeated this twice), and that there were to be no questions. He started talking, illustrating what he had to say with a video of a blonde girl displaying some facial expressions. Erving immediately raised his hand. Ekman pretended not to notice, but paused and without looking at Goffman said: 'In case anyone has misunderstood what this session is about – it's a workshop, not a discussion, you're here to learn how to use the FACS.' Goffman lowered his hand, and Ekman continued. A few minutes later Goffman raised his hand again, as Ekman talked us through the muscles around the eyes of the blonde girl on the video. You could see that Ekman was getting slightly angry, it was hardly a micro-expression of anger, more a full-blown display, but again he didn't look at Goffman directly. Instead, he repeated his earlier message. 'In case anyone has misunderstood what any of this session is about – it's a workshop, not a discussion, you're here to learn how to use the FACS, not ask any questions. Does everyone understand?' It was much louder this time, directed at no one in particular, and he added 'any' to the basic message. He went back to the video, and Goffman lowered his hand. But a few minutes later he raised it again. Ekman was fighting to control his anger, I can still remember the redness in his neck. He stopped abruptly and looked directly at Goffman this time. 'Erving, you've obviously got a burning question. This had better be good. So what do you want to know?'

Goffman cleared his throat. 'I was just wondering, Paul, are all the girls in California as attractive as she is?' and he pointed at the video screen. And this very serious, studious and highly-selected group of scholars in the audience collapsed with laughter. Ekman looked furious and struggled to regain his composure.

Jens explained to me later that the girl on the video screen was Ekman's ex-partner, and emotions might well have still been raw. In later sessions, Goffman sat in on the classes with students and often destroyed some of the faculty with his devastating questions. He was particularly critical of highly technical approaches to the study of human social behaviour favoured by many of the faculty. He asked how detailed *objective* measurements of behaviour might be used to define whether two people are 'together' or not in different contexts. He was arguing for a different approach.

This, in some senses, was a pivotal moment. I loved the irreverence and humour of Goffman, so far removed from Cambridge, and his rule breaking and his role-playing (and, of course, his brilliance). This was an academic that a corner boy could identify with. It could have been Duck or Rob in there from the turn-of-the-road, having a bit of craic, disrupting the flow, taking that pompous fucker down. Down and fucking out. Or maybe even me, from a previous life. I laughed out loud, and then I started thinking. What had Goffman been doing? How might I understand his 'situationally improper' behaviour? Goffman had written about this very thing in *Behavior in Public Places*. He wrote:

> when an individual intentionally or unintentionally conducts himself in a way that others consider situationally improper, and shows thereby that he is either alienated from, or an alien to, the gathering, what other information can this provide them about his current condition – apart from what his impropriety tells them about his likely fate?
>
> (1963: 217)

But what was more important was what Goffman wrote next. He warned that 'we can see that an offence *as such* tells us very little about the offender. All those who exhibit alienation from a gathering may share nothing but their alienation' (1963: 220). In other words, he might well have been signalling a degree of alienation from the event, the seminar led by the world's leading forensic analyst of objective human facial expression, but one has to be extremely careful about moving beyond the analysis of the behaviour to an understanding of the causes of the behaviour, including his own behaviour. Was it an attack on Ekman's approach to analysing human behaviour, or Ekman the person himself (or the uses to which his analyses could be applied)? Can we ever hope to analyse emotional signalling in terms of frozen, isolated and deliberately encoded images as Ekman claims (Beattie 2016), when the whole point about human emotional expression is that it is situationally driven, spontaneous, and unconsciously produced? If a great academic starts with certain assumptions, including the assumption that we (the audience) need to learn the details of a particular approach to progress, when these assumptions are not being laid out and open to scrutiny, what else are you supposed to do, except to disrupt the proceedings? And in so doing alienating yourself from the academic gathering.

This was very familiar to me: this was the behaviour and style of the boys from the corner, challenge the fuckers, and I loved it.

I thought that this was Goffman's deliberate ploy, an obvious act of defiance, the manifestation of his pedagogy to teach us all (staff and students) something about the analysis of human behaviour. He was conducting a test, an experiment. Goffman had also written:

> In such cases, certain kinds of involvement that are prohibited in the establishment may be presented as acts of interpersonal defiance and be understood as such. Sometimes such affronts are means of testing the limits, to determine how far the guardian can be pressed; sometimes, apparently, the offender may act in this way to see if the guardian will be true to him whatever he does.
>
> (1963: 228)

And his conclusion in that great insightful book of his that ranged across disciplines, that ranged across arts and science (it went wherever it had to in order to gather up insights – an experimental study in psychology here, a play there, a fragment of a novel somewhere else – maybe Kevin Connolly wasn't right when he said that you have to choose), was that

> Situational requirements are of a moral character: the individual is obliged to maintain them; he is expected to desire to do so; and if he fails, some kind of public cognizance is taken of his failure. But once this character of situational obligations is granted, we must see that a study of them leads off in many different directions. We may expect to find many different motives for complying with them, many different reasons for breaking them, many different ways of concealing or excusing infractions, many different ways of dealing with offenders.
>
> (1963: 240)

The study of situational obligations and how some people break these obligations leads in many directions, and prompts the search for a range of motivations and consequences. Goffman seemed to be opening a door on human behaviour, to allow us to search for the diversity of natural experience, action and response, beyond the laboratory.

Perhaps, he was giving me a license to do something a bit different – to study diversity of experience, to use whatever means I had to, to try to write about things in human terms and not just to describe it abstractly, objectively and scientifically – to attempt to understand rather than predict human behaviour (as difficult as that itself was). To write something that everyone could understand.

Political and personal contexts

After the NATO Advanced Study Institute, I didn't go back to Harvard or Cambridge or Gothenburg, but back to Sheffield and my life: to Carol in the kitchen trying to cut some meat with her one hand in our rat-infested university-owned flat, part of an old coach house, just across from the posh 1970s Hallam Towers Hotel. We lived in the damp hollow opposite, damp and infested, and hidden from view. Jens came to stay one night, and insisted in sleeping in front of our electric fire, which he kept on all night. 'Why do they make academics live like this in England?' he asked. Life had not yet materially improved (even my mother was shocked by the way that we had not yet moved on from Legmore Street). But within a few years, Carol and I had saved up a deposit and moved to a little terraced house in Crookes in Sheffield, to a street full of steelworkers and miners.

The broader context for me now was the UK during a time of change in the late 1970s and early 1980s, a challenging time, a raw time, a time of rapid evolution, a throwback to a more primitive era perhaps. The era was heralded by the election of the Conservative government of Margaret Thatcher in 1979 and the rapid 'deindustrialisation' of the North of England that followed, with the closures of the mines and the steelworks, high unemployment, minimum job security, and a change in the very nature of society itself; a harsher, more brutal environment for all those caught up in it. These were times when truth and lies in everyday interaction were particularly salient because if you could no longer believe the State, or no longer depend upon your neighbours, friends, and colleagues in quite the same way, as society crumbled around you, who could you rely on? You had to be able to read people to survive.

These times now provided the backdrop to the psychological 'analyses' that I was carrying out, they affected almost every aspect of them, in subtle and not so subtle ways. It is often said that in the United Kingdom, the hard, industrial North of England really is a different country to the 'soft' south of the country where the government, big business and the financial institutions reside. Two 'countries' that in the years in question seemed almost to be at war with each other. These were times of momentous political and social change after the Conservative victory in 1979. The working class in the North of England voted Labour (or did then), so this was a government not of their making, a government that they did not choose. The signs were there from the start.

The philosophy of this new government was to be of free market capitalism, the individual, self-reliance, self-interest, the entrepreneurial spirit, competition, competitive markets, the anglicised version of Gordon Gekko's 'greed is good', reinterpreted and reformulated with literally biblical conviction (Thatcher 1995). 'No one would remember the Good Samaritan if he had only had good intentions, he had money as well', Mrs Thatcher famously said in an interview in 1980 where she defended increasing inequality in the UK with the statement: 'It means you drag up the poor people because there are the resources to do so'; where the expression 'drag up the poor people' variously evokes images of drowning sailors in sinking ships, or urchins dragged by the scruff of their necks out of their hiding places (although one might well point out that she had sunk their ships in the first place, or caused them to hide away out of view, as a way of fusing both metaphorical interpretations in a way that might horrify George Orwell). The political goal of Margaret Thatcher was that the UK armed with this new economic and social philosophy might regain its 'rightful position' in the world. Mrs Thatcher, the grocer's daughter from Grantham (coincidentally somewhere in the middle of the country but that does not guarantee either impartiality or balance), said famously that there was no such thing as society (or the entitlements that derive from it) in an interview in *Woman's Own*. She effectively said this not once, but three times in this interview. It is worth pointing this out in case it might be thought that this is a famous quotation that has been taken out of context, or misinterpreted. It would not, after all, be either wise or desirable to start a semiotic argument with a case of misjudgement and poor interpretation. She said: 'I think we have gone through a period when too many children and people have been given to understand "I have a problem, it is the government's job to cope with it!" or "I have a problem, I will go and get a grant to cope with it!" or "I am homeless, the government must house me!" and so they are casting their problems on society and who is society? There is no such thing! There are individual men and women and there are families' (with two more mentions to come).

The North relied on heavy industry and manufacturing, particularly steel and mining, which were becoming increasingly 'uncompetitive' without government help. The steel industries started to close with enormous consequences for the region. Sheffield was called 'Steel City' for good reason. Unemployment rose rapidly. The number of people involved in manufacturing in the UK fell from 7 million to 4.5 million between 1979 and 1993. Unemployment rose by an extra 1.59 million in the first ten years of the new Conservative government. Many argued that the real unemployment figure was much higher because the government changed the definition of unemployment nineteen times in that period. This was a period of what political economists call 'negative deindustrialisation'.

The miners had brought down a previous Conservative government through the famous miners' strike of 1974, with the former Conservative Prime Minister Edward Heath going to the polls with the slogan 'Who governs Britain?' The answer was a hung parliament and Heath resigned. Thatcher from the beginning was determined to break any subsequent miners' strike (and it was clear from the start that she aimed to take the miners on, so a national strike was inevitable). The strike came in 1984–85, led by Arthur Scargill, the President of the National Union of Mineworkers, who Thatcher called 'the enemy within' ('more difficult to fight [than the Falklands War] and more dangerous to liberty'). What was lost in the end through this bitter industrial dispute, and the iconic and pivotal Battle of Orgreave, where miners and mounted police faced each other on a bright summer's day in June 1984, with numerous casualties on both sides and many arrests (although the charges were later dropped), was not just the coal industry itself, and the jobs, and the pride in manual work, but the mining communities. No such thing as society indeed, or mining communities, and a lessened sense of community anywhere in the North. It was all now to be just about the individual.

These individuals, alone and isolated, were now my neighbours, and here was I, sitting on pages of data of human interaction, all from the lab in Cambridge. I published my paper, 'Sequential temporal patterns of speech and gaze in dialogue', in the journal *Semiotica* in 1978. I was interested in how patterns of speaker eye gaze are influenced by the semantic planning phases of temporal cycles identified through relative hesitancy and what happens to the fluency and coherence of speech when eye gaze at the listener is not averted at these critical junctures. I studied how speech-focussed hand movements coordinate with these planning cycles and how the more complex movements occur at different parts of the temporal cycles compared to the less complex batonic movements. That was my academic background; this, I suppose, was my world, the world that I was still trying to hold on to.

Then I watched Thatcher in an interview with Denis Tuohy in 1979, and my life lurched again. My attention was not drawn to her threats and promises, her arguments, her 'vigorous defence of our proposals for trade-union reform', as she later described in her memoir, *The Path to Power*. I was interested in her nonverbal communication, of course, her gestures, her filled hesitations, the basic temporal structure of the interview, the turn-taking, the interruptions, the simultaneous talk lasting five seconds, and where this all came from. Two people talking at the same time – 'simultaneous speech' in any conversation, let alone a television interview, is very striking. This was what people noticed about this interview, this is what they remembered – this bossy, domineering woman who wouldn't let her poor interviewer get a word in edgewise. But I wanted to understand how and why this simultaneous speech was arising. What were the specific mechanisms? Perhaps it was my Cambridge training taking over. There are always different levels in human interaction, that's what they taught me down there, and I was drawn now automatically and subconsciously to the most fundamental level – the base level of structure and organisational principles, the mathematics of social interaction, not, of course, the level of everyday humanity.

I analysed the interview (my co-authors Anne Cutler and Mark Pearson focussed on the phonetic analyses) looking for sequences and regularities, trying to discover how the contested simultaneous talk had arisen. I discovered that it was she who was interrupted, rather than her interrupting the interviewer. That's not how it was viewed by the public. When I listened to the tape carefully, I thought that I heard something in her speech and then I noticed something in her body language (Beattie 1982b). I thought that she might be subconsciously cueing in her interviewer with a series of what the American psychologist Starkey Duncan (1972) had termed 'turn-yielding signals' (when I stopped the tapes at certain critical points, naive judges agreed with the interviewer that she had indeed finished her turn at these points). More specifically, she cued them in with a rapid fall in pitch at the end of a clause, both falls in pitch and clause endings are effective turn-yielding cues. With these so-called 'turn-disputed' utterances ('turn-disputed' because the interviewer came in at these points, but she continued to talk) she didn't let her pitch drop too low (there was a trough of 167 Hz compared with 141Hz for genuine turn-final utterances, where she had actually finished and relinquished the floor), but what she did do was let her pitch drop very quickly on these turn-disputed utterances (a span of 463 milliseconds for this drop). She also sometimes terminated an iconic gesture. However, she rarely used filled pauses, like 'ums' or 'ahs' (she only used four in the whole interview). Filled pauses are effective floor-holding devices – they protect the floor for about 600 milliseconds afterwards. Instead she made time for cognitive planning by extending the length of certain syllables or drawling. Drawl is another turn-yielding cue, and Duncan had found that the more turn-yielding cues displayed by a speaker, the higher the probability of the listener (or in this case, the interviewer) trying to take the floor.

I, therefore, had evidence which seemed to suggest that her idiosyncratic interview structures depended upon interviewer-initiated interruption which she then contested (leaving the interviewer a little puzzled). The locations of these interviewer-initiated interruptions could be mathematically predicted on the basis of prosodic and speech-based turn-yielding cues in her own speech. In other words, the high proportion of simultaneous speech was not simply a case of her underlying personality coming through in these interviews, rather this *joint* behaviour was a product of a more complex interactional sequence (although her underlying personality might well have had a role in how the breakdown in turn-taking was finally resolved). My guess was that her speech training from a voice coach at the Royal National Theatre in the years previous to this, which had successfully lowered her pitch and apparently encouraged her to drawl rather than use filled pauses to make more time for cognitive planning, was largely responsible for this.

I published my detailed micro-analyses of Thatcher's interviews and associated turn-taking problems in the science journal *Nature*; I called it 'Why is Mrs Thatcher interrupted so often?' (Beattie et al. 1982). I attracted some very positive publicity in the media for this work (including brief mentions on the front page of the *New York Times* and *the Sydney Morning Herald*) as a twenty-something academic and would-be semiotician, and offers poured in. The Iron Lady, I argued, was born in these micro-political battles rooted in various paralinguistic phenomena and body language. That, at least, was my thesis, and I was applauded for it.

But I am sure that many on the streets of Sheffield, where I was now living, would have been horrified at my academic focus on this interview, a focus on the nonverbal and prosodic mechanics of the verbal interaction rather than on the harsh political message – the threats to the trade union movement and her unqualified support for the police – 'The police do a fantastic job and we support them in every way possible' (interestingly, this was one of the turn-disputed utterances in the interview because Tuohy tried to take the floor as Thatcher said 'job', and yet Thatcher continued talking). Perhaps, worse, I was now making a career out of not seeing the broader reality of the interview or of life. After all, it is one thing to feel liberated in moving from the sound-proof rooms in the Psychological Laboratory in Cambridge, with the egg boxes covering the walls, to the academic offices and seminar rooms in the same building where tutorials and seminars take place to make my observations more ecologically valid, it is quite another to take my insights into that real world where I was now living. It is one thing to 'explain' Margaret Thatcher's domineering behaviours in the pages of *Nature*, or to an academic audience in Cambridge, it is quite another to attempt to explain my thesis to the unemployed steelworkers and miners, now living in her individualistic and self-reliant 'non-society', where the only kind of Good Samaritan worth knowing was the one with the pockets of his thawb stuffed with readies. How did my semiotic analyses fare in the wider culture? How did they translate to life on the street with the steelworks and the mines closing or closed, where it was all about the individual and sharp tooth and claw competition, where society, we were told, no longer existed, not even in these great traditional Northern communities where neighbour had traditionally looked out for neighbour? How did her message about self-reliance and self-interest (and greed and inequality) percolate down? What truths did they hear? What home truths? What mishearings? What did I actually know? Had I ever studied behaviour on the street itself where most human action takes place? Had any of my psychology colleagues? Our knowledge was premised on a thin and shaky empirical base, and, at some level, we all knew that. That's what makes the application of psychology so fascinating and so precarious. You have to one day leave the lab and survive with the little that you do know.

You may have the imagination or the foresight to think that it was always going to be very hard for a young psychologist to take his Cambridge research into this new territory, and that it is indeed dangerous, perhaps very dangerous, to proselytise about reading truth and lies in body language in less constrained and less controlled contexts than the Academy or the laboratory. For me it was a process of major discovery with many shocks along the way, as I set out quite alone to apply my newly acquired knowledge of nonverbal communication to other people's lives, where the unemployed steelworkers and miners were fighting to survive without society, now that the Iron Lady was firmly in charge. And where it was indeed obvious to anyone who chose to look around that she was now stamping her iron heels on all of them, until nobody knew which way to turn.

The piece in *New Society* on Carol had emboldened me. I left the lab for a while, I had to. I decided to attempt to write about human social interaction and life at another level, the level of individual experience. I didn't have the skill, expertise or scholarship of a Goffman (who always was a unique talent), I just had to write about what I saw. I had no training in this. Indeed, my training ran counter to this, with its focus on operational definitions and reliability of measurement. There would be little way of checking reliability in some of the situations I found myself in. No psychologist would have followed me down that street or into that dive or boxing ring. These were the places that I ended up.

I started in my own street two doors down with a tape recorder: I wanted to say something about situation, and then I went further afield, but rarely leaving Sheffield to begin with. I didn't need to. There was enough despair on my doorstep. But was I leaving psychology? That was what I was now having to ask myself. I didn't have a name for what I was now doing: 'ethnography' sounded too grand, 'reportage' too trendy, 'journalism' too banal. Goffman was whispering in my ear.

I used his book, *The Presentation of Self in Everyday Life*, to help me understand my observations – the unemployed still trying to be somebody, when everything had been taken from them. Goffman used a dramaturgical metaphor to analyse social life. He said: 'All the world is not, of course, a stage, but the crucial ways in which it isn't are not easy to specify' (1976: 75). People establish and maintain a 'front' – that part of the individual's performance which acts to define the situation for those who observe it. Hard-working men, grafting away, even when they were unemployed. Fred Smith, the unemployed steelworker (in the next chapter), took his breaks out of doors when he was decorating his house. At the end of the day he sat, with the grime still on his face, on his front step, at the exact time the employed were returning from their work (Goffman calls this 'dramatic realization' – 'While in the presence of others, the individual typically infuses his activity with signs which dramatically highlight and portray confirmatory facts that might otherwise remain unapparent or obscure', 1976: 40). I met a number of unemployed 'big spenders' in Sheffield in those years, pretending to have money that they didn't have, ten bob millionaires the ordinary punters called them, when they finally got wise. One drove an old Rolls Royce, and he kept it on the road by siphoning petrol from other cars. He had a VIP card to the top nightclub in Sheffield, it was free of charge to big spenders like him but he never bought a drink. He described himself as the 'man with the five-octane smile' and he brushed his teeth constantly, even in the multi-story car park below the club (he kept a toothbrush and a bottle of water in the car just for this), to maintain the image, the front, so that he could play the role of the big entrepreneur, making it, the fan of Margaret Thatcher and free enterprise. He lived in a council house, or did until his wife found out what he was up to, offering young women jobs in his company, the company that didn't exist. He was always on the lookout for a good PA, he said – one who was willing and able.

But this was always going to cause problems with psychology. Brian Butterworth used to pick out phrases of Goffman's back in Cambridge to illustrate sloppy sociological terminology and definition. I just wanted to write about the people around me and their worlds, their uncertainty, their fears, their desperate attempts still to be something. I recorded everything on my tape recorder, chatting to them in their living room, in clubs, in the back of a van as they drove from Hull to London to work on a building site, in a park where a bare-knuckle fight was about to take place, 'black-on-white', they said excitedly. Then the police tried to arrest me. I went out with a burglar as he cased up houses in a street that I suggested and he selected a house. I asked him how he would get in and I climbed up with him. I told him that he couldn't take anything. It was my own house (but he didn't know that). Mine was the obvious target because of where it was situated by a jennel (or alleyway). A few weeks later the house was burgled for real; the children were asleep in bed, and Carol was furious.

The irony was that while I was spending my time hanging out with burglars and boxers I was awarded the Spearman Medal by the British Psychological Society for 'published psychological research of outstanding merit'. This, needless to say, was for my other work.

I hadn't lost my interest in the spoken word and its nuances for giving meaning to our lives. I wanted to get close enough to them to get them to open up. So I took up boxing and trained with some bouncers in Brendan Ingle's gym in Wincobank. 'Don't let them use you as a punch bag,' Brendan admonished. This was action research, I was observing the world and the behaviour, and I remembered that old ethnographic maxim, knowing when to ask a question is as important as what you ask, and, you might add, so is where you ask it. The work was published in *New Society*, and then *The Guardian*, *The Observer* and *The New Statesman*, and in a series of books (Beattie 1986, 1987, 1988, 1990, 1992, 1996, 1998, 2002). I wanted to write it in a way that people, including politicians and policy makers, would understand – it was jargon free. I didn't try to flag up *any* academic credentials, I assumed that they weren't relevant, but I tried to spell out the experiences of the desperate unemployed, still trying to be something, in this new economic wilderness. And, needless to say, my own background: Paddy from the backstreets of Belfast helped enormously in getting on with my interviewees, many of which became my friends over many years.

As the young lecturer at the University of Sheffield, Dr Geoffrey Beattie, I was often asked whether I knew the other Geoffrey Beattie, the one who wrote for *The Guardian* and hung around with the unemployed, the pimps, the burglars, the bouncers and the lone sharks of Sheffield, and all of their multifarious victims.

I said that I'd met him in passing, and that he seemed alright, but I wouldn't bring him home with me. I said that you could never trust a man like that, you would never know what he might get up to.

Chapter 4

Other lives

Figure 4.1 Copyright Hugh Mckeown/Belfast Archive Project

Continuing this argument against psychologism we may say that our actions are to a very large extent explicable in terms of the situation in which they occur. Of course, they are never fully explicable in terms of the situation alone; an explanation of the way in which a man, when crossing a street, dodges the cars which move on it may go beyond the situation, and may refer to his motives, to an 'instinct' of self-preservation, or to his wish to avoid pain, etc. But this 'psychological' part of the explanation is very often trivial, as compared with the detailed determination of his action by what we may call the logic of the situation; and besides, it is impossible to include all psychological factors in the description of the situation. The analysis of situations, the situational logic, play a very important part in social life.

Karl Popper (1945/1983: 353) The Autonomy of Sociology

Karl Popper is widely regarded as one of the greatest philosophers of science of the twentieth century. His view of science is clear, in the words of his editor David Miller: 'knowledge evolves through a sequence of conjectures and refutations, of tentative solutions to problems, checked by searching and uncompromising tests'. Critical to this is the concept of falsifiability – all scientific conjectures must be restricted to those that are empirically falsifiable. This concept is what distinguishes empirical science from metaphysics and pseudoscience. Psychoanalysis, according to Popper, is not a science because it cannot be falsified – everything can be ultimately accommodated within the theory. Popper's concept of falsifiability as the defining feature of science is what he is best known for, of course, but Popper was a brilliant writer and thinker across a range of domains, and the quotation above is especially relevant to this chapter where I explore the situations of certain people way beyond the psychological laboratory, and hint at the situational logic that guides their behaviour.

Summertime in Brick Street

Summer had to come to 'Brick Street' some time and the mist eventually did lift from the Rivelin Valley so that you could see the grey slab flats of Stannington (they turned out to be brown and white, but they had looked grey all year). Swallows appeared overhead, dipping for flies. Boys with fishing nets set forth. Funny, I thought that sticklebacks had gone for ever, but they obviously knew different. Old familiar smells – hot tarmac, rain on warm pavements – returned to haunt the memory and tease the imagination. Steel City was heating up after a year of wind and rain. Cold Steel City to chill the bone and dampen the spirit, but now the chill had gone.

But Brick Street was different this summer. The noises were different. The feeling was different. People were getting up later. There was no bustle. It was now a street of people who didn't work. Some were retired, some hadn't got jobs yet; but most had been made redundant. Work was never really discussed. People were bitter. Casual enquiries about work or job prospects could hurl you into an endless spiral of accusation and complaint. 'Thatcher.' 'Foreign steel.' 'Bloody recession.' Most people only fall down this well once. Some things are better left unsaid; everybody knows that everybody else knows who's to blame and that's all that matters. And anyway, there were more important things to talk about – the decorating, the price of houses, the weather. This summer, especially the weather.

The women seemed to rise first. Two old retired dears brought their milk in first. They lived side by side and hated each other. Both were in their 70s, both were widows and both natives of Sheffield. One had a son, one hadn't got anyone. Mrs Hill's son came to visit her once a week in his S-registration Polo. He would sit for an hour in her house on a Sunday, then leave. If it was a good day they would drive for an hour. But one Sunday he had his two corgis with him. He was supposed to be taking his mother to Chatsworth for the day but, Mrs Hill said, 'There was no room with the dogs in the back. I don't mind. It would have been too cramped. It's a good day for just sitting out anyway,' and then she went off to the bingo. Her luck was in – she won a tenner. 'It pays me to go,' she said.

Mrs Hill's neighbour, whom she always referred to as Mrs What's-her-name (despite the fact that she had an excellent memory), was new to the street. She had bought the terraced house after her husband had died – it was a step down for her from lower-middle to upper-working. She had lived in Sheffield all her life, but not in this street. Mrs Hill didn't like her – she didn't like strangers. Mrs Hill left her living-room curtains undrawn well into the night and watched the comings and goings. Mrs Hill patrolled up and down her living room pretending to tidy it but really she was just watching the street. Her black and white television was always on. (Errol Flynn in the afternoon, Magnum at night.) Mrs What's-her-name also watched the street, but from behind drawn living-room curtains and after she had gone to bed she liked to watch from behind the bedroom curtains (Mrs What's-her-name was from a higher social class). You didn't have to page the oracle in our street; you just asked Mrs Hill. She knew who was moving and why; she was good on the price of houses, she was top on adultery and divorce. She told Mrs What's-her-name the spicier bits, but they were both a bit deaf, so they shouted. It was strange to hear yourself talked about in this way, but of course they thought they were whispering – it would have been too embarrassing to tell them. Mrs Hill went to the shops at 10 am and 3 pm. Mrs What's-her-name went at 11 am and 4.30 pm. Mrs What's-her-name also went somewhere at 7 pm, although no one knew where. Mrs Hill had tried to wheedle it out of her but Mrs What's-her-name's lips were sealed. Mrs Hill suspected that she took a drink.

Mr Smith and Mr Forrest were another unlikely pair. Both were steelworkers, both redundant for two years. Both bitter. Mr Smith was in his forties. His wife was a clerk; his daughter had just left school but hadn't got a job yet. Fred Smith had been decorating his home all year. Now he had reached the outside, he was replacing the window frames and varnishing the door. He started at about 9 am and took breaks every few hours out in the sun. He didn't sit out in the sun before he started, but only after he had

worked for a couple of hours and at the end of the day he didn't wash immediately, he liked to feel he had been grafting. He could then sit and enjoy the
sun for a bit – he'd earned it. He liked this stage of the decorating, its hard
work, plenty of graft; all the poncey bits done. He didn't know what he'd do
when the decorating was finished, though.

Mr Forrest, the other former steelworker, was fifty-seven, and lived at
the bottom of the street. In a street overlooking the Bole Hills and the Rivelin Valley – a street which was really exposed – Mr Forrest had the most
exposed house of all. The wind tore at his house, he was constantly replacing his tiles and his guttering. He had been made redundant just over two
years earlier. He didn't mind much at the time – his wife was very ill with
kidney failure. This summer she wasted and died. He always referred to her
as Mrs Forrest. 'Mrs Forrest is in a better place now,' he said. But he didn't
let her death get him down. He was constantly on the move, constantly busy.
He ran everywhere with his dog Suki. 'I could be out dancing every night,'
he said, 'if I'd got the brass.' He was always up ladders replacing people's
guttering, unblocking their drains, digging their gardens – he needed any
money people could afford to give him. He'd worked for a day for a couple
of quid. He got business by worrying people.

'The next time we have a good storm that drainpipe is going to come
right off.'

'Oh,' said Mrs What's-her-name.

'I could do it for you tomorrow.'

'Oh, all right then.'

And off he went, whistling his happy tune. He talked in the same kind of
shout as the old people because he was deaf from the years in the noisy steel
mill. The whole street shouted their private messages at each other. There
was little privacy here.

It was a funny, old-fashioned street. There was no graffiti, little vandalism.
There were too many people watching what was going on for these to occur.
Everybody knew everybody else's business. And yet the houses themselves
with their neat little gardens were very private. No posh houses, mind. They
were just stone terraced houses or fifty-year-old unfashionable, red-brick
terraced houses. Privately owned houses for the working class with the discipline and the thrift, once a way station for the economically mobile steelworkers reared in council houses. And houses for the retired folk when they
found themselves a bit of money.

But now things were different. Instead of standing on the parapets and
planning their advance into new unconquered territories, these people were
in a state of siege. Constantly reworking their decorations, their fortifica-
tions, constantly mending their guttering, varnishing their doors, constantly
polishing their J-registration cars. These people wouldn't be leaving their
castles and they knew it. They also wouldn't have to retreat, thanks to
redundancy payments.

So this summer, the sun was shining and the temperature rose but they were not tempted out. These were the working class, reared on discipline and hard work; sitting in the sun was redolent of idleness and waste. Sitting in the sun was skiving. And these were the people who didn't skive, who had timetables fixed and immutably etched on their brains, the people who thrived on overtime. But now the overtime had gone, as had the work. So they were poorer and a bit disillusioned. Some of them had lost all their aspirations and yet the little foremen in their heads still made them feel guilty for enjoying the hot summer sun.

And the sun was shining and the grey slab flats of Stannington across the valley seemed even closer. And the three-bedroom semis of middle-class Sheffield seemed a million miles away.

(from Beattie 1986)

The commuters

It was the middle of the night. A quarter past three to be exact, in a village called Holton le Clay, just outside Grimsby. The snow was falling heavily and the wind from the North Sea whipped it right across the road. It was a very good night for snow drifts, but very little else. Dave Cowley opened the front door of his little semi, and the wind blasted him in the face. 'Bloody hell,' he said. He'd left his wife wrapped up in bed, in the middle of her eight-hour sleep cycle. He was in the middle of his sleep cycle as well, and that was why it felt distinctly odd to be up and about. He pushed out through the blizzard, and into his mini-van. The temperature was way below freezing. Luckily the van started the first time. But the snow was starting to lie. 'That's all I bloody need,' he said, as he roared off, 'I'll have to push it a bit now with this bad weather, or I'll get caught up in the traffic, as I get near London.'

His housing estate was asleep, Holton le Clay was asleep, all of Grimsby was asleep. Nothing at all stirred. 'That's the bloody problem basically, it's dead up here now. The fishing industry's been killed off, and Grimsby was the fishing industry. Don't ask me why it died, that's political, and I'm not into politics, especially at this time of the bloody morning. But I've always been one of those that got on their bike basically. Just as well really.'

Dave made his way through the town, and into a cul-de-sac with more warm semis. There was one light on in the whole street. 'That'll be George,' he said. Dave pulled up. There was a slight delay as George made his way slowly through the blizzard and loaded his gear into the back of the van, between the portable bed and the empty buckets. 'The bed's in the back in case I can't find anywhere to kip tonight,' said Dave. 'I'm moving on to a new site today in Mansell Street near Tower Bridge. I haven't got any digs lined up yet.' George got into the van beside him, he was bleary-eyed and shivering. He wrapped himself in his donkey jacket.

'Wake me up when I get to London,' he said. George was fifty-five years old, 'and I feel it, I'm getting too old for this bloody game'. This game being commuting from Grimsby to London for work on a building site. Dave and George were both crane operators for the 'Expanded Piling Company' of Grimsby. George had been commuting like this on and off since 1957, Dave since 1971.

'But there's been one big change in the past five years,' said Dave. 'There's more blokes having to do it now. You'll see when we get on to the A1. You used to be able to do the 180 miles in two hours, but now the traffic is terrible near London. It takes nearer four hours now. You have to leave earlier and earlier to get there on time. It's dead in the North, that's the basic reason.'

'When I started out,' explained George 'you used to go down for a month or six weeks at a time. I never saw my kids grow up. I prefer coming home for weekends, but all this travelling is very hard on you. It's worse when you're travelling on your own though. This morning we're going in convoy with a couple of lads from Hull – they had to leave home at half two this morning.'

And sure enough, through the blizzard you could just about make out the other little 'Expanded Piling Company' van, with the snow settling in layers on its roof. Dave screwed his eyes up even tighter to try to see the van through the snow on the windscreen. 'And the worst thing is that with this weather we're going to have to push it all the way there,' he said.

Dave was thirty-eight, but he looked in fact much older. He had been getting on his bike for the past seventeen years. He did it, he said, for the job security. It cost him his first marriage. 'She found somebody else while I was away. But she wasn't a patch on Sheila, my second wife anyway. Sheila is more independent; she needs to be. She understands why I have to work away. Most building sites, you see, operate on a hire and fire basis. One week you've got a job, the next you're out. With this company, you've got a bit of security.'

For a basic week of 50 hours, Dave took home around £200. 'But the hours can stretch it a bit. I've had to work a 20-hour day before now, and once I had to work 27 hours on the trot. It can be risky work mind. One time my crane nearly tipped over on the Cenotaph, it's risky enough even without these long hours. But I've made as much as £400 in one week, absolutely fantastic wages by Grimsby standards, so I can't really complain. But you don't get money like that every week.'

With wages like that, he had been able to buy a three-bedroom semi in Holton le Clay for around £32,000. 'You'd get nothing in London for that kind of money,' he said, 'and don't forget within a few miles from my house I've got both countryside and seaside – Cleethorpes is only six miles away. I wouldn't swap it for the world. But,' he added after a moment's contemplation, 'the sea is a bit shitty around here, and to be honest if it wasn't for the people from Sheffield and Rotherham, no one would come to Cleethorpes for their holiday. I only go there for some decent fish and chips. But I'd never move to London. It's a horrible place, it's too fast and too expensive. I'm a big bloke, but when I go down the street, everybody's flying past me.' George stirred for a second and said: 'The people are all like ants, the way they pour out of the tube stations and that. Just like ants.' He curled up again, and his eyes closed – 'Five days a week in London is plenty, believe me.' Dave took over again, 'But that's where the money is, basically. If I'd bought a house in London when I first started working there, I'd be one of them now, I suppose – the rich. But I've left it a bit late. For me it's up and down this bloody road, week in, week out.' Dave squinted even harder at the windscreen, trying to follow the white line in the centre as it wound its way through the sleeping Lincolnshire countryside.

'The main problem with this job,' said Dave, 'is the travelling. I've had a few scrapes already. In 1976, I was off work for a year when I broke my spine in an accident on black ice. I was in hospital for four months. The bloke who found me just said, "I thought you were dead mate." I said, "Well, I'm bloody well not." I've never been so happy in my life to see the inside of a hospital. In '84 on the way back from London I went straight into a woman doing a three-point turn right in the middle of the road. There was a three-tier wedding cake in the back of her car, after the smash it was just trifle.' He guffawed with laughter, but George didn't stir. 'But luckily she wasn't hurt. Six weeks after that I rolled my car right over a hedge and into the grounds of a detention centre. My son Jason was beside me and he fell out of the car, luckily he wasn't hurt. There wasn't a straight panel on the side of the car though. I'd just bought it as well, but I hadn't got round to insuring it yet. It's just the law of averages though. You're bound to have a smash going up and down this road all the time. I think I've been pretty lucky so far. One of my best pals was killed a few months ago, I guess his luck just ran out. I've worked out a few ways of keeping myself awake on the drive – I'll sing at the top of my voice, or talk to myself. Who cares if people think I'm a nutter? Sometimes I have a shave when I'm driving, with an electric razor. I don't shave all week when I'm down in London. So when you start pulling your beard off with this thing, it keeps you awake alright. There's nothing more boring than driving slowly.'

The blizzard stopped rather abruptly as we headed toward the A1. The road was dry now as Dave started to accelerate. I couldn't stop thinking about his sojourn in hospital, as we started to drive faster and faster.

'It's not a bad life,' said Dave. 'In addition to your wages, you get £12.36 a day subsistence allowance. That's not bad – it's a quid over what most firms pay. You can usually get a bed and breakfast for around £14 a day in London in the Kings Cross area. The only problem is that we're out in the morning before breakfast and back in the evening after tea. We get fish and chips most nights, or a kebab. We live on that kind of food. Nearly everyone prefers working out of London; up in Morecambe you can get bed and breakfast and an evening meal for £8, which is very reasonable.'

'And a cup of tea for 15 pence.' Added George. 'In London it sets you back about 25 pence.' George shut his eyes again.

'The only problem is,' continued Dave, 'all the work is down in London. They're always pulling office blocks down and putting up new ones. I've built all sorts – the Lloyds bank building – that's a real space oddity, the extension to the Covent Garden Opera House. I've even drilled a hole in the House of Commons car park. I don't talk about my work much at home, and Sheila has only been to London a couple of times, so she's never really seen anything I've built. There's too much to be crammed into a weekend to have time to talk about it. We have to do the shopping at weekends, and visit all our relatives. My dad has farmer's lung disease, and if I don't take him out, then he doesn't get out. It's as simple as that. And Sheila often says that some things that you're dying to tell each other about during the week just seem trivial by the time the weekend comes around. Sheila would like me to work at home but she knows the score about the job situation up in Grimsby. Once you couldn't move down at the docks early in the morning, now you can drive straight through any time of the day or night. That says it all. You either go in search of work, or you stay on the dole and commit Hari Kari, and I don't fancy that somehow.'

We passed Lincoln Cathedral at around 4.30 am. Lincoln slept.

'I'm going to a new site today and I don't know what it's going to be like. If I can't get digs, I'll have to just kip down where I can – in the site office or whatever. I always say that after a few pints it doesn't really matter anyway. The truth is I don't even go out drinking much in London these days. After a day at work I'm too knackered. We used to go up in Soho and that sort of thing – into the sex shops. When I was looking at this magazine once, this bloke came up behind me and said, "This ain't a library mate." I'm big, but he was huge, so I legged it. But I'm getting too old for that sort of thing now. I usually go to bed before 10.00 pm. I bring a little portable telly with me and that's about it. Sometimes I'll go around some model shops in the evening – that's my hobby, you see. Now and again the blokes will bring a blue video to watch in the site office, but I'm more content with a good fishing book to tell you the truth.'

The A1 got noticeably busier near Leicester. It was, however, still pitch black. 'The other problem with this journey is that there are so few transport cafes open all night. But luckily there's one around here – time for a cup of tea,' he said and we pulled into Truckers restaurant. The other 'Expanded Piling Company' van was already sitting outside. Inside sat another Dave, who was a foreman, with Mark and Jim. Nobody talked, and somewhat incongruously the TV in the corner was broadcasting an American news programme about the Republican Primaries. 'You know, I'd prefer to work anywhere in the country except London,' said Dave the foreman – 'anywhere.' This was followed by a long silence.

We left the cafe at 5.45 am, and got back on to the A1. The road was starting to fill up. Dave still pushed the pace along. Dawn started to creep up as we entered Hertfordshire at around 6.20 am. Ten minutes later the A1 was solid traffic. London was still twenty-nine miles off. 'Five years ago this road would have been empty at this time,' said Dave, overtaking another mini-van full of workers. 'To miss the traffic jams now, we'd have to leave at 2.00 in the morning.' George started to wake up. 'Do you know what you're building at the moment, George?' asked Dave.

'No, but it's probably an office block, they're all office blocks – going up or coming down. It's always the bloody same.'

We started to drive through Mill Hill, it was now 6.45 am. A green Mercedes, with a personalised number plate, raced the van at some lights, and finding itself unable to leave the van behind, simply cut right in front of it. Dave muttered something, you could see that he hadn't really got the energy to shout anything stronger. 'It's like this,' said Dave, surveying the posh houses of Mill Hill, 'there's so much money floating about down here. I was on a job where they offered the resident £30,000 each not to complain about the noise. Thirty grand a piece. Straight up. There are some Cockneys on the site, and they're all the same – they've all got their heads screwed on alright. And look at all those wanted criminals on the Costa del Sol, they're all bloody Cockneys. They don't just go for the odd grand, they go for the whole bloody lot. They think big down here, that's why all the bloody money in the country has ended up down here. It's nothing to do with effort. Nobody worked harder than the Grimsby fishermen, and look what they got for their trouble.' George just squinted out at the roads paved with gold and litter, before getting out of the van at his site at Tower Bridge. 'See you on Friday,' he said.

It was now 7.25 am as we pulled into Mansell Street. It was still freezing, but thankfully there was no snow. I made my excuses and retired to bed. Dave started a day's work.

(from Beattie 1990)

The song and dance man

'Ooooooommmmmmppphh.' The noise erupted from the pit of my stomach. From way down low. It did not sound human. It was an involuntary response way beyond my control. Way beyond anybody's control. That's what I tried to tell myself. It was out before I could do anything about it, and there was no way to apologise or make amends now. That noise sealed my fate. Gary, standing at the side of the ring, laughed. I wanted to. I wanted to smile and to clown about to show that I wasn't taking any of this seriously. But I couldn't. It was all serious, and that was obvious even to the casual spectator. I was grimly determined. Just try saying that word 'grim' and watch how it makes your lips purse in an ugly manner. My lips wanted to hang open, bleeding, sucking in the air. It took all my effort to keep a face together. I was past caring whether it looked aggressive or like the face of somebody who should be respected. It was a grim mask.

To spare my embarrassment Gary kept glancing away, shouting to his mates still on the bag routines. But I could see him looking back towards me, looking out for little signs from my body. To see how I was taking it. To see what kind of man I was. I covered up. I watched the eyes of my opponent. I was looking for signs from him. Of what, I didn't know.

But I was already starting to slide down the greasy, phylogenetic scale of respect. If I had started the morning at the gym on my first day of boxing at the level of hamster or dormouse, I was now fast approaching the level of amoeba. I had been warned, you see, not to make any noise when hit. 'We have lads who've come down to train once or twice and they've taken a good shot and then they're down on the canvas.' Gary had warned me before we started. 'The rule down here on a Saturday morning is if you're hurt, you box on. If you're hurt, you don't make any noise – you don't make a song and dance about it.' But it was too late. I had made a noise, and not just any noise. I had managed to produce a low moan that had played its own tune on the way out. I had never heard that noise before, although I had seen it written down several times in comics when the filthy Bosch had been butted in the stomach with the handle of a gun by some Tommy or other. I was the filthy, cowardly Bosch. Or an amoeba. I didn't much like the thought of being either.

I was now watching my sparring partner's face for a sign of recognition of my rule infringement. I had broken the rule; I had violated the code of manly conduct in the ring. But there was no such sign, just that quiet look of satisfaction from Mick 'The Bomb' Mills of work well done. My song, which had started so softly and which had risen to some sort of crescendo, was music to his ears. There was a sign at the side of the ring that read 'Boxing can damage your health'. It was meant to be funny. I now knew it wasn't. I was trying to remember where my spleen was, and trying to imagine how it would feel burst. Or merely ajar, leaking. Seeping.

I was more determined now. It might have been just the impetus I needed. Sweat dripped into my eyes. It stung. I tried wiping it away with the edge of the glove. It left my stomach exposed. My vest was soaked with sweat. My biceps ached. Never had I imagined that a man, even a complete novice at boxing, who had been performing bicep curls more or less continuously from the age of eleven upwards, would ever have to endure biceps that ached. Not biceps, for God's sake; those curious muscles that run up the back of your arm, maybe, but not the obvious bicep. But just try that movement – out and back, out and back, out and back with the left arm – a hundred times, now a thousand times. Continuous defensive movement. I ached. All of this effort expended on my jab was meant to be effective. It was meant to keep my opponent at arm's length. But it was no defence at all. Mick walked right through them. His jabs, on the other hand, landed with great dull thuds on my upper arm and forearm with hypnotic regularity. My arms were stuck rigid in a defensive covered posture.

He bobbed and weaved as I tried to land one good punch on him. Just one, Lord, just one. I wanted him to respect me. I was desperate for some respect. But I knew that I was going to have to earn it. I wanted to start scrambling up the other side of that deep hole I had managed to dig for myself through my whimpering. But I was telegraphing my shots and he didn't even have to block them – he just had to bob and weave. He was about my height, five foot eight, but his forearms were of similar dimensions to my thighs. My shots were landing harmlessly on those great slabs of meat. And by the time they had landed they had no power whatsoever. As Mick had said earlier: 'Boxing looks easy enough, especially on the telly. You may even be able to land a good punch on a bag. But connecting well with someone who's moving is a lot more difficult.' It's all in the timing, and my timing was off. It was a simple as that.

The problem was that I always thought that *I* could have done a lot better, even with a moving target. I had always fancied myself in the ring, you see, although for the life of me I couldn't remember why. I had been brought up on boxing. My uncle had been an amateur boxer in his younger days, and on Saturdays when he and my father got back from the pub I would be invited to box him. Me and the dog both. Spot, our black and white fox terrier, would only ever attempt to bite him on Saturday night, when he reeked of Guinness. Spot would be on his shoulder biting his neck, I would be clambering over the back of the settee boxing his ears. My uncle was by then about five stone overweight, but it didn't matter. My aunt was always very proud of the fact that I had managed to give my Uncle Terence a black eye, never mind the scars that Spot managed to inflict. My uncle would sit hunched up in his suit, sweating, with the Guinness coming back out through his pores. The dog would distract him and then, 'wham', I got one in. My uncle would hurl the dog to the floor. 'You have to show them who's the boss,' he would say. My mother would agree.

'Your uncle is very good with animals. Your father's too soft. You have to be cruel to be kind.' We always worked ourselves up into a great lather, all salty sweat and sickly foam from the mouth of the dog. The dog would have to go and lie down in front of the electric fire afterwards to cool down, and then it would sneak round the back to drink the porter out of my uncle's glass. Only on a Saturday night. But all that was a lifetime ago. It was no preparation for this. A one-on-one. Man-to-man. No Spot to help me out.

Mick never stopped moving – this way and that. Impossible to pin down. My punches left my body hard and determined, but they fizzled out somewhere in the gap between us. Mick's glory days in the ring may have been behind him, but I say 'may have been' because there were still some people in Sheffield who were talking about a comeback for this ex-fighter, who was now a bouncer, but he was streets ahead of me. Untouchable. He was always a good crowd pleaser, and his punch had not left him – the boxer with the hardest punch since Randolph Turpin, Harry Gibbs the referee had said. They had warned me on the way to the gym that Mick could be a bit heavy-handed. I thought they'd meant he wasn't very tactful. Now I knew that it was meant in an altogether more literal sense. 'But,' they told me, 'he won't hurt you. He knows that you're a nobody. He'll have nothing to prove.'

Sweat was closing my eyes. I was working in the ring. Voices from within. Nothing to prove indeed. A nobody. Work! Acidic little drops in my eyes. Narrower and narrower. Imaginings. 'So the countdown for the end of the first and the steam is already showing now.' The steam was showing, rising from the solid thick torso in front of me. Steaming bulls on a cold winter's morning. No, raging bull. Majestic. How would I look in the ring if the camera was on me? How was my footwork? Just try a little shuffle. I looked down, and another heavy jab nearly broke my shoulder. Careful, steady now. Blocking. The raging of the beef brigade, steaming bulls. Steaming. Steam. Two steam trains speeding towards a head-on collision. A clinch, our heads collided. He compressed my arms at the elbows. Locked in tight. My breathing slowed. Like an animal caught in a trap. I didn't want to breathe on him. I didn't want my breathing to tell him anything. I felt his forehead grinding against the side of my head. I could hear the wet hairs rubbing. Short, spiky, wet hairs grinding against my temples. I tried to pull back. Then again. Stuck fast. Just that noise in my ears, and my elbows feeling as if they were about to shatter. No referee in this sparring. Just one-on-one.

Then the trap flew open; he let me go. Bored.

Everything on the proximal horizon was now a blur. He was the focus, the sole figure on which my attention was directed, and when he moved, which he did continuously, his whole body was a great white blur. Out of this haze, for that is what it had become, I just felt these slow, methodical blows. A man at work. Not sharp, stinging blows that might leave you annoyed or irritated but great, solid, dull thumps. Every time they landed on my chest I thought they might stop my heart. I had never heard of a boxer's heart being stopped by a punch before, but those moments in the ring I thought that this was a real possibility. My heart was racing and then, boom, it slowed. The involuntary noises coming from my body, as I was winded, reassured me that I was still alive. A sudden surge of energy. The body in full flight. Adrenaline pumping. A strange feeling of optimism. Noises from within and without. Alive and working now. Harder! Faster! I was listening for the bell that had to come, and hearing other voices.

'This is the most professional that I've seen Beattie.'

'Beattie was never intimidated, he got on with the job.'

'I'm proud of Geoffrey Beattie, because he did the job fantastic.'

Gary stood there saying nothing, too embarrassed to watch.

Out through the haze and way out somewhere in the corner of my eye I could see that we were now being watched by another bouncer with a T-shirt that said 'Kiss my ass'; I had dreaded this moment. I thought I might be able to survive in the ring with Mick, as long as there was no one there speculating, or just Gary, who was only half watching anyway, but now there was a crowd of two to egg him on. My heart was sinking fast. My wave of optimism had broken on the shores of this grimy, blood-stained ring. Paul, the bouncer in the 'Kiss my ass' T-shirt, and a black belt in jiu-jitsu to boot, who also happens to own a couple of fitness clubs, called across the room: 'You're not running, are you, Mick?' It was an inoffensive kind of question, really. My eyes told Mick to ignore it. They pleaded with him to ignore it. But his feet started to grind to a halt. My knuckles were already bleeding after the bag work. 'Left jab, left jab, right jab, left upper-cut, left hook' – the opening routine in the bag work. Ten times. It was the upper-cuts that had done the damage. It was the upper-cuts that had brought the knuckles of my two smallest fingers on my left hand into contact with the bag. After one routine they were bleeding. My hands felt tender. What damage could I inflict on him with those hands?

I had been talking to a climber the previous day who had just fallen off a rock face. He had told me that it was the longest one and a half seconds he had ever experienced. As 'The Bomb' drew to a halt, I could understand exactly what this climber meant. I remembered what Joe Louis had once said: 'You can run, but you can't hide.' But I couldn't even run. At least not backwards. Mick had let me go after him. I now had a little experience of moving forward and defending myself, but none whatsoever of moving backwards and staying upright, with those jabs coming at me.

The first blow came to my shoulder. It jerked my body around, as if someone had rotated me in a dance. He squared up for a second punch. 'Don't forget, no head shots!' shouted Gary. I covered my stomach and started to make an involuntary but quiet 'uuurrrrggghhhh' sound even before the shot had landed – in preparation, I think.

'Time!' shouted Gary, laughing. 'We never time rounds here. We play it by ear, so to speak.' I wasn't sure whether he intended the pun or not, but I was relieved anyway. 'He was just playing,' said Gary reassuringly. Mick and I touched gloves and I climbed slowly out of the ring. My legs were trembling. Mick started to shadow-box the air where I had stood. The air probably put up more resistance than I had. Steve climbed in beside him. Steve had also been a professional boxer, but he'd never had the same kind of talent as Mick. One of Brendan Ingle's old boys – a spoiler. He knew how to look after himself in the ring and that was about it. Now, he looked after himself on the door of a nightclub. He still had a full-time job as a sheet metal worker. He was no challenge to Mick. 'Bastard,' said Steve under his breath, as one of Mick's bombs landed within the first few seconds.

I had a chance to look around the gym. Old faded posters, heavy bags, sweat-stained floor. Everything hinted of work. There was a lot to be done. This was my first day of training. My sparring partners worked as bouncers at Josephine's nightclub, Sheffield's ultimate nite-spot, it called itself. They had been asking me for months to join them in the gym, but I had always managed to get out of it without losing too much face. I had said that I wanted to learn about boxing. They had told me there was only one way, and that was by stepping into a ring. This ring was famous. Herol 'Bomber' Graham, who had two cracks at the world middleweight title but had never made it in the end, had bobbed and weaved in that confined space. Kids would queue up to try to land a punch on him. The old slippery Graham would stand with his hands behind his back, dodging every one. Johnny Nelson, an up-and-coming cruiserweight, was honing his skills in those same few square feet. Then here was a young Arab boy, called Naz, with buckets of talent, or so they said. And here was I. The song and dance man with leaden feet. The ring was in Brendan Ingle's gym in Wincobank in Sheffield. An old church hall – St Thomas' – with a great wooden floor. A few rusty weights, and huge punch bags everywhere. One speed ball looked forlorn in the corner. On Saturdays Brendan let Mick and the lads borrow it for a workout. 'We all come from different backgrounds,' said Gary. 'Professional boxing, karate, jiu-jitsu, and there's Lloyd, who's been a professional heavyweight boxer and is now a body-builder. He's currently "Mr Central Britain". Mick Quirke is also a body-builder and he owns his own fitness club. Oh yeah, and then there's the DJ from the club where we work. That's him trying to skip over there. After the bag work today he took off his gloves and his hands were all red. He thought they'd been cut to pieces. It was the dye from the bag gloves! But it's good for us all to get together and know what we're all capable of.' Or not capable of.

Mick now climbed into the ring with Paul, the black belt in jiu-jitsu. Paul had something to prove. Mick winded him in the first few seconds. Unlike myself, Paul made no sound. Gary watched this bout with me. 'Everybody here has a lot of respect for Mick. You don't appreciate how good he is until you step into the ring with him. Although we only play at boxing down here on a Saturday, you've still got to think very carefully about what you're doing. It's a very good way of finding out what it's like to be hit. It's also a good way of getting rid of aggression. Working on the door of clubs, you rarely get called upon to do anything, and then when you do it's usually out of the blue. Some kid managed to get my coat over my head and put my head through a glass door in Dinnington a while ago. The kid had a big reputation in the area. Mick was working with me at the time, but he didn't help out. In fact, he was standing taking bets on who was going to win. But it was important for me to get the better of this kid. Mick knew I had to come through it on my own. It was like an initiation ceremony. It must have been harder for Mick to stand there and watch than join in. Mick could have punched holes in the kid. He's still very good. Although Lloyd is good and very, very big, he doesn't have the same kind of talent that Mick has. These regular training sessions down here let you get all of that kind of stuff sorted out. You soon get to know what kind of talent everyone has, and who to respect.'

I kept thinking of deer rutting, and status hierarchies in the animal kingdom, but what had any of this to do with mating, for goodness sake? The

DJ, who had trouble skipping and even more trouble with his upper-cuts, had his girlfriend and newborn baby along to watch, as if to emphasise the point.

'I've never done any boxing in the past, but Mick has taught me everything,' continued Gary. 'I regret not taking up boxing earlier. The nightclub where we work recently put up a glass case with photographs from all the other door staff's fight days. They had boxing photos of Mick and Steve, boxing and wrestling photos from Big Jim, and boxing and body-building photos from Lloyd. I had nothing to put in the cabinet. Mick says that although I'm thirty I should try a few fights in the ring. He says I'd be OK. It'd be something to look back on, something for the glass case.'

In the changing room with the paint hanging off in great dollops sat another Gary, an up-and-coming heavyweight boxer who works as a bouncer in a club in Nottingham. He was wearing a black T-shirt with 'Rhythm Killers' on the back. 'When you face up to guys like Mick Mills on a Saturday, then you know you can handle whatever comes off the streets the rest of the week. Training always makes me feel very calm afterwards.' I wished I could agree with him. I had by now realised that there were people out there who could punch holes in me. I think I had been happier in my ignorance, but I kept my mouth shut.

This was my initiation. I sat in the changing room examining my body. My upper arms and forearms were black and blue. Bruises were appearing on my back as if the pain and injury had been conducted right through my torso. Mick laughed. I promised faithfully that I would become a regular down in the gym on a Saturday. I told them I wanted to understand boxing – what it felt like, where the boxers came from, why they did it. Mick told me that I had started well. 'You mean I know what it feels like?' I asked. He wiped his face with the back of his glove and looked at me with little expression in his eyes. There was no sparkle there, no real warmth, certainly no respect. Perhaps a little curiosity. He had a look at me before he replied. 'I wouldn't go that far, but at least you know what a sickener it is to get one in the stomach. Boxers have to get used to sickeners. So at least you've made some kind of start.'

(from Beattie 1996)

Selling jewellery on the never never

It was a normal-looking jeweller's shop in the suburbs of Sheffield, just up the hill from the university. Inside the shop – the nerve centre of the operation – you could hear the laughter out the back. Behind the jewellery, behind the glass cases, behind the gold and silver. Somebody was telling a funny story. The laughter dampened down. Then it erupted again. Great guffaws of laughter. Bodies curled up in spasms of mirth, behind those four walls. Behind the thick blue velvet curtain. I edged closer. The voice had a

Black Country accent. 'I've sold vacuum cleaners to people without a carpet in the house.' The laughter started again slower this time, but quickening. The pitch rose in volume. 'I sold a woman two ironing boards – one for upstairs. She only had a £100 credit limit, so she couldn't have the iron.' This time the laughter sounded harsher; it came out like 'tak, tak, tak'.

'I've sold a woman velvet windows for every window in the house including the toilet.'

This time there was no response. 'Velvet windows?'

'Velvet curtains, I mean.' He had fluffed his lines, and the laughter never came. I could see in now. The man with the Black Country accent had a ruddy complexion. Too much time out in the biting wind, knocking on doors, canvassing – as they put it. His partner sat in a leather chair. Balding with a paunch, wearing a brightly coloured shirt. A large Rolex glinted on his arm, thick gold rings on two fingers of each hand. Two women were doing the accounts in an adjoining room. Brian, the owner of the shop, watched as the £50 notes changed hands. He listened intently to the tales from the field. His employees had been out there and survived.

It was his turn in the round of stories. 'I remember Ron telling us about having to go back to this customer who had complained about his carpet, which had a hole worn in it. He went into the house and said: "What have you been doing here, then? It's not for walking on this, you know." The punter said, "Oh, I'm sorry." So Ron said, "You've worn it out because you're supposed to pick your feet up when you walk. You're not supposed to shuffle along it."' The laughter crackled as Brian shuffled along his imitation of the gait of the hapless punter.

In the background you could hear the quiet but confident tapping of the calculators as the figures were being totalled. 'A very good week,' said Brian. 'A very, very good week,' said the bald man with the Rolex in a parody of the AA advertisement.

We were in the back room of a jeweller's shop in Sheffield. The jeweller's car, all £50,000 of it, sat outside the shop, looking just slightly incongruous in front of a shop that size. The shop, despite its tasteful jewellery, didn't look capable of sustaining a car of that sort. And it didn't. It was the back room that paid for the car, the back room with the little charts on the wall and the rows of noughts after each figure.

This little room was the centre of a highly successful company selling jewellery in what it called a 'direct sales operation'. In the past they had sold other items in a similar fashion – duvets, ironing boards, sheets, Hi-Fis, carpets, vacuum cleaners, even frying pans. But now they were concentrating on jewellery. Brian explained to Mark how it all worked. Mark was hoping for a job there. The company worked hand in glove with a credit collection company. The idea was simple and very neat. Agents from the credit company would go out on a weekly basis to collect outstanding debts from clients. They obviously got to know their clients very well. A representative

of the jewellery company would then accompany the agents to certain targeted customers – customers who were paying off their outstanding credit.
'But only to the very good payers, or to the "crème-de-la-menthe" [sic] of
the good payers, as we put it,' explained Brian. The jewellery would then be
offered to the customer on the never never. They showed Mark and myself
an attaché case containing all the gleaming, glittering merchandise. Rows
of gold horseshoes and coats of arms, and rings inlaid with semi-precious
stones. ('*Semi-precious* covers a lot of bloody things,' explained one of Brian's salesmen helpfully. 'It's better than saying the stones aren't real.') All
this temptation to clients already in debt.

'We're doing a social service to the public,' continued Brian. 'We sell
directly to some disabled customers who can't get out to the shops. We
bring a jewellers shop right to their own doorstep in some of these highrise
flats they live in.'

'And don't forget that ninety-nine per cent of our customers couldn't go
out and borrow a tanner from anybody else. And if a customer decides
not to pay, there's not a lot you can do about it. If a guy's unemployed and
you take him to court, the court won't have a lot of sympathy for the guys
who've got him into debt. The court will end up telling him that he'll have
to pay you off at 50 pence a week. We're in a business where we have to
take a lot of risks. You can't go in with a hard edge, because they're your
customers.'

Brian blew on his coffee. 'And believe me there are some right evil bastards out there, who just want to screw you for what they can get. They'll
borrow money, they'll take your jewellery, they'll take anything that's going
with no intention of paying any of it back. Then when the credit company
says that they have to pay up, they'll try to return the goods. We had one of
our agents ring up and say that his customer wasn't going to pay because
she was dissatisfied with the ring we'd sold her – the stone must have been
loose or something because the bloody thing had fallen out. So we got the
agent to send the ring back in. The stone was still there, but the ring was so
dirty that you couldn't see the stone. It was all misshapen as well. We've had
rings returned when the punters have obviously punched somebody with
the ring on their fingers. These are the kinds of people that we have to deal
with.'

Two more salesmen arrived back. A case of jewellery lay open on the
table. One of the salesmen stood well away from the attaché case, as if it
might contain a hidden, unexploded bomb. 'I hope that's not the case that
the dog tiddled on last week,' he said. 'Perhaps you should sniff it and see.
How did you let things like that happen? The worst thing that ever happened to me with a dog was when this little Jack Russell ate one of my rings.
I put the dog's name down on the voucher. My boss at the time went mad.
But what else could you do? Anyway, we got the ring back after a week,
although the label had disintegrated.'

They all laughed. These were people on a high. You could see that everyone here was a winner. The jewellery company had a group of customers targeted for it, plus the introduction from someone who was almost a friend of the family, and the credit company got its customers to continue to borrow. The jeweller got his money directly from the credit company, which in turn took a hefty commission. The credit company had, however, to collect the debt, but this was their business. Sweet. Very sweet. Everyone was a winner.

Except, perhaps, the customer.

A customer buying a £300 ring over 120 weeks would pay £204 on top of that for credit, and this is an individual on a low income and already in debt. 'But the customers themselves care little about the interest rate being charged. All they're interested in is how much per week the ring or gold chain or whatever will cost them,' explained Brian. 'This £100 ring will cost them £1.60 a week over two years. We always say in this game that we leave all the multiplication up to the customer. It's not our problem, after all. But you couldn't walk into a High Street shop anywhere in the world and get a ring like this for a fiver a week.'

I looked at the ring with the horse's head on it. 'It's Red Rum, I think,' said Brian. 'You see, many of our customers are unemployed. But we always say that the unemployed are often better managers of money than those in work. They know exactly how much is coming in. They might be paying between ten and thirty quid a week to the credit company, for all sorts of things – household goods, car repairs, plus, of course, to clear previous debts – but they know they have to meet the repayments, because they've nowhere else to go for credit.'

'We're basically salesmen, we're not their financial consultants,' explained one of his salesmen. 'Our customers often tend to be at the very bottom of the heap. You should see some of the houses that our men have to go into. I've been in a house in Winsford in Cheshire where the mother was selecting a £300 diamond ring and the six kids were sitting around having dinner out of a jumbo tin of processed peas. I've been to houses where you can see piles of disposable nappies chucked out the back and left to dissolve in the rain.'

'I've been to houses where I wouldn't crap in the bog,' said Brian, not wishing to be left out of all this. This notion that the customers are somehow different from themselves, somehow alien, is very important to maintaining the spirit of the team. 'It's a different planet out there,' added Brian unselfconsciously.

Mark and I left that cosy little office with Brian for a look. It was a bitterly cold night on the other side of the town. Brian parked his jeep at the end of the street. Some teenagers on the corner eyed us suspiciously. This was a regular call. Brian was on his own tonight. He was pleased that Mark, with his boxing skills, was with him. He poked his head in through the broken window between the kitchen and living room. The house may have been poor, but still it had a colour TV, a video recorder and a library of video-tapes, including, incongruously, *Jane Fonda's Workout*. Brian was welcomed into the house like an old friend of the family, which he undoubtedly was. Angela's husband was not about. 'He's off again,' said Angela. Brian told her not to worry. 'You've got some new curtains since I was last here . . . I've got some goodies here for you to look at.' Angela's father sat beside her. Things, you could say, were not going too well for the family. 'I was married forty-nine years, eleven-and-a-half months. If she'd just lived another two weeks we would have made our golden wedding anniversary,' said the father. Brian was settling in – 'It's like coming home, you know, coming here. When I sit down on this settee I don't want to get up again.'

'I always have a right good laugh when Brian comes round,' said Angela. 'It's one of the few good laughs I ever have.'

Angela's son woke up at this point. He ate some ice cream out of a plastic bowl. A pile of coins had fallen into the bowl; the coins remained there as he ate the ice cream. Angela said she wasn't interested in any jewellery, until the case was opened. The rings sparkled brilliantly in those surroundings. 'Ooooooh, come here, let's have a look, then.'

'Try it on,' said Brian. 'Now let me tell you how much that would be a week if you were to buy it. That would be a week if you were to buy it. That would be £4.08 a week. Very reasonable, eh?' Brian turned to Angela's father. 'We've got some nice men's tackle here, if you're interested.' He unfurled the gold chains in their velvet case with a practised flourish. The old man sat up straight for the first time. 'Try it on,' said Brian. The old man fingered the chains as Angela started pouring her heart out to Brian, mainly about financial worries.

'I'm more like a social worker sometimes,' said Brian as he climbed back into his jeep. 'Some of our customers are really decent people in hard times, and it's all very sad, but what can you do?'

If Brian was the social worker, Billy was the clinician. 'You can't afford to get involved,' he said. His technique was quite different. 'I'm a master at this game. It's all done as a series of moves. Watch me.'

The frost was worse the following night. The punter looked as if he had just been roused from a deep sleep. He looked like the sort of man you wouldn't like to upset. Probably early forties, but could in real time be younger. 'What are you trying to sell me this time? Not more bloody rubbish, I hope.' This was Billy's cue. Mention 'rubbish' and Billy is right in there.

'Not rubbish, sir. Certainly not rubbish.' Billy had explained to me previously that selling works on objections. 'I've got some smashing jewellery for you today, sir, and a little bit special it is.' Billy was now ushering the punter, the agent and myself all into the front room of the little house. This house was a good deal more orderly than the previous one. Billy was in charge, and we could feel it already. The wife emerged from the kitchen. Billy had told me that the first thing you must do when selling is to assess the situation – see what priorities the customer has got. The wife had obviously just finished washing up, so there were no problems there. The telly was blaring in the background, but they'd obviously only been half watching it. The situation was 'ripe', as Billy liked to say.

As the agent sorted out the financial transaction, which was ostensibly the real purpose of the visit, Billy started to open his attaché case. All that glittering gold. He had their attention, their undivided attention – well, almost. 'Is anyone watching that?' said Billy, pointing at the television, and then without waiting for an answer he nipped across and switched it off. There was a stunned silence for a moment. The television probably acted as a backdrop to every conversation that had ever taken place in that front room, at least since the time when someone like Billy had last visited.

'Now, madam,' said Billy, 'if I said to you that you could have whatever you wanted from this box free of charge, what would you have?' There was another slightly stunned silence as everyone in the room tried to work out whether this was a genuine offer or some elaborate ploy. 'I'd have one of those rings. I love rings and so does Frank there.' Frank nodded enthusiastically. If there were any rings going free, he wanted to be in there as a potential recipient of any largesse. So Billy now knew that it was a ring they were both after, and he knew exactly what they could afford. 'Ripe,' I thought I heard him muttering, but he may just have said 'Right'. Billy guided them through the rings. Rings were no longer £180 or £220, they were just a couple of pounds a week over two years.

It was now just a case of selecting the items. 'What job do you do, Frank? Lorry driver? Right, then. You don't want anything with a stone in it, that's for sure. It'll make your finger go black.' Frank nodded and his gaze shifted to the solid gold horseshoe rings.

Billy started to chuckle. 'You know, I once said the very same thing to a blackie. It took me a few seconds before I realised what I'd just said. I apologised and told him that it was just a figure of speech. "No offence taken, mate," he said. You can't be too careful, though, can you, Frank? You have to watch what you say to them. Now, what about this smashing ring here with the horse's head on it? Are you a gambling man yourself, Frank? I like a bit of a flutter. I'm sure that's Arkle. Just think – you could be wearing a racing legend on your finger for years. It could be a family heirloom. Leave it to your kids, Frank, there's a little bit of history on that ring. And don't forget the price can only go up, especially with inflation. That ring's only £180.'

You could see that Frank was far from prepared to carry out the necessary mental arithmetic that would tell him exactly how much this nag's head ring at £1.80 a week over two years would eventually cost him. He didn't care. One look around the house told you that here was a family very short of heirlooms. Ripe.

It was now Alison's turn. 'I would have thought something with one of these ruby or emerald stones would be right up your street, madam,' said

Billy. 'They are real, aren't they?' asked Alison nervously. 'A friend of mine bought a ring with fake stones in it a while ago. She'd been taken in, but I'd never fall for that.' Billy adopted a tone of some seriousness. He wanted to sound sincere, scholarly. 'They're what you call semi-precious, love. They keep their value very well, do semi-precious stones. They're a really good investment.' But it was time to get off that track double-quick. 'Here, let me try to guess your ring size, love. "P", I reckon. Is that pretty close? Now try this one. Didn't I tell you? A perfect fit. That one's only £1.20. What do you think of it, Frank?'

Before we had made the call, Billy had drawn Mark and myself a graph of the whole procedure from going through the door in the first place to finding the egress double-quick at the end. Even I recognised where we were now on the graph. We were, at that very moment, sliding down the hill, on the other side from the sale. Billy had now only to do the paperwork and then we were out. His rule was to talk about anything other than the sale at this stage. A little bit difficult with two customers still mulling over the concept of *semi-precious* on the same settee as him. 'Aren't you going to put the kettle on, then, love? We're all parched in here, and I'm sure that Frank could then, love? We're all parched in here, and I'm sure that Frank could do with a cuppa. Isn't that right, Frank?'

Friday was the day when all the salesmen came back from the field with their tales of survival out there with the punters. They swapped stories and compared sales. 'Now, Bob, are you going to explain to us all how you managed to lose an £86 gold chain? I wouldn't have thought that a salesman with thirty-three years in the business would have fallen for something like that?' The rest of the salesmen laughed.

'Well, it was like this,' said Bob. 'I went to this jewellery party at this house, where there were fourteen scantily clad women. Now, you can't sell to all fourteen in one go, especially because they were all new to credit. So I had them in three at a time in the kitchen. I'd already sold a grand's worth of stuff when this eighty-six-quid gold chain suddenly went missing. One of the birds had obviously tried it on and then let it drop down her bra. What could I do? I couldn't very well line them all up for a strip search, now could I? Even if I'd wanted to. I've always believed, by the way, that you should never get involved with customers like that – even when I used to sell sheets and bedding. Business comes first, you have to remember that. Some of the reps I've known haven't been as disciplined as me. There was one rep I used to work with who had five kids in five different houses on the same estate. Straight up. But I've always put the sale first. My old boss used to say, "Never get your fishing tackle out when you're trying to make a sale", and I think that's a good philosophy of life. So I wasn't interested in any strip search at this jewellery party. So I played on their sympathies instead.

'I told them that it was a hundred-quid chain, and that the money would be coming out of my commission. Then I watched their reactions. One bird asked if it really was worth as much as that. You see that gives you a clue – she must have seen the price on the ticket by that stage. Then the same bird asked, "Aren't you insured?" That gives you another bloody clue. So I say, "For the whole case, madam, not for a single item. So who wants to hit me on the head and take the whole bloody lot?" You see, I'm still working on their sympathies. And it worked. One of the husbands, who had turned up by this stage, then ordered a £300 chain. So I'm in profit, even if I have lost a chain.

'But this is small-time thieving. It's a dangerous game walking around some of these places with thirty-six grand's worth of stuff in an attaché case. I can tell you. I've had a few near misses over the years. I was in this block of flats in Birmingham one time and I was the only white face to be seen. My heart's pounding, and I'm gripping my case. There are these four big black guys in the lift with me, and I'm already thinking that I've been set up. There had been a single order, you see, from one of the flats on the top floor. So this big black guy turns to me and says, "Which floor are you going to, Doctor?" You see, I was wearing a pinstriped suit, a collar and tie, and was carrying this attaché case. So I played along with it.'

A close friend of Bob's, however, who also worked for the same company, was not so lucky. He had been mugged in Moss Side in Manchester. As he emerged from one house he was hit over the head with an iron bar and knocked unconscious. He was off work for a fortnight. 'And the worst thing about it,' said Bob, 'was that he was treated like a bloody criminal by the police for a fortnight. The police always seem to assume that it's an inside job, even if you're lying in the gutter with your brains smashed in. They think that you were involved in it somehow or other. My pal's carried all his jewellery in a sports hold-all rather than an attaché case since the mugging.'

Bob had a theory about the violence that goes along with such robbery. 'The problem with muggings is that the people who do them always get so hyped up beforehand. They think that they're going to have to do you, so even if you offer to hand over the case of jewellery they end up doing you just the same. If anyone tried to mug me I'd hurt them, for the simple reason that I know they'd end up doing me anyway, so I might as well leave my mark on them. That way, they'd have to go to hospital sooner or later, and you stand at least some chance of getting your gear back. If you end up losing your gear, then you know that you're going to be the number one suspect and that's not very pleasant, believe me. That's the negative side of the business, but on the plus side there's the thrill of selling, although you have to have a sense of humour for this job.

'I've got a joke for every occasion. OK, try this one: What do ostriches, pelicans and poll tax collectors have in common? . . . They can all shove their bills up their ass. I've been using this joke on some of the estates where the poll tax isn't too popular. Or did you hear the one about this fellow who went to the ticket office at the train station, and said, "Two tickets to Nottingham, please" (in that very nasal, blocked-up voice from the TV advert). So the guy from the ticket office says, "What you need is some Tunes." And the other guy says, "Why, do they cure cerebral palsy?" I use this joke all over the place. You need a good sense of humour in this business.'

Bob has spent a lifetime in direct selling, and telling jokes; it has not always been jewellery, although he reckons jewellery is easy. 'The basic argument with jewellery is that you have it forever. It will give you years of pleasure, even after you've forgotten what you've paid for it. You buy it now and you even get two years to pay it off, so it's cheaper than it would be in two years' time. You get a new jacket, on the other hand, and the same time next year it's out of fashion. I've sold everything. I used to sell Calor gas heaters. They produced so much condensation that one woman rang the water board because she thought she'd got a leak. Then it was fitted suits. You should have seen the state of some of those suits – hanging right off the poor bastards who ordered them. One salesman couldn't fill in the forms correctly with all the details. I put it to him, "Have you ever seen someone with a fifty-six-inch waist, and a forty-inch chest?" Then it was safety rings for children to wear in the water, which came in the shape of ducks. With these particular rings, when the kids went into the water the ring turned over. There were all these complaints from parents that their children had been nearly drowned with them. Then it was the furniture, now it's jewellery. It's all the same to me, to be honest. But the truth is with jewellery we get a lot of respect from the police for carrying this much jewellery around with us. I was in an accident last year, when my car went down a ditch. You should have seen this copper's face when I told him what was in my attaché case. He climbed down and got it for me. When I told him where I'd been with the gear he told me I deserved a medal. Well, it's all a service to the public, I told him. Somebody has to be prepared to do it.'

(from Beattie 1996)

Bare knuckles in the park

I heard the word the night before in a nightclub. It was to be a fight, the like of which I hadn't seen before. Bare knuckles, anything goes, a fight to the bitter end. It was Big Steve who gave me the word. 'Bring your camera if you like. You'll get a few good shots.' It was his older brother who was fighting. He wasn't with Steve in the club. 'He's in bed, resting,' explained Steve. 'What's it all about?' I asked. I was told not to worry about that. It was a grudge match. The nature of the grudge was never explained. 'But he's fighting a blackie,' added one of Steve's entourage, trying to give it a bit of extra sparkle. 'Just remember to bring your camera,' said Big Steve again. 'We want you there to record it for posterity. One of my pals is going to video-record it for me. We'll have something to look at when we're old men, something to look back at when we're past it.' The venue and the time were whispered in my ear. I was a little surprised by both. I thought that he might be setting me up.

It was a bright, sunny spring afternoon and the park in the posh west side of the city was full of children, ducks and lovers. The sunshine had drawn them all out. A circus tent had been erected in one corner of the park, and the children were congregating down that end. At the opposite end by the duck pond stood three men in their late twenties or early thirties. One wore shades and a bright yellow Levi jacket. He had the build of a bouncer. He and his friends were obviously waiting for something. It just wasn't clear what. They didn't look like the type to waste a few hours in a park, even on a sunny afternoon. They looked like the type who should be bobbing and weaving in some dark corner somewhere. The sort who don't get up until lunchtime.

They sounded lost. 'Are you sure this is the right spot? It's the only needle thingamajig in the park. It must be here. I bet your other man doesn't show, anyway.' The man in the yellow jacket with the fifty-two-inch chest seemed to be thinking aloud: 'This is going to be a right waste of time.'

'A right waste of bloody time,' echoed his friend, as another young couple with their nice, neat middle-class children in tow walked past in search of the ducks.

'I've better things to do on a Saturday afternoon than this, you know,' said the man with the huge chest and shades. Suddenly a cavalcade of cars approached along the road at the side of the park. 'Ey up, something's happening,' said the man in the shades. But you couldn't see his eyes to determine whether he thought that what was happening was positive or negative. A series of cars pulled in and from each poured groups of men of the most unlikely shapes. One was at least six foot six and twenty-two stone. None of the men looked far behind in terms of build. I could only guess at their occupations. They were clearly not men to mess with. Out of the last car emerged two females, with unlikely shapes of a different sort, and tight-fitting clothes accentuating their shape. The men poured into the park; the females hung back gingerly.

Two men seemed to be leading the group. One was smaller and older than the other. 'He's ready,' said the large one. It was Big Steve. He winked across at me. 'Fit and ready for the fight,' he said again reassuringly. His older brother wore what looked like an old casual shirt, khaki-coloured combat trousers and trainers. 'I came down this morning and swept the concrete slab where they'll fight,' said Big Steve. 'I bet it'll be as slippy as fuck,' said his brother. 'I'll be slipping all over the fucking place.' And at this point the performed a few mock slips, before going into a hand spring. 'He may be forty-five and he may not have had a proper fight for fifteen years but he's as game as fuck,' said the man in the yellow Levi jacket. And the bare-knuckle fighter stood in front of the assembled throng demonstrating his kick-boxing technique. 'Whamo,' he said as he kicked the air. 'Whamo.

I may not have had a proper fight for all those years, but you never lose your ability. Isn't that right, brother?' Big Steve just nodded. 'My whole family have natural fighting talent, natural talent. None of this steroid crap.' Big Steve added after a slight pause. 'I fucking hate steroids. You see all these bastards walking around full of them.' The man with the very large chest, indeed the unnaturally large chest, dressed in the yellow Levi jacket, winced.

Steve's brother did another handspring on the grass. I wasn't sure whether he was warming up or giving us all a demonstration. But a demonstration of what? A demonstration of the fact that although he was forty-five years old he could still do handsprings on the grass? Or were these moves he was going to make in the fight, the fight where anything goes. Even handsprings.

We all waited patiently. Mick Mills had been one of the first to arrive. I just hadn't noticed him. He had been sitting on a memorial to Queen Victoria. He looked pleased to see me. 'I hope you've not come to fight in those clothes, Geoffrey. They might get a little bit dirty.' They were all laughing, including Big Steve's brother. I suppose that it was a way of relieving the tension. I just happened to be a convenient target, the fall guy. 'Things may get a little bit out of hand, and you're poncing about as if you're going out for the night. I mean black trousers and an orange bomber jacket. What the fuck do you think you're here to do?' It hadn't occurred to me that I might be involved in any of the fighting. My imagination did not stretch that far. They were all roaring with laughter, but they got bored quickly. It must have been the tension. I asked Mick what he knew about it all. 'All I know is that it's a bare-knuckle fist fight between our man and this black kid, who's twenty-four. It's a bit of a grudge fight, really. The dispute's been going on for months. It flared up again in a casino in the middle of the week. There was no way it was going to be settled amicably so they agreed to settle it here today at two o'clock. Big Steve asked us down here to show a bit of presence, to back him and his brother up. Big Steve's well respected in this town, in fact he's got the hardest reputation in the whole place. But it's his older brother who's involved today. The rest of the family will have to stay out of it, if the blacks do, that is. If they get involved it could be really dangerous, because some of them could be carrying knives and that sort of gear. It could be a war down here today.'

It was now five minutes past two, and the seriousness of the occasion seemed to be lifting. The birds were singing, for goodness' sake. Big Steve's brother continued to loosen up with a series of kicks and handsprings. I thought he might wear himself out. The hard men with the fifty-inch chests continued to greet each other and remake old acquaintanceships. 'What time did he ring you at?' There was a certain pride in who had been contacted first. It was a measure of each individual's personal worth. Then it was time for other chitchat – 'Did you have a lot of trouble on the door last night?' I overheard one boxer talking to his friend – 'I know somebody who's put two hundred quid on the black kid not showing. My pal says he hasn't got the bottle for it, and look at all us mugs standing about here on a Saturday afternoon. I bet we look like a right circus.'

There was almost a party atmosphere, growing as every second passed. The other kid was late. 'No bottle.' You would have had to be deaf not to have heard the whispers. 'No bottle.' But suddenly the whispers stopped. 'Just look down there. It's like something out of *Zulu*.' And there across the park walked this large group, nearly all black. Just one white guy with a shaved head and an Alsatian dog and girlfriend in tow. There were over thirty of them, nearly all big just like the other group. 'This is war,' said one. 'Jesus, they've even brought their families for a day out,' said another. The bare-knuckle fighter momentarily stopped his kick-boxing and stripped off his shirt. He wore a black singlet under the top. 'There's the black kid down there in what looks like brightly coloured pyjamas.' And sure enough one well-built black guy with a shaved head walked up to the concrete slab. 'Right, brother, you're on,' said Big Steve. One of Big Steve's pals with a camcorder made his way down to the slab to record the whole thing for good measure.

The two fighters faced each other from opposite ends of the slab. This was a fight from a different era. They circled each other slowly. The white fighter appeared to be smiling ever so slightly. The other one looked extremely serious. This was, after all, a fight with no rules. This was a fight that nobody would stop. The large contingent of spectators would see to that. I noticed that some kids from the park had crowded in for a better view. One little girl with long blonde hair was playing with the toggle on her hooded sweatshirt. It seemed an age before any punch was thrown. The black fighter missed spectacularly with one. The white fighter smiled again. The crowd grew impatient. 'Go on, get stuck in, stop fannying about.'

'Go on, get stuck in.'

'*Go on, finish it.*'

'*Go on.*'

'*Go on.*'

The first punches landed with dull thuds. A boot made the same kind of dull noise on a groin. Blood was already appearing on the white fighter's face. The two bodies locked together and tumbled on to the ground. The brightly coloured pyjamas pushed and heaved and toiled their way to the top of the dusty heap. The crowd swarmed in. 'Don't touch them.'

'Leave them to it!'

'*DON'T FUCKING TOUCH THEM!*' A black fist was still free to work inside the hold. It smashed into the white guy's face. His teeth sank into his ear.

'He's going to bite his fucking ear right off.'

The group of blacks opposite were going wild, sensing that their man was winning. 'Finish him off. Fucking do him proper. *Do him!*' shouted one in dreadlocks. The blood poured out of the older guy's face. The black guy standing over the pair of them took the initiative.

'He's had enough.'

'Do you want to call it over?' he asked of the battered and bloodied white fighter. No words were spoken, but then again perhaps none needed to be. It was obvious who had won. The black guy in the bright pyjamas got up slowly. Big Steve was trying to smile. The large contingent of blacks walked back through the park. The whole thing had only taken seconds from start to finish. The large gang supporting the white fighter looked crestfallen.

'He got too excited before it started,' said Big Steve. 'He'd got nothing left when the fight itself started.'

Big Steve's brother slowly got up off the ground. His face was covered in blood. There was a deep bite wound by the base of his ear. It looked like the ear might have come off if the fight had been allowed to continue. 'How bad is my ear?' he asked his brother.

'Not too bad,' his brother replied. 'It'll look better once it's been washed.'

'That was a load of bollocks,' said the fighter. 'It never really got going.'

'Never mind,' said Big Steve. 'These things happen. Don't worry about it.'

The group made its way back slowly to out of the park. Mick was disappointed. 'That was fucking crap. I've seen better fights than that in my local boozer.' The large gang seemed very disappointed with their man's performance.

'If I'd fought like that last night I'd be in hospital today,' said one with some teeth missing.

Suddenly a number of police cars screeched along the road. Police wagons and other vans. Police wagons and other vans with dogs hurtled across the park. 'Don't run,' said Big Steve. 'Just make your way out. Don't look up, for fuck's sake. Just try and walk right past them. If they ask about his ear, just say that he was climbing a tree and fell off.'

We shuffled out of the park. 'Stop right there!' shouted the senior officer on the scene. 'What's been going on? What's happened to his ear?' We were like the deaf and the dumb. We just walked in a straight line. The police did not try to physically stop this group of large, dangerous looking men. I kept my gaze focussed on the ground in front of me. Without glancing up, I turned instinctively to the right of the gate. Unfortunately, my car was parked somewhere along the road on the left. I seemed to be out on my own. I had stuffed my camera up inside my bright-orange bomber jacket. I walked quickly, trying not to run. I got to the end of the road and turned right, trying to double-back on myself to get to the car. A large van of police screamed to a halt beside me. My bright jacket must have stood out a mile. They asked me what I had been doing in the park and what I had inside my coat. 'You've been photographing the fight, haven't you?' they asked. I said that I had been photographing the ducks. They asked for my name. When I said, 'Dr Beattie', they said, 'Go on, Doctor, sorry for bothering you.'

I saw Big Steve that night in the same nightclub as the night before. He was in a foul mood. His brother had been beaten and his friend who had been given the video-camera to operate had forgotten to turn it on. He told me that there was going to be a rematch, but this time it was going to be in a barn somewhere, with no possibility of any interference from outside. He said that his brother had taken some tablets for a bad back and that these tablets had weakened him. 'That's why he lost. It was just because of these tablets, you see.' I thought it would be unwise to dispute this. 'The next time he'll win and win well.'

Before I left he asked me if I knew how to operate a video-camera.

(from Beattie 1996)

Work today, paid today

I had been told to turn up at five o'clock in the morning to be first in the queue for work. I would be paid at the end of the day. It was an American concept apparently. Work today, get paid today. It represented the casualisation of labour in this great country of ours. But there had been a storm the night before in Salford and the wind and rain had been lashing against my window. I had started to drift off to sleep but the rain had begun to sound like a fire crackling. I know that this is an unlikely image, but that's how it sounded. Like a fire just outside my window, threatening and irregular enough to keep me awake. I got up a bit later than I had intended, bleary-eyed. It was just after 5 am. I had to walk. There was no sign of any buses at that time of the morning so I didn't want to risk waiting at the bus stop, and there were very few souls about in the freezing rain to ask about the times of buses. So I set off in the rain, impossible to dodge the puddles in the pock marked streets, but there was time for one last selfie, as I paused by the zebra crossing, my eye lids still blinking with the tiredness.

I got there after six, but I wasn't the first to arrive. I looked around to get my bearings. One man in his late twenties sat huddled under his coat in an armchair. A girl of perhaps nineteen sat on a settee. She had tinsel in her hair. They were watching *Goldfinger* on a large screen, drinking coffee. James bond was enunciating 'Pussy Galore' very carefully. 'Poooooosy,' said the man peeping out from beneath his coat, sensing my presence. I couldn't see his face. I must have smiled because he said it again. You have to be careful, you don't want to cause too many ripples in a place like this, with faceless men.

I went up to the reception desk and registered for work. A surprisingly cheerful young man with clean shiny hair and nice even teeth explained to me that I would have to complete a safety questionnaire. 'It's alright,' he said. 'It's multiple-choice.' He told me to fill it in at a large table. I assumed that it would be very easy – after all, the work was hardly going to be demanding. 'When are drugs permitted at a job-site?' it asked. 'Never' was the first answer. I was just about to tick 'a', chuckling quietly to myself at the idea that some people might think that you are permitted to bring a large lump of hashish to a building site, when I noticed that the second answer was 'Only when prescribed by your doctor'. 'What is the most common site injury?' was the second question. 'What is the safest way to carry objects up a ladder?' 'How should you carry a power-tool?' I had no idea, so I guessed.

The young man behind the counter smiled at me benevolently when he gave me my score. 'You got sixty-five per cent, but don't worry. Oh, and you got today's date wrong.'

'I'm sorry,' I said, trying a wry smile. I always thought that it was part of my charm. 'I get dates mixed up sometimes. I've often got a lot on my mind,' I said. He looked at me as if he felt a bit sorry for me. I couldn't help noticing that my Irish accent had grown noticeably stronger. I don't know why. That soft Northern Irish lilt comes and goes. It seems to have a mind of its own. But I didn't try to explain this to him. I wanted to stop while I was ahead.

He didn't tell me any of the correct answers. He just told me to take a seat, and help myself to coffee and a doughnut. I sat next to the girl with the tinsel, who didn't look at me. 'This film is crap,' said the man from below the coat. 'So is the latest James Bond film. They're all crap.' The girl just nodded once while exhaling. She had reddish hair, and a pale, pinched face. She looked like she might suffer at times from some sort of acute but undifferentiated anxiety, a gnawing anxiety that might stop her interacting with people in a pleasant way.

I could hear American voices from behind the counter. Young men with co-ordinated shirts and ties. Immaculate at this time of the morning. I noticed that there was a sign above the full-length mirror on the far wall. I went over to read it. I stood there in front of this mirror, looking at myself, padded against the cold of a Salford morning, with a thermal vest below my sweatshirt and an old leather jacket. Not fashionably old, just unfashionably old: 1991 rather than 1950. Something to wear on a building site. My eyes were red from sleeplessness caused by the crackling noise of the storm the night before. The lower lid of my left was twitching. I had never seen this happen before, and I found myself staring at the little spasms of the lower lid.

'Would you hire this person?' the sign above the mirror read. I laughed to myself. I knew the answer to that one.

I sat down and sipped my coffee. I read the other notices on the walls. 'No guns, knives or other weapons are allowed on the premises'. 'Anybody caught drinking before or during work will be terminated'.

They wandered in individually. Young men with shaved heads and the remains of attitude. The young man behind the counter knew most of their names. Most of them were regulars. Two teenage girls came in together and immediately went outside for a smoke. A man sat down beside me and we started talking. He had a South African accent, he stuck out a mile. He told me that he had to get out of his home country. Luckily, his wife was entitled to an Irish passport. 'There's a rape every twenty-six seconds at home,' he told me. His brother had been hijacked. 'He was stripped naked and kicked to pieces. That was when we decided to leave.' The man had been in the quality assurance field in South Africa. Last week he was cleaning aircraft seats with high-pressure hoses for £14.15 an hour. But life was better here, he told me. His wife could walk the streets at night. 'There are some gang-related shootings in Salford, but it's nothing compared with back home. You're very lucky here,' he said. 'You should count your blessings.'

I laughed politely and went back to looking at the big screen, counting my blessings. Goldfinger was raiding Fort Knox, and Pussy was co-ordinating her team of foxy girls. The man under the coat had got a laugh once so he tried again, 'Poooosy Galore'. Nobody responded this time, so he pretended to go to sleep. I sat and waited. I noticed that a lot of those who had arrived after me had been sent out on jobs before me. *Goldfinger* was ending. Mr Bond, at least, was on the job. I assumed that I was being passed over because of my score on the safety quiz and the fact that I didn't seem to know what date it was. Or perhaps it was because I could claim none but the most basic of labouring skills.

The girl with the tinsel put on a new film. It was Judge Dredd with Sylvester Stallone. She seemed to be in charge of the film selection, but her pinched face meant that few would be inclined to challenge her. I found myself watching the film. 'Would you care to explain that, Citizen,' said Judge Dredd who was judge, jury and executioner all rolled into one. I wanted to know why I was still there. I went to the toilet but there was no toilet roll. I came back to my seat, feeling slightly soiled. There were only two of us left now: me and some latecomer. I tried to start up a conversation but he wasn't interested. I asked what the work was like here. 'Shit,' he said. 'I'm only staying to half nine and if nothing comes up I'm going home,' he said. I too thought about going back to bed. It was nearly nine o'clock. I had been there for almost three hours. Then I got the call. It was all first names. "It's factory work, Jack," said the young man with the open smile. 'It's warm and dry and not that bad. It's putting zips on jackets. To be honest with you, the firm wanted women, but we don't have any. I've just sent a car load up, but one of the staff will give you a lift.'

I went out the back and jumped into the small car with an American who had thick, heavily lined skin, like the skin of a lizard. He was under pressure because they had sent a group the day before but they had not made the target. It was a rush job before Christmas. Some jackets had the wrong zips and they had to be fixed. 'We're bailing out China,' he said in a way that only an American could. 'That's why the cock-up occurred. Are you ready for this job today?' he asked.

'I am,' I replied.

'Are you really ready for it?'

'Definitely,' I replied. I noticed that there was now no trace of my Irish lilt. I was becoming posher by the minute. I wanted him to notice that there was something different about me. It was pathetic really, but I wanted to stand out like I did when I was a student on summer jobs on building sites. But I didn't. On the drive up, he didn't once ask me anything about myself. I was just another hard-up punter. We raced through town following another of the American employees in his car because he wasn't sure where the factory was. He was crunching the gears. 'I'm not used to this kind of little tin car,' he said.

I asked him about the agency. 'Well, in the States we get a load of homeless working for us,' he explained. 'They queue around the block for a job, but you lot in Salford are a lot better off. You all have houses.'

I nodded vigorously. 'Indeed we do,' I said. I was now emphasising my vowels like a classically trained actor.

I asked about the rate of pay, but he said that he couldn't remember it offhand. And then he returned to the stresses he was under, with the guys letting him down. 'I could train four monkeys to do this job,' he said. But I wasn't sure where that left me, the wise monkey who speaks no evil, who keeps his counsel, who just listens, the untested monkey who said nothing.

We arrived at the factory in a part of Manchester that I didn't know, but there was trouble already. The man who like to say the word 'poooosy' didn't want the job when he saw what it involved, and he wanted a lift back. The two Americans were discussing whether he *deserved* the lift or not. I was led in past the regular workers who looked at me with cold condescension. I sensed my place. It was all in the way they looked. The guy who had been huddled under his coat was walking up and down, a little agitated. 'This is a crap job,' he said. 'I'd rather play with my dick than work here.' The two decided that he should be taken back, and he was led away.

I was shown the ropes by Phil, who had been there for a week. 'It's fiddly,' he said, 'and boring as hell, and the pay is shit. But apart from that . . .' Our boss, sensing the mood, decided to stay for an hour to motivate us. He talked about us bailing out China, and then talked about us bailing out the company.

'Do we get extra if we make the quota?' asked Phil.

'We'll see,' said the boss.

He positioned me right beside him and offered to race me in the assembly of the jackets, and for some reason or other I agreed. I could tell by the looks of the others that they thought that I was a bit soft in the head for going along with it, but I agreed to try to fasten fleeces to jackets, file down the zips, fold them and bag them quicker than him. The boss talked incessantly throughout. I beat him, and his retort was, 'Gee, if you and the rest of the guys keep that up all day, then we might be out of the woods.

'You see, guys,' he said, 'this can be fun.' He was quite serious. I could see Phil making wanking movements with his hand. The boss stuck it out for about forty minutes. He left us to it, after suggesting that Phil should be the new boss for the day. 'I'll do it for £6 an hour,' said Phil.

'We'll see,' said the American. 'We'll see.'

Our gang stood in a huddle away from the rest of the factory. You could tell that nobody really trusted us. It was hot and, as I had dressed for a building site, I had to strip off to my thermal vest. It wasn't yet 10 am and I was feeling done in already, red-eyed and yawning. I started chatting to one of the lads with a shaved head. Kev told me that he had stayed up all night decorating his girlfriend's flat because he thought that he might not get any work that day. He was worried about getting through the day.

The girl with the pinched face and the tinsel in her hair worked away on a bench in the far corner. She had a personal stereo and seemed to be in a world of her own. Occasionally she danced, sometimes she burst into song. She was taking selfies as if she was dancing in a club, or at a Christmas party, with all that tinsel around, every time the coast was clear.

A few of the Salford lads formed a clique within our group. They told each other tales of gangland Salford as they fiddled with zips. One of them, who had been a professional boxer, was talking about his form, 'five wins out of twelve; it's better than it sounds', and then he told us that he had told off the Salford godfathers for giving toffee to children.

'The kids might get confused and accept it from perverts,' he explained. 'Your man agreed with me and admitted that he was in the wrong. It's just as well for me, otherwise I'd be dead meat.'

Another told the story of how he took his daughter to visit his mother in hospital and passed armed officers guarding another Salford gangster who was recuperating in hospital. 'Daddy,' his daughter said, 'the gun you keep in the cupboard at home is bigger than his.' They all laughed, but they made sure I was listening. Big men reduced to this.

'If I'd invested my money when I was younger, I wouldn't have to do this crap,' said the man with the gun at home.

I noticed that three of them had iPhones that didn't go off once that day. After the introductions, nearly all the talk was about money. I kept myself to myself for obvious reasons. 'Do you know how much you're getting today?' Phil asked me.

'Not really,' I said.

'You'll be lucky if you clear twenty quid. So slow down, for fuck's sake. You're not on piece rate,' he warned.

Every time U2 came on the radio, Kev with the shaved head shouted over, 'I bet you like U2. They're Irish as well.' And just in case I missed them, he'd shout a warning every time they came on.

Management in suits passed us, occasionally making friendly little quips our way, and Phil, Steve and Darren would smile back and whisper 'fuck off, cunt' under their breath in one single exhalation. We were told at lunch time that if we all went to the chippy our half-hour for lunch would commence as soon as we put on our coats. Only two could go. I ordered fish, but it wasn't much of a chippy because I was told there wasn't any fish. 'You can have chips or chicken or a sandwich. That's all,' said the girl with the tinsel very loudly over the music from her personal stereo.

We had our lunch together in the canteen as the regular workers carried in food and drink for their Christmas party. Phil kept asking them if we would be invited. Some said they would ask the boss, but you knew that we weren't welcome. You could just tell. 'If I was a woman,' said Steve, 'I'd be a fucking millionaire. I'd lie on my back and make fucking millions.' According to one of the regular factory workers, who supervised us, one of our lot that week had been an escort. 'And a lesbian,' he added for good measure.

The day seemed like a month. I have never looked at my watch so many times or felt that an hour could last an eternity. I always thought that time flew. Not here it didn't. In the afternoon tea break we got the leftovers from the Christmas party and a can of lager each 'to take home with us'. We all drank them on the spot. Then they huddled by the back door to smoke some dope and blow the smoke out into the cold, wet air. The smell inside was still unmistakable. The men in suits pretended that they didn't notice as they hurried past. The lads made some effort to fan the fumes away, as if they understood that some effort was all that was required, from what was clearly perceived as the dregs of society, the hopeless cases.

We knocked off at 5 pm. The young lad in charge of us said that we had done loads of jackets that day. He also told us that the factory paid £6.55 an hour. We were on £4.15; the agency pocketed the rest. I felt that we were being watched as we left the factory, as if we couldn't be trusted not to attempt to relieve the boredom of the work with a few fleeces under our coats. Sometimes, I feel that you can understand the motivations that under-lie petty thieving. A couple of the guys picked up a fleece each and stuffed them inside their coats. I declined. 'What's the matter, Paddy?' one asked. 'Are you good living or something? Or chicken?'

'Just chicken,' I said. 'That's me. Chicken Jack.' And they all laughed at me.

Phil raced us back to the depot where we queued for our money. I got a cheque for £23.10. The rest got two quid less because they had money deducted for the lift to the factory. They forgot to deduct mine.

Our American boss was back at the depot, beaming away. We told him that the factory was pleased with our performance. Phil asked about our bonus for making the target. He told us to hang on and he went into the back room. He emerged 'with something for each and every one of us'. He gave us a Kit-Kat each and told us that because we had done a good job we would be picked first on Monday for the zip factory. 'You'll be first away,' he said. I heard Phil whispering, 'Fuck that for a laugh.' I pock-eted the Kit-Kat and made my way out into the freezing cold Salford night almost exactly twelve hours after I had started the day. My left eye was still twitching. I don't know why.

(from Beattie 2002)

Undercover

Writing these pieces made me reconnect with something that I had once known. Occasionally, reviewers of the books would comment on this, they would try a little bit of psychoanalysis in their reviews – Beattie goes out there in the grim streets of the North of England to reconnect with his past, to rediscover his working-class roots in the dignity of the working class.

The work was well-received. *New Society* published a review of the first collection, entitled *Survivors of Steel City* (Chatto & Windus). The reviewer wrote:

> Here's richness . . . some of his evocative chapter openings would not disgrace the old master, Ed Mc Bain. . . . This book is a splendid example of sociology as it often could be but rarely is: Imaginatively presented, lively, well written and easy to read, but without ever losing integrity of purpose or its capacity to illuminate and inform.

The Listener said that the book was 'engrossing', *Marxism Today* described it as 'sharp and clear'. The review in *The Psychologist* said that 'the strength of Beattie's work is in the ethnography. An achingly direct sympathy with losers.' *The Sunday Times* reviewer wrote about *England After Dark* (Weidenfeld & Nicolson) 'Geoffrey Beattie is a psychologist who lectures in social psychology at Sheffield University. He is also a gifted journalist with a genius for making people talk, for giving them rope and finding that they were often hang themselves. . . . It is a view of Britain unknown to most of us and Beattie's perceptive and non-judgmental eye is perhaps the best filter through which to see it.' *On the Ropes: Boxing as a Way of Life* (Victor Gollanz) was hailed as 'a boxing classic' (*Publishing News*), 'one of the two greatest books on the modern fight ever written' (by *Loaded*), and described as 'breathtakingly good' by *Scotland on Sunday*. *The Daily Telegraph* wrote that

> Beattie can write about the low-life of boxing like no one else. . . . [He] has got the smell of the gym in his lungs. He breathes resin, sweat and soiled towels. He even goes three rounds himself with Mick Mills. He writes for adults and quite beautifully. Not since I first went ringside with the late Ring Gardner have I so enjoyed a book on boxing.

But this all sat uncomfortably with my academic training and my day job. *The Sunday Times*, at least, recognised that there were two of me, although they never commented on the curious juxtaposition. I certainly never felt like a professional sociologist or ethnographer. And as for the 'achingly direct sympathy with losers', I never thought of the people I was writing about in that way at all. These were people who had found themselves in difficult circumstances, they were losing out, that was clear, but it was not a character trait – internal, stable and 'global' (as in affecting everything they do), linked to the definition, 'A person who is always unsuccessful at everything that they do'. These were people who were desperate to show me that they weren't losers in that more general sense, they were fighting back – finding new ways of being somebody, breaking the rules, using humour, taking it out on others, taking it out on me, the Blarney Boy, half in and half out.

'What exactly are you?' 'What would you call yourself?' they would sometimes ask, puzzled by my Ph.D. but wanting to hang out with them. This work wasn't necessarily helping me find a way back, to reconnect with my working-class roots, it was telling me in a straightforward and forthright way why I didn't belong there either. I knew early on in Brendan Ingle's gym in Wincobank that I could never box in a more serious way. At the beginning of the boxing book, I had thought about trying to train as a professional, and basing the book around my first professional fights. That's before I felt the relentless physical pain and realised that I couldn't deal with it. Yes, of course, I could take a couple of punches and show off the bruises on my head and shoulders, or my biceps swollen by all that protective movement. But I couldn't do that day in, day out, just as I couldn't drive from Grimsby to London every week, or cope with months or years of skulking around supermarkets because I didn't want to bump into old acquaintances from the steel mills because of the embarrassment of my current unemployed status. I may have subconsciously wanted to reconnect, but I was always faced with unanticipated emotions, feelings and fragmentary images, that made me feel slightly uncomfortable (and even slightly repelled, disgusted even) by what I sometimes saw in this dog eat dog world, even if it wasn't of their making.

I had been part of something once, a gang, and I can get a little sentimental about that, friends who would always have backed me up, no matter what. I have worked for years in universities, and I can't imagine one friend or acquaintance from all my time there, in that professional world of mine, ever stepping forward in that way, putting themselves at *any* risk of physical harm on my behalf (a ludicrous thought, I know, looking for that in academe, as if academics fight! They're far too passive-aggressive for that). And in this new twilight world of mine I know that I had found something in guys like Mick Mills who would have looked out for me, and did. But often I didn't like what I was seeing or hearing from them in this new world with endless tales of dog fighting and macho values. I never wanted to reconnect with this in a more permanent way. I had worked so hard to get away from it.

And if my writing had any merit, it was this – this approach-avoidance conflict that psychologists ponder about endlessly. Drawn to something, but then (deep down inside perhaps at some Dostoevskian level) repelled by it. Its 'a non-judgmental eye' (in the words of *The Sunday Times* reviewer) because you're not on one side or the other, not through choice, rather that's where the push and pull has left you, trying to make up your mind, postponing any judgement about the way things really are.

And life back in Belfast went on much as before – my mother kept me up to date. More friends were murdered – she would give me the details, but she could never really remember whether they were my friends or my brother's. She would tell me about seeing Duck carried out of the park again, 'on the drugs'. Nobody seemed to be prospering.

Then in the mid-80s, they pulled the old house down. I was busy at the university, probably thinking away, busy as always.

'The workmen had to help me out,' she said. 'It's bad when you have to rely on strangers.' She left a pause for me to comment. There was just silence.

Eventually, she filled this deadened silence, full of expectation, her telling facial expression quite invisible to me now. 'The workmen were lovely but they never gave me the time to get out. Everything was bulldozed away. They told me that there wasn't much point in bringing the carpet from my old house or most of my clothes. Everything was damp; everything had mould all over it. I left a lot in the old house, including the sewing machine, which I didn't mean to leave. I had to get out in such a hurry in the end. After over sixty years it was such a last-minute thing. I was born in that house, but I never looked back when I left, not once.'

This was going to be the new fresh start.

'When I got to the new house, I went straight to the bathroom,' she said. 'I bought a new flannel and a sponge. My friend Sadie bought me a brand new back scrubber. I had some fancy Yardley soap and talcum powder that your Aunt Agnes had bought me for Christmas a few years ago. I'd been keeping it for the new house. The only problem was that it had been sitting getting damp in the old place. I didn't want to unwrap it until I had got a bathroom of my own. By the time I got the packet open, I realised that the talcum powder was damp right through.'

But she still left it sitting out in the new bathroom in the new house, a hundred metres or so from the old one, even if the talcum powder was a funny greeny-blue colour.

'It's an expensive make, you see,' she explained, 'only the best for my new house and my first bathroom. I'm very proud to have a bathroom after all these years.'

She was in her mid-sixties when she had her first bath in her own house.

Chapter 5

Endings and beginnings

Figure 5.1 Copyright Mariusz Smiejek/Belfast Archive Project

> To turn oneself into a stone becomes a way of not being turned
> into a stone by someone else. . . . Thoroughly to understand one-
> self (engulf oneself) is a defence against the risk involved in being
> sucked into the whirlpool of another person's way of comprehend-
> ing oneself. To consume oneself by one's own love prevents the
> possibility of being consumed by another.
>
> R.D. Laing (1960/1973: 51) The Divided Self

I am reminded that R.D. Laing wrote this book when he was twenty-
eight years old (and Laing himself often liked to remind his readers

of this). But this fact makes the book astonishing, it is clearly a work of precocious genius with a vision and understanding that goes so far beyond his years. There is much to dispute about some of his interpretations (and even more to dispute in some of his later work) but this extraordinarily bold attempt to offer an existential-phenomenological account of some schizoid and schizophrenic persons makes for compelling and engrossing reading. It is, however, not just about making the experiences and behaviour of the schizophrenic person comprehensible, but about making *all* of our experiences more comprehensible than they might sometimes seem.

Home again

I arrived one Friday morning at a home on the Antrim Road in Belfast that looked a little run down and shabby, and got some directions to my mother's room and there she sat, small and vulnerable, the bathroom a few feet away, the television in the corner, a remote in her hand. She never had a remote before, and she flicked across the channels. 'I'm not staying here,' she said. 'I want to go home.'

The Social Services had suggested that she come over to England and live with my family, but she had argued strongly against this. 'They're all out all day at work. He's got this big dog with grey hairs on his face. My friends are all here.' So they had arranged for her to go into the home just for a few weeks, they said.

We talked about my family and my dog, the dog she loved to hate. She told me that she had read that the Japanese were bringing out mobile phones for cats and dogs and she suggested getting one for Louis, my dog. 'So that you can talk to him,' she said. 'I sometimes think that you prefer talking to that animal than talking to me. I can't stand the way you kiss that creature.'

I asked her what it was like in this home and she just repeated that she didn't want to stay. 'And the staff are nearly all Taigs,' she whispered. 'But do you like them?' I asked. 'I don't trust Taigs,' she replied. 'But do you like them?' I asked again. 'They're all dead-on,' she said and we both laughed. 'It's bloody daft, isn't it? I grew up with Taigs, I worked with them all my life, it's these bloody Troubles, they make you think stupid,' she said.

She talked about old times and me and Bill when we were young. She always said that all she ever wanted was for us to be together. 'I remember coming over the Hightown one night, with your father and you and Bill in the car, and I was scared because it was dark but then I thought that we were a family all together and that if we went off the road and we died then we'd still be together. And then I realised that I wasn't scared anymore.'

But I suppose at that very moment I realised that there was a corollary to all of this, that if we were not together, then she would feel even greater fear than everybody else and I felt terrible inside because here she was completely alone in that room. I tried to cheer her up by telling her that I had seen a sign saying that there was going to be a party that afternoon in the home, a Country and Western singer was coming in and that I would take her down to it. 'You're not going to leave me down there on my own, I hope,' she said. I told her that I would stay with her. 'Have you had your run yet?' she enquired. 'I don't want you disappearing for one of those long runs of yours.' I told her untruthfully that I had already had my run. She made a huffing sound. I told her that I had seen quite a nice-looking man on the way in to distract her, and she looked quite excited. I fetched her a small hand mirror and she sat there doing her lipstick and brushing her hair forward, heavy with grey because she couldn't get near a sink to dye it. But she still looked well. I complimented her on her appearance. 'Well, your da always said that I was the best-looking girl in Ligoniel, and he had an eye for the girls so he knew what he was talking about.' I got her zimmer frame and lifted her into position on it. She always laughed when I manhandled her like that; it was a girly sort of laugh. We got through the door with difficulty.

A woman was coming out of the room opposite, much younger than my mother. A face that was heavily made up, the make-up covering deep cracks and lines. She could have even been quite young, it was hard to say; she looked like a very heavy drinker. The wall stopped her from falling. It could have been the drink or something altogether more permanent. 'Is that your son?' she asked. 'Coming to take you out once a week, so that he can feel good about himself, so that he can feel like a big man.' The words were a little slurred; her backside was pushed outwards towards the wall for support. There was a fury in how she asked the question. 'Oh no,' said my mother, defending me. 'He doesn't live here. He's come all the way from England to take me out. He's a professor over there. He's very busy.'

'Too busy for his own mother?' the woman asked, and then not hearing any immediate response, said 'Oh, have I put my foot in it?' My mother nudged me with her elbow and I knew what that meant, we had no time for people like this. My mother glared at her. The woman lurched from one wall to the opposite wall in front of us, and stood there as if she had been crucified, her arms out to her side, unable to move and watched my mother, bent over the Zimmer frame, move towards the lift and the party downstairs.

We smiled at each other on the way down in the lift, and my mother said that it was terrible what drink does to people. In the party room old people sat in a circle like children, drinking out of paper cups filled with sherry or orangeade. I sat in the seat next to my mother. The woman to our left looked a little distressed. 'She's only forty-four,' said my mother. 'I don't know what the matter with her is. I think she's had a stroke.' I noticed that this woman was gesturing in short, batonic, stabbing movements down towards her lap; she obviously couldn't speak. There was a wet patch between her legs that was spreading; her grey slacks were damp. I found myself staring down at the wet patch, and then looked away feeling ashamed.

The much older man on the other side of her knocked the table to attract the attention of the woman serving the drinks, who went over to him. 'Do you want a drink?' she shouted. 'Orangeade or sherry?' He knocked the table twice. 'I think that means orangeade,' she said and laughed to the rest of us. The woman in the light grey slacks was still gesturing. You could smell the urine now.

One of the care assistants came up to me. 'Do you want a wee sherry?' she asked. 'No, thank you,' I replied. 'What about a wee white wine?' 'No thank you.' 'A wee sherry then?' 'No thanks.' I could see my mother looking over. 'I hope that you've been for your bloody run and that you're not going to spoil this party for me.' The woman beside us was still gesturing. 'It's a terrible pity,' said my mother, gesturing towards her, 'and she hasn't even had her life yet.'

The Country and Western singer had started, and some very elderly man took one of the care assistants by the arm for a dance around the floor in this room reeking of stale and fresh piss. I noticed that my mother was looking on in envy. 'He's a great mover for a man his age. A great mover.' I went to the toilet and I glanced back and I saw the look of undisguised envy in my mother's face, she was like a teenager at her first dance; she would have loved to have got up, if it wasn't for those ankles of her, and danced that dull afternoon away. I came back and sat with her for a few minutes and then told her that I had to go for my run. 'What did I tell you?' she said. 'I knew that you were lying, I can always tell. You and that bloody running.' I told her that she would be alright and that she would enjoy herself, and I left her trying to catch the eye of the grey-haired octogenarian who was moving so gracefully across the old carpet in front of so many admiring female eyes.

A few months later, after my mother had been back in her own house for a while, my Uncle Terence phoned me with bad news (my Aunt Agnes had died years before). He had already been in hospital for three weeks and was due to have a kidney removed. Then the operation was off. That was all I knew. 'Postponed or cancelled?' I asked, as if it was a football match. Then I heard the words down the phone. 'Scan', 'tumour', 'growth.' It had to be spelt out to me. Me with all that education, as he liked to say. I went to see him a week and a bit later in a hospital in Stoke-on-Trent; he had moved up to Stoke after my Aunt Agnes had died to be closer to his sister. I had a tape recorder in my carrier bag. My father died suddenly after what was supposed to be routine surgery. My brother died in that climbing accident. I didn't want to let my Uncle Terence go without the chance to talk to him, about our home in Northern Ireland, about the changes there, about the Peace, about my father, a man I can hardly remember, and how I was becoming the spitting image of him, at last. I wanted to tell him that I had just been appointed to be the Head of the Department of Psychology in Manchester, the oldest psychology department in the United Kingdom, and that all those years sitting studying at the card table in the front room in Legmore Street had paid off.

His girlfriend, Marjorie, brought me to see him. My mother always referred to Marjorie as his girlfriend. It's a strange term given that she was eighty-two and he was seventy-seven. Terence and Marjorie had been inseparable for twelve years or so, after my Aunt Agnes died. My mother was always a little resentful of his second relationship.

'Look who's come to see you, Terry,' Marjorie said. 'So you got here then,' he said, looking up at me. 'You've arrived at last.' He was always commenting on me being late for everything. 'What time do you call this?' he would say, after I had driven across England to see him. 'The Beatties are always late,' he would say. My mother likes to tell the story of the day the whole street thought that we were dead in our beds because the woman who rapped us for work and school couldn't raise us. 'The Beatties would sleep all day,' he liked to say, 'if you let them.' He was an early riser.

He was sitting on a chair beside the bed, his bad leg up on a stool. He was just my uncle but he was always more than that. Terence taught me to fish the streams coming of the mountains around Belfast, to fish with my hands. He would stand with his legs balanced on wet slimy stones in the middle of the bubbling mountain streams above Ligoniel and say: 'Get your hands in under the rocks and tickle them. Tickle their bellies. Trout love having their bellies tickled.'

I never caught anything that way, but he did, even though I claimed to have had the odd tickle. However, I did once manage to pull a large dying trout out of a wide, weedy river one bright sunny afternoon in England and he photographed me holding it out in front of me, the fish splayed across my open palms. 'Did you really catch that with your hands?' asked my brother when he saw the photograph. 'Really?' My brother didn't believe that you could catch brown trout like that in the middle of summer with your bare hands. He never really believed me even though he had the proof in front of him. My uncle threw the dying fish back into a deep inlet in the river and it flopped about in the thick brown water as if it couldn't right itself. But then its fins moved slowly and it disappeared. 'It wasn't dying,' said my uncle, not quite convincingly. 'Or it couldn't have swum away like that.' But it didn't swim so much as sink.

Terence had boxed when he was younger, but it was only old people like Isaac the barber who could remember his boxing days. When I knew him he was always five stone or more overweight, always on a diet, and every Saturday night when he and my father got back from Paddy's at the bottom of the street my dog Spot and I would be invited to take him on. He would sit down in the chair by the window in our front room, heavy with drink, waiting for his supper, and beckon us towards him. 'Come on, get stuck in,' he would say. The dog would jump up on the back of the chair and bite him in the neck and on the back through his jacket; I would club his large, heavy head with my fists. I can hear the noise of the dog now, that low roar from deep inside that would break up into a higher pitched biting sound and then a yelp when Big Terry caught him with his hand. 'Give that dog a good skite,' my mother would say. 'It's getting carried away.'

The dog would only ever go for the Big Fella like that when he could smell the drink from him. So would I. Not long after my father died, Terence left for England. So every summer I went to Chippenham to live with him and get some holiday work, and he would slap sun cream on my back with those large manly hands to protect me from the suns of Southern England as I set off for another day on a building site in Bath or Bristol. He had left Belfast because he always said that his promotion was blocked in the Civil Service because of his religion. He was the Fenian in the Belfast of the 60s. The days of Unionist rule. He moved to England and got his promotion. I followed him for the school holidays and came back to Belfast knowing all about Ska and Reggae, and things that never seemed to reach Belfast in those days. It was natural (in a way) for me to go back across the water for university when the time came. I always think that Northern Ireland lost two of its own.

He sat on the chair by his bed in hospital, full of a confused fury. 'I want to go home,' he said. He asked me how the family was, but he seemed to be distracted, as if he couldn't wait on the answer. He had asked the doctor, who had given him his diagnosis of cancer, how long he had got left, but the doctor had told him that it was hard to say. All the talk was about who could look after him at home. All the talk was of the future. The illness was not mentioned. The old man in the next bed called over to me. My Uncle Terence told me to ignore him. Terence told me that the old man was an attention seeker. The old man said that he wanted me to fix his sleeve. I went over to him. 'Leave it,' shouted my uncle. 'Could you help an old soldier?' asked the other patient. I guided his arm into his sleeve and buttoned up his shirt. The nurse told me afterwards that the old man had had a stroke.

A confused looking woman with a funeral-slow gait shuffled into the entrance of the ward. 'We call her the rooster,' said Marjorie, 'because of the way she moves her head.' The rooster peered in. 'Ignore her,' warned my uncle. Her unsteady steps took her right into the ward. It was the male ward. 'She shouldn't be here,' said my uncle. 'Out, out, out,' he bellowed at her. Her face showed not the slightest recognition of the message or its intensity, but she changed direction slowly like a large ship in the middle of the sea and walked away in a large unsteady arc.

'I need to get home,' said my uncle. 'This isn't the place for me.' I tried talking about work and my promotion because he loved hearing all about where my education had got me, but he was far too distracted. He asked Marjorie and me to move the stool from below his bad foot and he shouted at us for doing it too slowly. He still had his personality.

By the time I returned ten days later, he had been moved to a side ward. I was now prepared for the fury and the distraction of the previous visit. This image had intensified in my mind. I found the ward easily and glanced into all the other side wards with the doors open, hoping to catch a glimpse of what I might find when I got to his. There was a man lying on his bed in a foetal position. It seemed symbolic in a blatant sort of way, but who says that the meanings of life, the real meanings, have to be subtle. Entering and leaving the world, curled up and waiting for delivery into the next.

Terence lay back in bed, his head lolling to the side. His girlfriend was feeding him yoghurt, which leaked out the side of his mouth. He already had the look of death about him. There was a vacuum where his teeth once were. 'Terry O' Niell', the misspelling read above the bed. His left arm rested across his chest. A throw was folded above the pillow. A drainage bag clung on to the side of the bed. 'Single patient use,' it said. A plant pot that read 'Rosanova' with a couple of dying yellow flowers sat above the sink. There were a number of cards on shelves around the bed. I noticed that two of them were identical. My second cousin, Ann, and her husband sat quietly for a while by his bedside.

You could hear the snippets of talk coming from the corridor as patients' relatives made talk with the nurses. 'He's a lot worse, his breathing, his colour'. Terence lay there, like a ghost already. His toes, peeping out from below the blanket, were like ripe figs. I noticed that his feet did not match. One was like greasy chicken, the other, bandaged with an amputated toe, looked different. Diabetes, cataracts, a bad heart, cancer of the kidney, cancer of the lung. You name it, he had it. My aunt and uncle liked to enjoy themselves. That's what they always said. Smoking and drinking every night in life. They didn't have any children, so they always said that they might as well spend their money enjoying themselves, in the only way that they knew how in the Britain of the 70s.

His girlfriend reluctantly said that she had to go. She had been there all day and was exhausted. I stayed in the room, pleased to be alone with him. I could hear the hum of conversation from down the corridor, occasionally a child's voice. I sat watching his chest rise and fall rhythmically but shallowly. His nose hairs needed trimming. A man passed slowly in a walking frame, then a nurse. She hardly dared smile at me, in case it might start up a conversation, which neither of us wanted. I did not want to ask her anything about my uncle, and she did not want to have to tell me anything. I have never seen a man go downhill so quickly; I didn't need any gloss on it.

My mind was on all the private deaths in my family. It was he who stopped me from going in to see my father in hospital the night he died. I knew it was bad news because he wouldn't look at me. He was there in our front room in Legmore Street much later when we had the service for my brother who lay below a pile of loose stones on that Himalayan mountain, but he crept up to our back room for a sneaky cry. I caught him up there with his back to the door. Shielding his sorrow. He never liked showing any emotion in life, except perhaps anger and impatience. But they are manly emotions. Sometimes I think that I learned a lot from him and not just about fishing and fighting with your bare hands.

I wanted to talk to him, but I didn't want to listen to my own voice in that quiet room. I glanced into the blackened mid-winter sky hoping to see some distant stars but all I could see were some lights through a fog out the back of the hospital. I thought about what kind of man I have become and what my children will remember about me in thirty or forty years' time. A few frozen moments, a cross word here or there, a holiday perhaps. Not much.

He was peaceful, barely conscious, asleep, but thirsty. 'Do you want some water?' I asked. There was no response. 'Do you want some water?' I repeated it much louder this time. 'Yes please,' he replied. He seemed to be lapsing into sleep or unconsciousness but he remembered to say 'please'. Marjorie had told me earlier that he would know that I was there. I held the plastic beaker to his mouth. He sucked at it like a child before it has got its first teeth.

I looked around the room, which I thought looked a little bare and then I noticed what was missing. He was always religious. He had all these little religious symbols when I was growing up. Symbols that I had to hide and shield from my friends back in North Belfast. But here there were none. He was given the Last Rites the night before but now there was no sign of any Virgin Mary or Christ on the Cross or anything much. Just a bare hospital room with a few cards and a few private possessions like slippers, but nothing more than that.

I wanted to discuss the peace process with him, now that things were different. But I was too late. I was always too late for everything. That's what he always said. We only discussed my father once, and that was about a year previously. He said that I had shown no inclination to talk about my father after he died. He said that I just pulled the shutters down, I just closed the door. I've closed a lot of doors since then.

And as for the Troubles, we never discussed them. He always said that one side was as bad as the other, and we left it at that. I don't think that I ever admitted to him that I knew that he was a Roman Catholic. We never openly discussed it. I had only been told a few years previously by my mother that he hadn't been allowed into the house of my Uncle Jack for nearly forty years. Forty fucking years. The years of fucking madness, I call them. Only then did I realise why my Uncle Terence wasn't there that afternoon of my father's funeral, as we all sat around the wooden dining table in my Uncle Jack's house (bigger than ours, suitable for a wake). He wasn't allowed to be there because of his religion. He was my father's best friend.

The rooster came to the door. She looked even more confused than the last time I had seen her. 'Everybody is going,' she said. 'I'd like to know where they're going.' I didn't know whether this was profound or not. She looked at Terence in the bed. 'I didn't know that he lived here,' she said. 'Maybe I will need it later on.' But I didn't know what she was referring to. Just a confused old lady. She shuffled off slowly.

I asked him whether he wanted some more water. 'Not just at the moment,' he replied. I learned to time my questions whenever there was a slight movement from him. A nurse came in. 'Are you his son?' she asked. 'No, just a nephew,' I replied. After she left, I felt myself smiling because I should have told her what I was thinking. 'He's a fucking Taig,' I said to myself, 'and I'm a fucking Prod from North Belfast. We're from fucking Murder Triangle; we kill each other over there. How the fuck could I be his son? Answer me that.' My polite smile had turned to tears before I got to the end.

I spilt some water over his pyjamas and he made a loud groaning sound as if I had scalded him with boiling water. This was my Uncle Terence. I asked him if he was in any pain. He just said, 'It's starting,' but he didn't elaborate, no matter how much I pushed him.

I knew that he had only hours to live, I could sense it, but the staff nurse persuaded me that he was stable and that nothing would happen that night. So I left for the long drive home, and he died three hours later. I never did get the chance to talk to him. Always fucking late, that's my problem. He could have told you that. Always fucking late. It was the day before Christmas.

Farewells

My mother came over to England for Christmas that year but she hardly talked about him, except to say, 'They're all gone now – your father, your brother, my two sisters, now your Uncle Terry. I'm next.' She seemed almost happy about it. She couldn't make Terence's funeral because she was travelling back to Belfast that day. She wasn't inclined to change her travel plans, and Carol had to stay behind to take her to the airport. But the morning of the funeral, my children Zoë, Ben and Sam trooped into her bedroom to show her how they looked in black. She sat up in bed and inspected them, the boys in their black suits and white shirts borrowed from me. Zoë in a black dress and a black jacket borrowed off her mother.

She was used to seeing them in jeans and trainers. 'They look lovely when they're dressed up,' she said. 'Like you and your brother when you were young. I have to say that there's something about Protestants when they're dressed up,' she said. 'I hope you all look as nice at my funeral.'

We drove across the Pennines to a modern concrete-looking chapel in Stoke-on-Trent, the town Terence had retired to after he had left the Civil Service, to be near his sister. I had never been in a Catholic chapel before, and I looked around at the few elderly women scattered amongst the pews, who had braved the slippy pavements on that frosty morning to pay their last respects. I watched my son Sam cross himself in front of the altar, because the woman in front did it, and I laughed at this boy with pure Ulster Protestant blood, not really knowing anything about the rituals and symbols of religious affiliation. When I was his age, I used to watch out for people on the bus in Belfast crossing themselves as they passed the chapel at Ardoyne, just to know who was one of us and who was one of them. But I looked over at the coffin in front of the altar in that chapel, and thought of my Uncle Terence and remembered that he had blurred all this anyway in my own mind. How could I have turned on somebody I didn't know just because they were the same religion as the Big Fella lying over there? Some of it didn't make much sense to me. We moved on to the crematorium, Zoë and Ben mocking Sam gently in the back of the hearse for crossing himself, and then we watched the coffin slide behind the curtains and nobody spoke.

I rang my mother that night and she asked me how the funeral had gone and I told her about Sam and how he had crossed himself. 'Oh, God love him,' she said. I loved these old expressions that she used, the kinds of things that my age group never said. Things that would be lost, I suppose, within a generation.

I talked again about the night that he had died and I remembered that at one point in the hours before he had died Terence had sat bolt upright full apparently of surprise and shock. I had seen it in the films but I didn't know that this was based on anything. 'He's gone,' said Ann's husband. He had been introduced to me, as the husband of my second cousin, but not as a doctor, which he was. The doctor took his pulse and then changed his mind. 'No, he's not gone yet.'

My mother listened attentively. I told her again that I was sorry that I was not there at the end. 'It's just as well you left,' she said. 'People behave very outrageously when they're dying.' It was her word – 'outrageously'. 'They sent me out when your father was dying. They didn't want me to see it.' And again she told me the story of my father playing with her ring as he lay there in that coma for a week, squeezing her hand when she asked him to, but not able to speak. It was my image of dying, even though I had not experienced it first-hand. The person, my daddy, trapped in this helpless body for seven days, unable to move, unable to communicate properly. It was like being buried alive. The story, which was meant to comfort me, had terrified me as a child and it still terrified me. It was what death meant to me.

I told her that I would have liked to have been there at the end for my Uncle Terence. 'And what about for me?' she said. 'You'll probably miss mine. You're always bloody late for everything.' I told her not to be so silly and that she had a lot of life left in her.

Three months passed. She said that she was feeling a bit down. 'I'm fed up,' she said. So that weekend I went over. She hadn't been that well, but there was nothing new in that and we went out to a different restaurant every night. She insisted on the Bellevue Arms on the first night. It represented something to her; it represented Carol's father and mother out every Saturday night, out enjoying themselves when she was stuck in the house on her own, with what was in the glass for company. It represented the good life. I never liked it. Thick juicy steaks awash in their own juices, the juice sloshing off the plate. She was sick in the restaurant that night. She couldn't eat. I fetched her some paper hankies and watched the runny sick gurgle out around the pink hankies, which she had stuffed in and around her mouth. There was a young family on the next table, looking intently at her, and then looking away, pretending they couldn't hear her stomach retching. The children played 'I-spy' to distract themselves. I, for once, did not feel ashamed. I felt almost useful, and not paralysed by my normal social embarrassment when things go slightly wrong. She was boking. That was her word for the sounds she was making.

The next night we went down to Groomsport and I helped her out by the front door of the restaurant and left her standing in her Zimmer frame while I parked the car, but when I got out I could see her being helped up by two men. The wind had blown her over and she had hit her head. But she said that she was fine and she spent most of the night talking about the lovely fellas who had helped her up. I left her on the Sunday night, to get back to my work. We talked on the phone and she said that he had had a lovely weekend, apart from that old sickness in her stomach. She couldn't stop boking.

This all seems like such a long time ago now. That Thursday morning after the fall and I was back in Manchester, I got a phone call from Carol in Sheffield. My mother had had a stroke. Carol and I flew home and got there in the early evening. We sat with her through that long, long night. I prayed constantly for her to regain consciousness, to get better. I promised God everything if he would just show mercy. I promised to change. Work would no longer come first. I would spend time with those I love.

In the morning I watched her heart rate drop slowly until pauses started occurring in the beating of the heart, and then the pauses lengthened. I held her hand. 'Can you see my brother?' I said. 'Bill is there waiting for you. Can you see Bill?' I hoped that she was entering a tunnel with light at the end. I was trying to reassure her. She always told me that my father could sense her presence until near the end. I wanted her to know that I was there and I was trying to tell her not to be frightened. But I was terrified of her dying, of her leaving me behind. The pauses lengthened and lengthened until a fine line developed on the monitor in front of me, and I realised that my mother has gone. I tried to think of her words, I tried to think of what she would say. 'We're all going to die sometime,' she would say. She was always very matter of fact about it. 'I'll be with your father and your brother again. It doesn't bother me. We will all meet up again. Don't you worry. It's only natural.' She said that about everything – it's only natural. Why are men such selfish bastards? It's only natural. Why do people want to skive at work? It's only natural. And here she was – as she had long predicted, dying, although she had always said that I would never be there for her. She always said that I would be late.

But perhaps, I was. Perhaps it was she who had waited for me. Perhaps she knew me that well.

A past hidden

The next morning Carol told me that she was going back to England to fetch our children for the funeral. I was alone in my mother's house (the 'new' house, the one on the Ligoniel Road opposite the library) for the rest of the weekend, with my mother's slippers beside the table, her Zimmer frame waiting there at the top of the stairs, and the whiskey, half drunk and half-watered behind the bread bin. I knew that I would have to clear the house out. I walked around looking at all the things she had collected over a lifetime, knowing that I would have to go through it all item by item.

In a kitchen cupboard I found a manila envelope stuffed with articles I had written, some of them academic papers, about pauses and phonation and cycles of semantic planning as speech is being conceptualised and I wondered what my mother had made of these. The address was at the bottom, 'The Psychological Laboratory, University of Cambridge'. You could imagine her showing them to her friends. The words in the papers would have meant little, except perhaps for the address. 'Oh Cambridge, he's awfully clever, your Geoffrey.' One was the article about Carol losing her arm in the accident. She had kept them all safe; I always thought she threw everything out.

She had collected a lot of cheap ornaments and photo frames over the years. My children bought her £2.99 photo frames with white shells in a sea-blue background, or photo frames in plastic mahogany that folded out like a book, as presents at Christmas or birthdays. There was an exotic-looking brass tea caddy sitting on top of the record player in the kitchen, a record player that had not worked since I was a boy. It had old records from the 1960s piled up on the turntable: Manfred Mann, the Kinks, Roy Orbison. The record player was used as a cabinet because it had legs and a wooden casing around it. The tea caddy looked as if it was from the Middle East, but it was actually from Debenhams. I had bought it for her as a present, ostensibly from Turkey. No doubt she had shown that proudly to her friends. 'All the way from the Kasbah,' she would have said. 'He carried that all the way home to Belfast for me.' I thought it was a harmless deception.

The previous weekend, I had gone to Boots and bought her some Complan because she could not eat. The box lay in the cupboard with just the one sachet that we had shared together used up. We spent ages trying to remember the name of the drink I had taken in my early teens after I had started running. It was just a food supplement but I thought it would turn me into some sort of superman.

I moved around the house from room to room, peering into the wardrobes and her cubbyholes, just looking at the amount of stuff, that's what she would have called it – 'stuff'. I realised that nearly all of her personal belongings would have to be either given away or thrown out. There was a cubbyhole in the front bedroom, the bedroom where I stayed when I was with her, packed with her clothes. I burrowed in these to smell her old perfume and I noticed that this cubbyhole was much deeper than I had ever imagined. She could never have got in there in the last few years of her life, and perhaps not even before, she was never that nimble. I pushed past the shoes and the dresses and the coats and there at the back was an old suit-case. It had probably been pushed in there by the workmen when she had first moved to the new house. The lock didn't work so I pulled it open. It was crammed full.

There lay my old school text books, and my physics lab books, Bill's school cap and reports from Everton Secondary School, details of a panto-mime at St Mark's with Bill in the line-up and a yellowed bit of parchment lying at the bottom, my grandfather's discharge papers from the army. All of the things that I thought had been bulldozed into the debris, back in the old house. I tried to imagine Bill in his cap in his first day at Everton, but that image could not be evoked no matter how hard I tried. *The Adventures of Tom Sawyer* with that cover where the beautiful blond Tom bites the apple, and the little black boy in the group has those big white eyes and what appears to be red lipstick. Two sea gulls on the spine, which used to peek out of the bookshelf in the backroom in Legmore Street. The First Latin Composition Book, from form IVA, with some hand-written pages inside in what must have been my own neat writing. 'He is afraid to escape – *timet effugere*'. 'I hope to see you – spero me te visurum esse'. And that old musty smell of damp from the old house transfused in each and every page. It was like being back there for a moment.

There were details of my grandfather's army record on that discharge paper – he served twelve years in the army. My mother had always said that her father was a big man: 'Oh, much taller than you or your father', she liked to say, but this bit of yellowed paper informed me that he was five foot eight with a dark complexion and brown eyes and black hair with a mole close to his right nipple. I wanted to show her my find. I needed to tell her about it. And at the bottom of the case was a bronze-coloured badge with a number of capital letters in the shape of an arc, the clasp was broken: the letters spelt out 'INNISKILLING'.

I went downstairs and put on the TV, the TV that she had bought second-hand off old Joe, and which had never worked properly since she had got it. I sat there, with that yellow parchment from the War Office in my hand and the little badge, listening to the buses shuddering past the door, racing up the Ligoniel Road the way that they always did, and I started to weep like a wee child, knowing that the whole street could probably hear the racket from this house with its walls as thin as fucking paper. The next day I went around knocking on the door of her old friends, giving out some of her clothes. My mother and I had been up to Macro earlier that week and she had got some new gear; it had not been worn, and her friends who had known her all her life accepted it gratefully. 'It's still got the label on,' Vera, one of her neighbours, said. I was pleased that they were having it. My mother had got a new wardrobe of clothes when her friend Lena had died. She could hardly fit Lena's clothes into her own wardrobe. I suppose that morning I felt that I was celebrating some aspect of working-class life, a group who do not seem too sentimental when it comes to material things like clothes or ornaments after they have died. She would have wanted me to give them away like this. There was just one thing that she wanted me to keep. Her gold locket with flowers on the front, and small hazy photos of Bill and myself at my wedding, torn down to size, pushed into each half. That was our family heirloom. That was what we would pass on; it was always intended for my daughter Zoë. Her ornaments went to the Mothers' Union thrift shop up at St Mark's.

I just kept back what she was to be buried in because she was always a great one for the style: I selected something nice.

And as for the funeral itself, she always told me that she never wanted to be carried in case I dropped her. 'You can be very careless,' she always liked to say. 'You've always been a very careless boy.' But I never passed on this wish. We stood outside St Mark's waiting for the coffin, there was just to be one lift, down to the front gate, and my eldest son Ben and I linked arms, with George, my cousin and Tom, my cousin Jacqueline's husband, behind. She would have been proud of how the four of us looked in our black suits and our white shirts. We Ulster Protestants always look good when we are burying our own. When we lifted her out at Roselawn there was a slight decline down to my father's grave, which I had never really noticed before. Our steps quickened on the wet grass, and Ben and I gripped each other hard to keep the coffin steady, but for a moment I was sure that we were going to drop her. And as we laid her to rest, I thought to myself that she was right about most things, when it came down to it. Let's face it; she was a very shrewd woman. And she was gone.

Chapter 6

Reckonings and reconciliations

Figure 6.1 Copyright Mariusz Smiejek/Belfast Archive Project

This man is a human psychologist: what does he really study men for? He wants to gain little advantages over them, or big ones too – he is a politician! . . . This other man is also a human psychologist: and you say he wants nothing for himself, that he is 'impersonal'. Take a closer look! Perhaps he wants an even worse advantage: to feel himself superior to men, to have the right to look down on them, no longer to confuse himself with them. This 'impersonal' man is a despiser of men: and the former is a more humane species. . . . At least he thinks himself equal to others, he involves himself with others.

Friedrich Nietzsche (1889/1974: 76) Twilight of the Idols

Nietzsche was a brilliant writer as well as a brilliant philosopher. His style of argumentation can sometimes seem a little unorthodox, perhaps even a little unusual, but it is more often than not profound. Sometimes you find yourself laughing out loud as you read it (but this might just be me). His views on Darwin's evolutionary theory and the 'struggle for life' are that this fundamental proposition has been asserted rather than proved. 'It does occur,' he writes, 'but as the exception; the general aspect of life is *not* hunger and distress, but rather wealth, luxury, even absurd prodigality – where there is a struggle it is a struggle for *power*' (1889/1974: 75). Nietzsche commented often on psychology and psychologists (and interestingly on Dostoevsky – 'the only psychologist, by the way, from whom I had anything to learn') and his comments in the quotation above are perhaps worth bearing in mind in the context of this particular chapter.

The double bind

I miss her terribly, of course; she told me that I would. I can't say that she didn't warn me. 'Your mother should be number one. You'll regret not taking me out more', she used to say. Then the emotion and the tears would come. 'I'm way down the list; I think that you care more about Louis than you do me.'

Louis was my boxer dog and the object of great envious resentment. 'I cannot believe that you let that dog kiss you, you let it slobber all over you,' my mother would say, and I always thought that this complaint was occasioned more by jealousy than by concerns over personal hygiene. Sometimes I felt that Louis could also sense her resentment.

I would ring her every afternoon. I would be sitting in my bright, airy office in a university over in England, the laughter and the chatter of the students on the corridor outside filtering through, in this busy and self-important world. She would be sitting in front of the television in her front room, in the middle of the day, retired from the mill now, alone. She missed the work and the company; never wanting to retire in the first place. The laughter filtering into my office made it sound like I was at a party. 'I'm not living anymore, I'm just surviving,' she would say. 'I'm lonely all day; you're having the time of your life.'

I would feel those sharp pangs of guilt that you can anticipate but can't avoid. They cannot be dulled even with full expectation, and mental preparation. I had my life, my family, my children, my career and my busy, busy schedule but she never understood how universities worked or how you build a career. 'What time do you have to be in at?' she would ask. 'No time really unless I've got lectures or tutorials, but I have to get stuff done. It's extremely competitive.'

'So you can go into work whenever you like but you only come over here to see me once in a blue moon. I'd be ashamed of myself, if I was you.' I tried to get back home as often as I could and she would visit at Christmas, Easter and the July fortnight, but it would never be enough. When I did visit, I would often bring a computer with me and that would be the basis for the first argument, as I hoisted the bulking computer in through the front door. 'You're here to see me, not work. Put that bloody thing away, or I'm not even going to go out with you.'

She knew that I would try to mix visits home with work-related activities and occasionally it worked better. I would take her with me. We went together to a literary awards evening sometime in the 1990s. One of my books had been shortlisted for a literary prize. My mother had a few drinks at the posh reception and talked to Brian Keenan, the former hostage, who talked in a whisper after all those years locked in a Beirut cellar. 'Speak up, Brian,' she kept saying to him. 'I can hardly hear you; speak up, Brian, for God's sake.' Brian kissed her when they announced his name for the prize for his book, *An Evil Cradling*. 'He deserved it,' she said to me, 'for all those years sitting in the dark in that bloody cellar. He told me all about it. I told him that I knew what it was like. I said that I never get out either.'

We saw Andrew Motion across the room. He later became the poet laureate. He had published my first non-academic book (*Survivors of Steel City*) and I'd had a drink with him in some pub in London near his publishers. I told my mother that I knew him. He nodded almost grudgingly as he passed. She noticed it too, and then she glanced at me to see my reaction. 'He's not a very good friend of yours then, is he?' said my mother. 'I notice that you haven't got many good friends, not like when you were a wee boy and all your friends would hang about our hall laughing and joking.'

We walked across town afterwards to a piano bar and she told the man playing the piano that it was her birthday to get a free bottle of champagne, even though it was not strictly true (or even approximately true). He played 'Please Release Me' for her as a special request. Some girls at the next table on a hen night were getting a little rowdy, one wanted to kiss me because she was getting married. 'Leave him alone,' said my mother. 'The young hussies these days have no shame.'

A few years later, we both went to another awards ceremony held in the City Hall. My novel, *The Corner Boys*, had been shortlisted for the same prize. I had been told that Chris Patten would be there to hand out the award, and that the Republican politician Gerry Adams would be attending the function. 'I'll have one or two things to say to old Gerry,' my mother had warned me, 'after what he's put us through. There's no two ways about that. I'll have a wee word in his ear alright.' She was looking forward to the event, but I was worried about what she might say: all that day she had been getting excited talking about prize-givings of the past. 'When you and your brother were young,' she said, 'you won all the prizes in St Mark's from the Junior Training Corps and the Church Lads Brigade. My neighbours used to tell me that it wasn't worth going because the Beattie boys won everything that was going.' I had to get out of the house so I went shopping and then I realised that I was going to be late so I rang her from town and told her to make her own way there. I would go straight from town.

I stood at the back door of the City Hall waiting for her, and saw the Call-a-Cab car drive in past security. The driver nodded at me, as if he recognised me, and got my mother's wheelchair out of the boot. She was still chatting away to him. 'Do you remember playing "foot in the bucket" when you were young?' she asked him after he had opened the door to let her out. 'That's the problem with young people nowadays; they don't know how to keep themselves amused.' I pushed her into the City Hall slowly and carefully. The other guests all stood around in the centre of the room, holding their wine glasses delicately. I noticed that the men all seemed to be wearing grey suits, and all the women elegant black dresses with silver brooches. Then there was me in my puffer jacket and my mother in her pink anorak, with Top Shop bags, from that day's shopping, balancing on her wheelchair. She was wearing the wig that the dog liked to chase around the house. 'I'm starving,' she said, after we had pushed through the crowd. 'I haven't had any dinner. Go and get us some of them whatever they are.'

I went in search of food and got my mother a large glass of white wine. 'I'm thirsty,' she said. 'I haven't had a drink all day.' The speeches were starting, there were television cameras dotted around the room and, every now and then, some small circular area would suddenly light up in intense, white light. Chris Patten's report on the future of the RUC was just about to be released and the cameras were there partly to capture a few comments from him. The other contestants and their coterie of friends stood in a group in the middle of the floor. The women, in their expensive dresses adorned with silver bracelets in intricate Celtic patterns, looked appreciatively up at him, while my mother was concentrating on the food in front of her.

The waitress with the nibbles had found us on our own, stranded from everybody else. 'I'm starving,' said my mother to her, 'these little things don't fill you up.' 'Here you are love,' said the waitress, handing her a larger plate, as Patten started to speak. 'This is my son,' said my mother. 'He's up for the prize tonight, you know, but he won't win it. You have to be in the know to win prizes, and he doesn't know anybody.'

'Yes, but it's nice to be invited,' said the woman with the nibbles.

'Of course,' said my mother 'that's what I tell him. You should be proud just to be invited to the City Hall.'

'Exactly,' said the waitress.

'Have you met Gerry Adams?' said my mother.

'Oh yes,' said the waitress, 'he's a regular. Him and Martin McGuinness, they're never out of here, that is when they're not up in Stormont running around as if they own the place.'

My mother was sitting in her wheelchair making blowing noises. 'Who would have believed it?' she said. 'They're running the country and there's no two ways about that. They got everything they wanted. The Protestants got nothing.'

I stood there against the wall. I noticed that there were black stains up the outside of the arms of my jacket. I spent some time just staring at them and trying to rub them off with spit. The waitress had gone to get her some more wine.

'You're too backward,' my mother said to me. 'Go and talk to those men over there. Tell them that you're a professor.'

The waitress had returned with more wine and more food and overheard this.

'Is he a professor?' asked the waitress.

'He is indeed. But you couldn't tell to look at him,' said my mother.

'Are those his bags?' said the waitress. 'In the old days you wouldn't have been allowed in here with bags like that.'

'Does Gerry ever try to bring big bags in with him?' asked my mother and they both started laughing. 'Is Gerry not coming then?' asked my mother, who I think was disappointed in some strange way.

Chris Patten looked in our direction. It was probably the laughter that attracted his attention. He said something about my novel. I couldn't hear what it was.

'What's in those mushroom patés?' asked my mother.

'Mushrooms,' I said.

'What else?' she asked irritated. 'Do you know, you can't get a sensible answer out of you sometimes.'

The waitress went off to fetch some more drinks. We were still standing in the same spot. I made some pretence and then pushed my mother's chair so that she was now facing the wall, with her back to Chris Patten. 'I can't see,' she said. 'There's nothing to see,' I said. The waitress had returned. 'Are you not watching what's going on?' she asked. Chris Patten was just about to announce the winner. 'And the winner is . . .' he said.

I didn't hear the name but I knew that it wasn't mine. 'Never mind,' said my mother. 'Never mind,' said the waitress. 'Have some more of these lovely mushroom patés.' We could hear the chatter from across the room. 'What time does the bar close?' asked my mother. 'It's open as long as you like,' said the waitress. 'Within reason,' she added. 'Let's have a few more wee drinks then,' said my mother. 'And for God's sake go and speak to some of those people. You're never going to win a prize like that if you don't speak to people,' she said. 'That's his problem, he never speaks, except to bloody women. But then he's had a lot of practice at that.'

I wandered off to find a toilet and I tried smiling at one or two people unsuccessfully. My mother had decided that it was time to go. 'By the way, is there a wee phone around here for us to call Call-a-Cab when all this drink finishes?' she asked the waitress. 'We don't want to be stranded here all bloody night with nothing to eat.' I went to ring Call-a Cab but they were engaged, so I just hung about by the public telephone at the back door and then I bumped into a female TV producer from Dublin who just smiled at me and asked me if I had enjoyed the proceedings. It turned out that she was there to make some arts-based programme about the evening for RTE, but that all the interviews she needed were now in the can. I blurted out that my book was on the shortlist. It was too late to be relevant to anything; it was a moment for chitchat, nothing more. 'Really?' she said, and I looked at her expression and I regretted saying it even more. 'It's a pity that we didn't get to talk earlier. Oh, here's my car, I'm just off.' I smiled at her and walked off before doubling back to ring Call-a-Cab once more. Luckily I got through this time.

I pushed my mother out into the back courtyard of the City Hall to wait for the taxi. She smiled over at the security man and he smiled back at her. 'I think that your man thinks that he's scored,' she said. I wasn't sure whether she was joking or not, so I pretended that I hadn't heard. We hung about outside in the cold night air, a woman in a wheelchair and a man in a grubby coat. It was the professor and his proud mother going back home to the turn-of-the-road from the literary prize-giving, the professor who had departed from his working-class roots, but had not quite arrived anywhere else yet.

These are the moments I remember; I cling onto them because that is all there is. They are even sadder at the time of year I started writing this, with Mother's Day approaching. I would send her flowers every Mother's Day and ring her to make sure that they had arrived. 'They are lovely,' she would say. 'I've shown them to all my neighbours, they're all very jealous', and, at that moment, I would feel ecstatic. Then, she would add: 'It would have been much nicer if you'd brought them in person.'

Of course I would love to pick up the phone today, and just order the flowers and then ring that old number of hers in Belfast just to hear her say . . . anything. She was right a lot of the time, and sometimes I wished that I'd listened more in that busy, busy life of mine.

I wrote about my mother and our relationship for the *Belfast Telegraph*. One elderly lady from Belfast wrote to me to say that 'despite the kinds of things that were said between the two of you, it was obvious that you loved each other', as if this could ever have been in doubt. 'That's just how mothers sometimes talk to their sons,' she wrote, 'and vice versa. You were just as bad as each other, but the love shines through. I wept when I read your wee article.'

But why is this? Why do we say these sorts of things to one another? Why do we feel constrained to deal with each other in these sorts of ways? We say things that we know are going to be are hurtful and wait for those messages to land. My father died when I was young, but when I said hurtful things to her, especially during my adolescence, driven no doubt by an unarticulated anger over his death, she knew the most hurtful thing to say back. It was always the same. 'If your father was alive today, he'd be ashamed of you.' I can picture her saying it now: I can hear the tone in her voice and see her face, contorted in that blend of sadness and defiance, but still somehow looking up for the effect on me, the coup de grâce.

These sorts of conversation were like an arms race, escalating turn by turn, and this, we both knew, was the nuclear option.

Of course I remember how it felt and what my response was, sadness, despair, anger, frustration, guilt, usually contained, but sometimes I would lash out verbally. However, I never contested it. I felt unable to comment on the truth or validity of the statement, on my father's perceptions and interpretations of me as a developing adolescent. I could not bear to talk about my father because it was just too painful, let alone talk about how he might feel, if he was alive, which he clearly wasn't. There was none of 'How would he feel about you?' or 'Perhaps we wouldn't be arguing like this if we were not both consumed with grief that we are unable to deal with.'

Sometimes I was more composed. I would go to hug her and put my arm around her, and she would stiffen (it wasn't over just yet), so I would take my arm away, and she would say: 'I know you don't love me, you always loved your father more than me. You can see it in all our wee photos by the seaside, you're always sitting next to him, not me.'

And I would stand there, staring straight ahead, unable to move, hardly able to breathe, as she sobbed right in front of me, within arm's reach. However, my arm could not reach forward of its own volition. I could not walk away or move forward. I just stood there watching a woman getting older through grief, and knowing that if I was not the ultimate cause of that grief (my father's untimely death surely was), that I was also not, in any way, part of the solution. Even when I went off to read psychology at university over in Birmingham, across the water, they say in Belfast, to emphasise the great distance of a few miles of sea, I knew there was no escape.

I came back home at Christmas at the end of my first term, talking excitedly about psycho-genetics and learning theory, Pavlov's dogs, Skinner's rats and Konrad Lorenz's ducks. Maybe it was the mention of the ducks that did it, maybe she was expecting me to have learned something about human emotions, or human sadness and loss, or maybe it was my description of the way that the ducks had imprinted on Lorenz himself. Maybe that was the final straw. 'They just never left him,' I said enthusiastically, with awe and naivety. 'They just followed him everywhere like he was their mother.'

And she cried. Not at the wonders of science, or what we can learn from imprinting experiments, or even how ducks and children can vary, but how 'carried away' I was with my new life, how all I cared about was 'number one', and how psychology doesn't necessarily give you any insights into anything that matters.

A year or so later, I read Gregory Bateson's classic book, *Steps to an Ecology of Mind*. I wanted to understand some of the intellectual background to the new thinking about madness in the works of R.D. Laing and others. This was all the rage; schizophrenia was now to be regarded as a breakthrough rather than as a breakdown, in the universities at least. She wasn't impressed.

'Have you ever been to Purdysburn?' she asked. 'Or do you know anybody who's had to be put in there and shocked until their head sizzles? Well, I have and that's no bloody breakthrough. You could have fried a bloody egg on old Mary's forehead.'

I was pointed towards Bateson at university; Bateson as the intellectual giant. 'The vision of Blake,' my earnest, heavily bearded philosophy lecturer said one afternoon. 'One could see all of life in a grain of sand, one could understand all of human experience in the most basic atom of conflict in communication. He discovered the "double bind", that simple little twist of communication that changes everything. That was the starting point for Laing. Schizophrenia is only partly in the genes, it's mainly in the environment, and particularly in those close interactions between family members. It is the family that's really dangerous. Bateson knew that.'

And he leaned back in a heavily worn brown leather armchair, a chair which no doubt violated every university rule of standard office furniture, drew heavily on his Gauloises, and then expertly expelled the smoke into the vacant gap in front of him, where three of his second year tutees sat, desperately trying to avoid eye contact, either with one another or with him. He closed his eyes briefly and almost whispered as if confiding to us, 'To see a World in a Grain of Sand/And a Heaven in a Wild Flower/Hold Infinity in the palm of your hand/And Eternity in an hour.'

The tutorial felt like an eternity. He opened his eyes again, as if coming out of a long sleep, and took one more long drag on his cigarette. 'So what are your families like?' he asked. There was silence. I looked down at my boots, and noticed that there was some grass at the end of the left boot. It was sticking out at an odd angle, stuck in that gap between the upper and the sole. It had probably been there for some time. 'Do any of you have a schizophrenogenic mother?' There was still silence, so I pulled the grass out slowly and flicked it onto his beige, coffee-stained carpet.

'A castrating mother who is going to fuck you up. You might not know just yet. You might not *know*, after all, what is knowledge, but you might be starting to sense it.' I started choking on his cigarette smoke, louder and louder, so loud that he couldn't continue.

He looked straight at me. 'Some might see your *disruption* here, as highly significant,' he said directly to me. 'Ask your psychology tutors about defence mechanisms. Ask your psychology tutors whether rats have them?' And he laughed loudly at his own joke. 'Perhaps that's why they only study rats over there. They're afraid of what real psychology might reveal to them.' The tutorial finished early.

Despite this, or maybe because of it, I borrowed Bateson's book from the library and read it carefully, in private. In reality, it was not a disappointment.

It seemed to explain everything; it's scope was magnificent. It was indeed the world in a grain of sand, as William Blake would have said. It explained how madness is a rational response to an irrational situation, how irrationality is constructed in talk, how certain family members propagate this irrationality through their behaviour. And all of this boiled down to one simple behaviour, the double bind, an utterance or a series of utterances that put the recipient in an 'impossible' situation, because of an inherent contradiction in the communication. Any possible response was wrong. What jumped off the page for me was the description of the behaviour in question. I knew that I had seen it before somewhere:

> A young man who had fairly well recovered . . . was visited in the hospital by his mother. He was glad to see her and impulsively put his arm around her shoulders, whereupon she stiffened. He withdrew his arm and she asked, 'Don't you love my anymore?' He then blushed, and she said, 'Dear, you must not be so easily embarrassed and afraid of your feelings.' The patient was able to stay with her only a few minutes more and following her departure he assaulted an orderly and was put in the tubs.
>
> (Bateson 1973: 188)

The fact that the young man in question had been suffering from acute schizophrenia made this all the more poignant. He had been driven mad because of this conflicting communication, literally mad.

Bateson goes on to write that

> Obviously, this result could have been avoided if the young man had been able to say, 'Mother, it is obvious that you become uncomfortable when I put my arm around you, and that you have difficulty in accepting a gesture of affection from me.' However, the schizophrenic patient doesn't have this possibility open to him. His intense dependency and training prevents him from communicating upon his mother's communicative behaviour, though she comments on his and forces him to accept and to attempt to deal with the complicated sequence.
>
> (Bateson 1973: 189)

I could almost feel a chill when I first read these descriptions of a double bind. But, like every undergraduate, I saw examples of every psychological topic that we studied, from manic depression to delusional thinking, in my own life. My life at that time was full of chills. Our psychology lecturers had warned us to be careful about this extrapolation process; you need to examine the evidence more carefully, they explained. My heavily bearded philosophy lecturer, however, told me to be bolder. 'Recognise your experiences. Fight your intense dependency. Liberate yourself from the shackles of the family. Don't become a victim.'

I went home and listed the double binds in my own life. Some were easily recorded, as I talked to my mother on the telephone, or on one of my visits home, and I found myself surreptitiously reaching for my notebook:

'I want you to work hard for your exams. You never make time for me.'
  'Why don't you come home in the summer? Remember, there's nothing over here for you to do.'
  'You were such an affectionate boy. Now you just pretend to be affectionate – when you want something.'
  'What are you writing own in that notebook? Why don't you pay any attention to me?'

Some, however, were not solely verbal, but were harder to record, they were highly subjective. They were embodied in the conflict between the language and the nonverbal behaviour, but they were very reminiscent of what Bateson himself had described.

I wrote slowly and carefully for my philosophy lecturer:

I go to hug her, she stiffens, then sighs. I take my arm away, and she looks mildly disgusted at my withdrawal. The look of disgust was a very brief expression, a micro-expression at best, that only I could have detected. The sigh, however, was quite audible.

But when I studied my list as a whole, I realised that although many of the utterances might be slightly contrary, they were hardly the stuff of pathogenesis. Or were they? Some were somewhat 'contradictory'. But was that enough? I dreaded showing my double bind diary to my philosophy lecturer. How would I defend the presence of the micro-expression? How could I prove its existence? Existential issues reared up in front of me, making me approach the book again, then avoid it, then eventually I picked up the book.

Bateson wrote: 'The mother's reaction of not accepting her son's affectionate gesture is masterfully covered up by her condemnation of him for withdrawing, and the patient denies his perception of the situation by accepting her condemnation' (Bateson 1973: 189).

So it is clear that the double bind is not just about two mutually contradictory communications, stiffening and sighing and then a micro-expression of disgust, for example, it is also about the son accepting the condemnation of his mother, agreeing to her version of reality. In other words, Bateson maintains that double binds are about control – not just of the course of the interaction, and not just about the interpretation and meaning of the acts that constitute the interaction, but about the very nature of the situation itself. They control the 'reality' of the situation. This puts the young schizophrenic patient, the recipient of the double bind, the 'victim', in his own existential dilemma, which Bateson explains as follows – 'If I am to keep my tie to mother, I must not show her that I love her, but if I do not show her that I love her, then I will lose her' (Bateson 1973: 190).

But this is clearly not how it felt for me. I just thought that she was being 'awkward' or 'difficult'. I felt no underlying existential dilemma. But I was being urged by my lecturer in no uncertain terms to persevere. 'Philosophy takes the commonplace and makes it difficult. If it seems clear, then you're not thinking hard enough. If it seems incomprehensible, then you're think- ing more clearly.' I blinked back at him. 'I see,' I said.

I went back to search for moments of simplistic clarity in Bateson, which may turn out, on further study, to be bordering on the incomprehensible. I only half succeeded.

Bateson attempted to specify in detail what features constitute these 'double binds'. He said that 'the necessary ingredients' are as follows: it must involve two or more people, usually (and controversially) the mother. I say 'contro- versially' because there did not seem to be any a priori theoretical reason why this should be the case. Bateson added a qualification of sorts: 'We do not assume that the double bind is inflicted by the mother alone, but that it may be done either by mother alone or by some combination of mother, father and/or siblings' (Bateson 1973: 178). In other words, the role of the mother either acting on her own or in combination with other members of the fam- ily seems clear and unambiguous in his thinking. And, interestingly, all of the clinical examples he cited in support of his theory involved the mother.

Second, it must be recurrent rather than a one-off: 'Our hypothesis does not invoke a single traumatic experience, but such repeated experience that the double bind structure comes to be a habitual expectation' (p. 178). Third, it must have a primary negative injunction issued by one member of an intense relationship to another. This may have the form of 'Do not do so and so, or I will punish you' or 'If you do not do so and so, I will punish you'. Bateson and his colleagues assumed that punishment 'may be either the withdrawal of love or the expression of hate or anger, or most devastating the kind of abandonment that results from the parent's expression of extreme helpless- ness'. Fourth, there must be a secondary injunction, a more 'abstract' com- munication that conflicts with the first and again 'enforced by punishments or signal which threaten survival'. He wrote: 'This secondary injunction is commonly communicated to the child by non-verbal means. Posture, gesture, tone of voice, meaningful action and the implications concealed in verbal comment may all be used to convey this more abstract message' (p. 178).

He also made the point that 'the secondary injunction may impinge upon any element of the primary prohibition'. If one were to translate the sec- ondary injunction into words, then it would translate as 'Do not see this as punishment', 'Do not see me as the punishing agent', 'Do not submit to me prohibitions', 'Do not think of what you must not do', 'Do not question my love of which the primary prohibition is (or is not) and example'. He also wrote that the secondary injunction may involve others acting in tandem with the mother such that 'one parent may negate at a more abstract level the injunctions of the other' (p. 179). The fifth feature is that there must be 'A tertiary negative injunction prohibiting the victim from escaping the field' (p. 179). Bateson added: 'if the double binds are imposed during infancy, escape is naturally impossible'.

Therefore, this set of features specify a double bind in this classic paper grandly called 'Towards a Theory of Schizophrenia'. However, not all of the features need to be present and this is one of the most curious features in their account when the description of a recurrent pattern of communication is turned towards a focus on the perceptions of one of the two individuals involved (the 'victim'). Bateson writes that the complete set of ingredients is no longer necessary when the victim has learned to perceive his universe in double bind patterns. 'Almost any part of a double bind sequence may then be sufficient to precipitate panic or rage. The pattern of conflicting injunctions may even be taken over by hallucinatory voices' (Bateson 1973: 179).

This makes the formal identification of double binds and their possible instrumental role in psychopathology that much more problematic because their characteristic defining features do not actually have to be present.

So was this the incomprehensible element that my lecturer had urged me to pursue. A double bind is a mutually contradictory communication that doesn't actually have to contradict, except in the head of the mad person. The double bind was now being framed as an issue to do with perception where critical aspects like the conflicting injunctions can be imagined through hallucinations. I thought that my double bind diary might not be as useful as I had originally thought.

However, the ambition of Bateson was not to be halted. He boiled it down later in the same paper to a simple recipe (to continue with his own metaphor of 'ingredients'). He said that the general characteristics of a double bind are: '(1) when the individual is involved in an intense relationship; that is, a relationship in which he feels it is vitally important that he discriminate accurately what sort of message is being communicated so that he may respond appropriately; (2) and, the individual is caught in a situation in which the other person is expressing two orders of message and one of these denies the other; (3) and, the individual is unable to comment on the messages being expressed to correct his discrimination of what order to respond to, i.e., he cannot make a metacommunicative statement' (1973: 180).

Bateson accepts that this can occur in 'normal' relations and that in such situations the victim will also behave defensively, but that with pre-schizophrenics (his word, but without the hyphen), they feel 'so terribly on the spot at all times' that they end up confused about messages and their intentions. They are, according to Bateson, particularly confused about the metacommunicative system – the system of communication about the communication. 'If a person said to him, "What would you like to do today?" he would be unable to judge accurately by the context or by the tone of voice or gesture whether he was being condemned for what he did yesterday, or being offered a sexual invitation, or just what was meant' (Bateson 1973: 182). Bateson says that in response some become concerned about hidden meanings behind every utterance (and he says we call this 'paranoid'). Some accept literally what is said, regardless of whether it is contradicted by 'tone or gesture or context', and laugh off these metacommunicative signs (and we call this 'hebephrenic'). Some choose to ignore all utterances and 'detach his interest from the external world and concentrate on his own internal processes' (and we call this 'catatonic').

It need hardly be pointed out that the criteria for the double bind here (from Bateson et al. 1956, listed on page 180 in the 1973 volume) had shifted somewhat from those specified earlier in the same paper (page 178 in the 1973 volume), as Schuham (1967) and others have noted. The second set of criteria include a statement about the *intensity* of the relationship and the victim's *motivational state* ('he feels it is vitally important that he discriminate accurately what sort of *message* is being communicated'). There would appear to be very significant differences between these two sets of criteria which raise important conceptual and methodological issues about how we go about making judgements about the intensity of relationships and the motivational state of the victim, and therefore very serious issues about the formal identification of double binds. But as Schuham also notes: 'It is not clear in this paper whether the authors thoughts these two sets of criteria to be equivalent or to apply to two independent situations' (1967: 411). In other words, it is not clear in the original paper whether or not Bateson and his co-authors foresaw these issues or not.

Of course, there is another major difference between the two sets of criteria, which has given rise to even more confusion in the published literature. In the first set, Bateson and his colleagues focus on the concept of 'level' of communication in the double bind. One criterion specifies: 'A secondary injunction conflicting with the first at a more abstract level, and like the first enforced by punishments or signals which threaten survival.' They also say that

> The secondary injunction is more difficult to describe than the primary for two reasons. First, the secondary injunction is commonly communicated to the child by non-verbal means. Posture, gesture, tone of voice, meaningful action and the implications concealed in verbal comment may all be used to convey this more abstract message. Second, the secondary injunction may impinge upon any element of the primary prohibition. Verbalization of the secondary injunction may, therefore, include a wide variety of forms; for example, 'Do not see this as punishment'; 'Do not see me as the punishing agent'; 'Do not submit to my prohibitions'; 'Do not think of what you must not do'; 'Do not question my love of which the primary prohibition is (or is not) an example'; and so on.
>
> (1973: 178–179)

In the second set of criteria, Bateson et al. focus on the concept of 'orders of message', as in 'the individual is caught in a situation in which the other person is expressing two orders of message and one of these denies the other' (1973: 180).

Schuham (1967) has pointed out that the concept of levels associated with double binds are associated with a number of quite different dimensions. Bateson et al. (in the first set of criteria) put most emphasis on the abstract-concrete dimension but the other levels, which have also been discussed in this same context, are the verbal nonverbal dimension, the communicative-metacommunicative dimension, the literal metaphorical dimension, the particular-contextual dimension and the content-relationship dimension.

Of course, what is even more confusing is that Bateson seems to assume that nonverbal communication necessarily represents a more 'abstract' form of communication than verbal language. But this can be seriously disputed. Some of the communicative effects of nonverbal communication may be more direct than verbal language (e.g. facial expression) especially in terms of commonality of production and interpretation (see Ekman 1992a, 1992b; Beattie and Ellis 2017). Kahneman (2011) argues that the interpretation of emotional facial expression is an example of automatic System 1 type thinking – automatic, fast and effortless ('As surely and quickly as you saw that the young woman's hair is dark, you knew that she is angry', Kahneman 2011: 19). Some forms of nonverbal communication are specifically iconic as I had noted from my research at Cambridge onwards (McNeill 1992; Beattie 2003, 2016), where the nonverbal gesture (the signifier) bears a similarity in form to the concept, object or action that they are communicating about (the signified). This would clearly make them less 'abstract' and much more 'concrete'. David McNeill (1992) has argued this consistently in the case of hand gestures. But he also argued that the mode of communication of gesture differs in other ways to speech, and not just in terms of iconicity, but again in ways that do the opposite of making them more 'abstract'. McNeill says that the method by which nonverbal gestures convey meaning is fundamentally different to the way language does this. Language acts by segmenting meaning so that an instantaneous thought is divided up into its component parts and strung out through time, as in:

The table can be [raised up towards the ceiling]

Iconic: hands are resting on knee; hands move upwards, palms pointing down, forming a large gesture, hands continue moving until the hands reach the area just above shoulder level.

The single event here is being described both by language and by the accompanying iconic gesture (the square brackets in the example above indicate the start-point and the stop-point of the gesture). The speech does this in a linear and segmented fashion, first identifying what is being raised ('the table') and then describing the action ('can be raised up') and then describing the direction of the action ('towards the ceiling'). The linguist de Saussure (1916) argued that this linear-segmented character of language arises because language is essentially one-dimensional whereas meaning is essentially multidimensional. Language can only vary along the single dimension of time with regard to the units out of which it is comprised. As the psychologist Susan Goldin-Meadow and her colleagues note in 1996: 'This restriction forces language to break meaning complexes into segments and to reconstruct multidimensional meanings by combining the segments in time' (Goldin-Meadow et al. 1996).

But the gestures that accompany language don't convey meaning in this linear and segmented manner; rather they convey a number of aspects of meaning at the same time in a single multidimensional gesture. The gesture above depicts the table (and its size), and the movement (and its speed), and the direction of the movement, all simultaneously. The important point is that, as Goldin-Meadow notes, the iconic gestures which accompany speech 'are themselves free to vary on dimensions of space, time, form, trajectory, and so forth and can present meaning complexes without undergoing segmentation or linearization'. So does this make nonverbal communication more abstract? Or less abstract because gestures are not necessarily divided into linguistic units with a syntax necessary for the interpretation of meaning? It is almost certainly the latter.

Speech also relies on 'bottom-up' processing, in that the meanings of the words are combined to create the meaning of the sentence. To understand a sentence, you have to start with the lower level words (hence 'bottom-up'), whereas in gestures we start with the overall concept portrayed by the gesture. It is this concept which gives rise to the meaning of the individual parts (hence 'top-down'). McNeill provides the following example:

> The gesture is a symbol in that it represents something other than itself – the hand is not a hand but a character, the movement is not a hand in motion but the character in motion, the space is not the physical space of the narrator but a narrative space, the wiggling fingers are not fingers but running feet. The gesture is thus a symbol, but the symbol is of a fundamentally different type from the symbols of speech. This gesture – symbol is global in that the whole is not composed out of separately meaningful parts. Rather, the parts gain meaning because of the meaning of the whole. The wiggling fingers mean running only because we know that the gesture, as a whole, depicts someone running.
>
> (McNeill 1992: 20)

The important point to remember here is that when produced by this same speaker, this wiggling finger gesture may well have a different meaning (McNeill points out, for example, that it was also used for 'indecision between two alternatives'). In order to argue that gestures are processed like language in a bottom-up fashion, you would need to be able to demonstrate that the three components which comprise the running gesture – the V hand shape, the wiggling motion and the forward movement – have relatively stable meanings in the person's communicational repertoire, which can be recognised and interpreted wherever they are used. But this is not the case.

Another important difference between speech and gesture is that different gestures do not combine together to form more complex gestures:

> With gestures, each symbol is a complete expression of meaning unto itself. Most of the time gestures are one to a clause but occasionally more than one gesture occurs within a single clause. Even then the several gestures don't combine into a more complex gesture. Each gesture depicts the content from a different angle, bringing out a different aspect or temporal phase, and each is a complete expression of meaning by itself.
>
> (McNeill 1992: 21)

Gestures also convey meaning in a different way because there are no standards of form with gestures. Standards of form are a defining feature of all languages. All linguistic systems have standards of well-formedness to which all utterances that fall within it must conform, or be dismissed as not proper or not grammatical. Gestures have no such standards of form. Thus, different speakers display the same meaning in idiosyncratic but nevertheless recognisable ways. As McNeill (1992: 41) says: 'Lacking standards of form, individuals create their own gesture symbols for the same event, each incorporating a core meaning but adding details that seem salient, and these are different from speaker to speaker.' This non-standardisation of form is very important for theoretical reasons:

> Precisely because gestures are not obliged to meet standards of form, they are free to present just those aspects of meaning that are relevant and salient to the speaker and leave out aspects that language may require but are not relevant to the situation.
>
> (1992: 22)

In the example below, each of the three speakers creates the spinning movement of the table, but they do this differently. One uses one finger, two use both arms, two use clockwise movements, one makes an anti-clockwise movement, two make two movements, one makes three movements (Beattie and Shovelton 2002). The point of this particular picture in the cartoon story is to show the chaos caused when Billy gets on a chair that now spins causing a table to spin. One of the gestures seems to focus specifically on the rapid speed of the spinning; one specifically on the extent of the spinning; and the third depicts both aspects simultaneously.

The signifier: the actual speech and gestures produced by three different narrators	The signified: the event referred to
[It like spins round] *Iconic: left index finger makes three rapid, small clockwise movements.* The table went [spinning] *Iconic: right arm moves in two large clockwise circles, while the left hand moves away from and then towards the right arm.* Wrecks everything [spinning round and round and round and round and round] *Iconic: both arms make two large rapid anti-clockwise movements.*	Billy Whizz causes a table to spin around

Therefore, iconic gestures and speech convey meaning in radically different ways, with speech relying on a lexicon for breaking meaning down into its component parts and a syntax for combining these various elements into meaningful sentences, whereas iconic gestures represent multidimensional meanings simultaneously in one complex image. Each speaker creates the iconic gestures spontaneously without relying on a lexicon with defined standards of form, and even consecutive iconic gestures do not combine into higher order units. Each gesture is complete in itself, and the overall meaning of what is being portrayed represented in iconic form gives the meaning to the individual components.

These gestures work in this multidimensional and iconic manner not just when physical events are being described, but also when they are being used 'metaphorically' in much of everyday interaction, for example, when the hands move close together to indicate the 'intimacy' of a relationship, the hand or hands move upwards to indicate 'higher moral standards', the hands move apart to indicate different positions on a burning political issue and so on. Whether this combination of attributes makes the nonverbal gestures more 'abstract' than speech remains to be seen. You could clearly argue the opposite, that the iconicity of gesture, and therefore the inherent relationship with the thing being described, allows communication to progress in a more concrete way than is the case with verbal language where words do not have these iconic properties. The gesture also represents meaning in one whole, without an abstract syntax for combining the meaning from the various sequential gestures. Again, you could consider this as more 'concrete' than what occurs with speech. The meanings of these gesture are processed 'effortlessly' alongside the speech itself (Beattie and Shovelton 1999a, 1999b; Holler and Beattie 2003a, 2003b). When the gesture does not match the speech, and this does happen in certain situations where, for example, people are asked to intentionally deceive (Cohen et al. 2010), or when a speaker's underlying, implicit attitude to something like the environment and their self-reported attitude do not match, and where they report that they are 'greener' than they actually are, then this can affect both the message received (in that the messages from both channels are integrated) and the perception of the person speaking (Beattie and Sale 2012). Those with mismatching speech and gesture are liked less and listeners are less confident that what they are saying is true. None of these sorts of considerations were ever considered, by Bateson, even though some early work on gesture (see Beattie 2003, chapter 4) significantly predates Bateson's own theorising about the 'concrete' and 'abstract' nature of speech and nonverbal behaviour.

One might well be tempted to conclude that nonverbal behaviours like gesture are significantly 'more concrete' than verbal language because of their non-arbitrary and iconic nature. Critically, gestural movements seem to be rooted in sensory-motor schemas, which are clearly very concrete indeed, and gestures do not rely on combinatorial rules, or syntax, to communicate their meaning.

Nonverbal communication could, however, be considered more 'abstract' in one particular way, and that is because it is not itself encoded in verbal language then its subsequent encoding into language (by way of description) does require a degree of abstraction from the primary mode of its representation. But that, of course, is more a point about analytic description rather than its mode of operation in everyday interaction.

Of course, another of the examples used by Bateson ('the implications concealed in verbal comment') can be more abstract than the straightforward interpretation of simple utterances, especially if the implications are relevant to the interpretation of the content of the language ('Do not see this as punishment') or relevant to the signalling and interpretation of the nature of the relationship ('Do not see me as the punishing agent'). What is implied by any utterance within the context of family interaction can be very abstract indeed as it may require knowledge of previous conversations, previous interactions and previous experiences to work out the implications of what is being communicated (see Garfinkel 1967). Thus, it might be very difficult for researchers (even researchers in their role as therapists with more detailed knowledge of the nature of the relationship) to ascertain exactly what is going on, and to determine exactly what is being implied at any point in time. Of course, that is not to deny that what is being implied by any utterance in a conversation is not critical to the action, it is just to flag up the difficulty in identifying these either from an emic or etic perspective.

Bateson et al. do not help matters here by quickly moving on (in the same paper) to the concept of 'orders of message' that deny one another. Are 'orders of message' meant to be synonymous with 'levels'? And is the specified criterion – 'the other person in a relationship is expressing two order of message and one of these denies the other' (1973: 180) – meant to be synonymous with 'a secondary injunction conflicting with the first at a more abstract level' (1973: 178). One criterion specifies *denial* as a core feature, the other specifies *conflict*. Of course, the connotations of conflict and denial would seem to many to be quite different. Denial, as a process, would seem to be a more active process and perhaps even more deliberative. Conflicting messages, on the other hand, surely are the stuff of everyday life. Teasing, joking, flirting, sarcasm, and humour all involve conflicting communications. Whether they also involve the more active processes of actual *denial* is more open to question, although they may, on occasion ('I wasn't really asking you out; you misinterpreted what I was saying' after a very flirty discussion of a good place for a lunch), be one explicit verbal denial following something altogether more ambiguous.

One other important issue about the double bind, as specified by Bateson and his colleagues, is whether or not the victim actually needs to be (consciously) aware that he is indeed a target of a double bind communication. As Schuham himself observes: 'If not, does this negate the pathogenicity of what the observer would describe as a double bind situation?' (1967: 411). Schuham goes on to examine Watzlawick et al.'s (1967) further elaboration of the essential criteria in this context. They argued that double binds are not simply contradictions or examples of conflicting communication where there are responses open to individuals, they said that double binds are about paradox, where 'choice itself is impossible'.

Schuham points out that this confuses the concept even more because it now establishes that it is the nature of the relationship itself that is necessary for inferring the existence of double binds rather than the communication patterns per se. Indeed, Watzlawick (1963) asserted that 'Indeed, it would be impossible to imagine any emotional involvement, such as for instance courtship, in which double bind does not constitute a core element' (1963: 145). This changes the focus from communicational patterns per se to a focus on the nature of the relationship – many relationships generate conflicting communications, only some generate genuine paradoxes. This makes certain types of research on the double bind (which just focusses on the identification of conflicting communication) even more problematic.

How problematic in the first decade after its formulation is clearly spelt out in the Schuham paper. He points out that 'The great bulk of the literature . . . consist of the presentation of case histories, transcripts of family psychotherapist sessions, clinical descriptions and anecdotes' (1967: 413). Schuham rejects this work on the basis that it cannot be accepted as scientific evidence to validate the theory in question. He found only five studies using a more scientific approach in that first decade after the theory was proposed, and the most important feature of these studies (quite simply) is that they did *not* involve analysis of actual real-life face-to-face interaction, which is what the theory was all about. They involved testing 'memory' for double binds, or behaviour in simulated games, tone discriminations, the resolution of metaphors, the analysis of letters, but no analysis of multichannel face-to-face communication. For example, Berger (1965) asked schizophrenics to estimate how frequently double bind communications had been made by their mothers and found that the schizophrenic group scored significantly higher than any other group. But, of course, this difference in frequency of identification could be attributable to different levels of sensitivity to these kinds of communications, or symptomatic of more general negative attitudes to the mother as part of a process of blame ('she should have protected me more, then I wouldn't be in this state'). Potash (1965) tried to elicit double binds in a game situation but found that withdrawal 'was neither exclusive nor differential to schizophrenics'. Ciotola (1961) tried to generate double binds in an experimental situation in which the discrimination of two auditory tones was impossible. The results of the study did not, however, support the hypothesis that schizophrenics would react worse to the double bind situation. Loeff (1966) presented emotional metaphors to schizophrenics and controls, but found that the schizophrenics were more influenced by the metacommunicative elements, contrary to Bateson's apparent prediction that they would have problems at this level. Ringuette and Kennedy (1966) asked five groups of judges to identify double bind communications in letters written by parents to their hospitalised schizophrenic and non-schizophrenic offspring. One group of judges consisted of three of those researchers actually involved in the formulation of the double bind hypothesis. The inter-rater reliability of the identification of the double binds was extremely low (inter-observer reliability for the experts was 0.19), and only one group (the experts) could differentiate the letters received from the schizophrenics from the letters received from the non-schizophrenics.

Schuham's conclusions on the basis of this ten-year review of evidence were extremely pessimistic. He said that there was little agreement about what communicative phenomena are unique to double bind communication and concluded that 'there is no evidence that double bind communication is exclusive to, or differentially associated with pathological communication processes and not associated with normal communication processes'. He went on to say that 'There is no evidence that the double bind phenomena has an etiological connection with the development of the schizophrenic thought disorder' (1967: 415).

One might imagine that this might have been the end of this particular intellectual journey and that the concept of the double bind might have fallen away. But in many ways it was quite the opposite. It became part of our everyday thinking and, in addition, Bateson's view of the mother and her potential to produce psychological damage in her offspring through the use of double bind communications seeped into other areas of pathology beyond schizophrenia. Bugental and her colleagues applied a form of 'double bind analysis' to interaction in families with 'disturbed' children. At least this time it was actual face-to-face interaction that was the object of study. The disturbed children had been referred by their school to a university psychology department with a variety of 'serious and chronic behavior and emotional problems'. They were matched with 'controls' on various measures and their patterns of interaction were analysed as they waited for five minutes for the study to begin and then when they discussed what they would like changed in their family. Double binds were operationalised as 'conflicting' communications, if the evaluative tone of the verbal content, facial expression or tone of voice differed on certain scales (the evaluation of each channel defined by a consensus of 4 out of 5 judges).

The conclusion drawn from this study was that 'A much higher proportion of the mothers of disturbed children was observed to produce conflicting messages than of the mothers of normal control children. No equivalent difference was found between the fathers' (1971: 9). The conclusions are couched specifically in the language of the double bind. The authors say that they have studied 'contradictory messages' that 'effectively constrain' the child from responding. The double bind, they seem to assume, can be operationalised in terms of conflicting channels and that this provides 'a fruitful avenue to an issue which has previously defied empirical analysis'.

The study, at first sight, appears to be a controlled investigation that yields statically significant data. Although, even then it is hard to justify the language used throughout the paper. Mothers of the disturbed children somehow become 'disturbed mothers' (a neat but not so subtle shift of usage) as in 'The conflicting messages produced by *disturbed mothers* included conflict between verbal content and facial expression, and between verbal content and tone of voice' (1971: 9). To illustrate this observation, the authors write 'one mother typically cooed all here (sic) criticisms, for example, "That's not n-i- ce", in a "syrupy" voice' (1971: 9). Why cooed? Why do they not say that the single mothers (45 per cent of the 'disturbed' families were one-parent, compared to 0 per cent of the control group), trying to control their sons (85 per cent of the 'disturbed' sample were boys) with behavioural problems sitting in a waiting room, attempted to exert a degree of control over their sons by commenting on their behaviour. But these single mothers knew they were being observed throughout, so they tried to soften their various comments and directives with a more positive tone. Why is this not a better description than one of disturbed mothers sending out contradictory signals, with Bugental et al.'s conclusion that 'This is consistent with the double bind hypothesis, but suggests that conflicting communication is not limited to schizophrenogenic mothers' (1971: 9)?

When it comes to control groups, the researchers did not seem to realise that the meaning of this observational situation in a university psychology department would be very different for the experimental and control groups (one set knew that they were essentially on trial). Neither did the researchers seem to realise that a sample size of eighteen in the experimental group and nine in the control group (you have to exclude participants who did not produce 'agreed upon evaluative communications') led to violations of the assumptions of the chi square test, with corrections for small numbers necessary, and that any small (statistically unreliable) differences that were observed could best be explained by single mothers at their wit's end, in the university psychology department with all of these judges judging their every move (for that is indeed what judges do).

'I said "Sit still, you little shit. Behave yourself for once in your life".' I would have liked this shouted so loudly and with such force and anger by the mothers in that experimental situation that the microphones themselves would have shaken. At least, that way the mothers wouldn't be seen as somehow causing their child's 'disturbed' behaviour through anomalous patterns of communication.

And isn't it interesting that the reality (and inescapable existence) of schizophrenogenic mothers is assumed despite the fact that the researchers note that the theory up to that point 'rests heavily on anecdotal evidence' (1971: 6). But presumably no longer in the light of this research (they vainly hoped). Now it was on the basis of *sound* empirical evidence.

This was an experiment which seems to be in search of a conclusion. It was all about generating yet more blame for 'disturbed' mothers, with little understanding, analysis or insight into human communication under the microscope. To equate channels of communication showing a degree of divergence in 'evaluative content' with the concept of the double bind is clearly just wrong, but clearly right enough in some people's minds to allow for the blaming of schizophrenogenic mothers not just to continue but to be broadened in scope. They're not just responsible for schizophrenia, they're responsible for so much else besides.

At this point you may start wondering what exactly is going on. In order to understand this, it is necessary to consider Bateson's work in a much broader context (as Hartwell 1996 did so successfully). This particular Batesonian view of the schizophrenogenic mother (identified through specific recurrent 'conflicting' communicational features) had its roots in much earlier research. Harry Stack Sullivan (1927) described schizophrenia as 'an unhealthy adjustment strategy' (see Hartwell 1996: 276). As Hartwell points out, once you conceptualise schizophrenia this way you are, in effect, 'providing theoretical justification for psychoanalytically trained psychiatrists like himself to treat schizophrenia' (Hartwell 1996: 276). Sullivan's view, deriving from his therapy sessions with a small number of male schizophrenics, was that schizophrenia was the result of certain types of early childhood experiences, particularly connected to early mother-child relationships. The concept of the schizophrenia-inducing mother was born in his work. Levy (1931) brought to the table the concept of the overprotective mother, a mother who, because she apparently resents her prescribed female role, and has significant unful-filled ambitions, stops her child becoming independent. According to Levy (1931) 'the wife is competent, takes responsibility readily, and is often derog-atory of her husband' (1931: 888).

Kasanin et al. (1934) then combined this focus on the importance of early mother-child relationships for schizophrenia from Sullivan's work with this concept of the overprotective mother, and concluded on the basis of observa-tion that the majority of schizophrenic patients had been overprotected and/or rejected by their mothers. Of course, you will notice that 'overprotection' and 'rejection' appear to be two opposite ends of the spectrum, but what appar-ently linked them in some mysterious way was the absence of true love. Instead the concept of 'pseudolove' was developed (Reichard and Tillman 1950: 256). Fromm-Reichman (1948) introduced the concept of the schizophrenic mother, stating that the position of authority in the family, held by American mothers, was 'the main family problem' and that their domineering influence could be disastrous to the psychological well-being of their offspring.

A fascinating (and horrifying) narrative was now rapidly developing in this time of social flux after the Second World War, in this period character-ised, in part, by the breakdown of the traditional gender roles of men and women, where men had gone off to war and women had stepped into the workplace. As Hartwell (1996) notes:

> What is interesting is not . . . unfulfilled female ambition but the attribu-tion of meaning given the maternal quality by therapists; it was patho-genic. Moreover, if a mother of a schizophrenic had begun to actualize her ambitions by rejecting the homemaking role or working outside the home this would also be 'schizophrenogenic'.
>
> (Hartwell 1996: 280)

Hartwell reports one case where a therapist (in the Karon and Rosberg 1958 study), who lived with a family in order to carry out clinical observations, reports that a request by the patient's mother to help with the housework was seen as evidence of the mother's schizophrenogenic tendencies through her 'emasculation of men' (Hartwell 1996: 281). 'Hostile rejection of the homemaking role' was one dimension in parental attitude tests to differenti-ate schizophrenogenic mothers from normal mothers (Shepherd and Guthrie 1959: 213–214). Lidz et al. (1957) described mothers of schizophrenics as failing to fill 'their wifely functions' – 'They were openly deviant in major areas of interaction and rather habitually disregarded or circumvented their husband's demands.' One 'paradigm case', according to Lidz and his col-leagues (from their very biased upper-call New Haven sample), was a former career woman from a wealthy family who hated housework, thus interfering with the child's understanding of masculine and feminine roles and thwart-ing the attainment of a secure identity (Lidz et al. 1965/1985: 76–77).

This is a major part of the background of Bateson's double bind theory. As Hartwell says, the double bind was

> a theory of schizophrenia that tied together divergent versions of the schizophrenogenic mother. . . . Incongruent findings, a hostile, domineering mother, and overtly weak mother, and a rigid, controlled mother would now be united under one theoretical umbrella. The Palo Alto team salvaged the disintegrating schizophrenogenic mother construct. They set the mother's pathological effect at the metacommunicative level.

> (1996: 286)

She also notes that 'The Bateson (1956) article became the most common citation of reports involving the schizophrenogenic mother. Maternal speech was now the focus of attention' (Hartwell 1996: 287). You can perhaps understand now why all of Bateson's examples involved just mothers, even though a theory of communication like this has no a priori requirement to so do. You can perhaps see now why some of its slippery terms had to be exactly so, to tie together such a set of contradictory findings.

Bateson's theory is all about approach and avoidance, as indeed is life itself. It is a fantastical theory that hinges on this single idea. Imagine living in a world where you could not understand the very nature of communication itself. The way that Bateson tries to tie in all of the various manifestations of schizophrenia to this one idea, and the recurrent embodied communicational features that seem to be at the heart of it, is both brilliant and preposterous. Brilliant in the sense that it explains so much with the simplest of assumptions. Perhaps the clearest instantiation of Occam's Razor that I had ever come across as an undergraduate (or I have seen since). Preposterous because the anecdotal evidence marshalled could not hope to support anything like a 'theory of schizophrenia'. But some ideas take hold, and they take hold for particular reasons, and sometimes we need to look outside psychology to understand these.

Of course, central to the whole theory is the relationship between verbal and nonverbal behaviour. So many of Bateson's examples hinged on these types of 'contradictory' communications. We have considered this already in a limited way in the case of gesture but there are other important domains of nonverbal behaviour that Bateson did specifically address. If we want to understand possible 'conflict' in communication, we need to focus on the relationship between these modes or channels of communication. Critical to this thinking was that language and nonverbal behaviour are designed to do different things. The focus on nonverbal behaviour (which is often taken to include both bodily communication and some vocal aspects of speech), as the significant domain through which human emotion is expressed, relationships are built and interpersonal attitudes are negotiated and expressed, has a significant history in psychology and in related disciplines. The argument has always been that language, the verbal channel of communication, is used primarily to convey factual or semantic information about the world, whereas the nonverbal channels have primarily social functions – 'to manage the immediate social relationships – as in animals', according to Oxford psychologist Michael Argyle (1972). Bateson himself wrote:

> It seems that the discourse of nonverbal communication is precisely concerned with matters of relationship. . . . From an adaptive point of view, it is therefore important that this discourse be carried on by techniques which are relatively unconscious and only imperfectly subject to voluntary control.
>
> (Bateson 1968: 614–615)

We can all say 'I love you', some of us rather too easily. It is quite a different matter to fake love nonverbally, or so Gregory Bateson seems to think. So the argument goes that we express relationships nonverbally because these types of communication are less subject to voluntary control, and therefore presumably more honest, and yet at the same time are more nebulous. We send out signals and yet remain unaccountable for their expression.

Bateson also states that 'nonverbal communication serves functions totally different from those of language and performs functions that verbal language is unsuited to perform'. He continues that 'nonverbal communication is precisely concerned with matters of relationship – love, hate, respect, fear, dependency, etc. – between self and vis-à-vis or between self and environment'. The argument therefore within psychology and other disciplines has been that nonverbal communication performs functions that language is unsuitable to perform and that verbal language, on the other hand, that peculiarly human attribute, is concerned with the world of thinking and abstract ideas and the communication of complex information about the world. This functional separation of language and nonverbal behaviour became something of an established orthodoxy in psychology. Argyle and Trower (1979) stated that 'Humans use two quite separate languages [language and nonverbal communication], each with its own function.' This is perhaps the most basic and therefore the clearest statement of how psychologists view language and nonverbal communication and their relationship. In a similar vein, Trower et al. (1978) wrote: 'In human social behaviour it looks as if the nonverbal channel is used for negotiating interpersonal attitudes while the verbal channel is used primarily for conveying information.'

This is the broad structure on which the double bind was premised. Bateson saw the connection of the two channels as being critical to the double bind. The double bind involves 'A secondary injunction conflicting with the first at a more abstract level, and like the first enforced by punishments or signals, which threaten survival' (Bateson 2000: 207). Bateson makes the point that this secondary injunction is commonly communicated through nonverbal means – 'Posture, gesture, tone of voice . . . may all be used to convey the more abstract message' (p. 207). Again, he makes the point that despite the obvious iconicity of many of these nonverbal messages, they are more 'abstract'. One way to understand this is when he considers elsewhere the use of various communicational modes in human communication. He writes:

> Examples are play, non-play, fantasy, sacrament, metaphor, etc. Even among the lower mammals there appears to be an exchange of signals which identify certain meaningful behaviour as 'play' etc. These signals are evidently of higher Logical Type than the messages they classify. Among human beings this framing and labelling of messages and meaningful actions reaches considerable complexity, with the peculiarity that our vocabulary for such discrimination is still very poorly developed, and we rely preponderantly upon nonverbal media of posture, gesture, facial expression, intonation, and the context for the communication of these highly abstract, but vitally important, labels.
>
> (Bateson 2000: 203)

So in this sense, Bateson could argue that they are more abstract. They tell you what kind of utterance an utterance is. I say 'I love you', and the nonverbal behaviour tells you that this utterance is

(a) A genuine declaration of my feelings
(b) A joke
(c) An unkind joke
(d) A provocation
(e) An attempt to get someone into bed
(f) An attempt to elicit the same words back, the first part of an 'adjacency pair' in the terminology of Schegloff and Sacks (1973)
(g) An apology.

It could potentially be any of these and the nonverbal behaviour is critical in 'this framing and labelling of messages'. This would suggest that nonverbal signals are especially powerful in the signalling of relationships between people. After all, 'I love you' as a genuine declaration of love and 'I love you' as an unkind joke would have very different effects on the nature of a relationship,

I have described before (Beattie 2003) how there are two sets of critical experiments that are seen to be critical in demonstrating the relative power of nonverbal behaviour over verbal communication in this interpersonal domain. The first set was carried out by Albert Mehrabian at the University of California in Los Angeles and published in the late 1960s (Mehrabian and Ferris 1967; Mehrabian and Wiener 1967). Mehrabian investigated the effects of consistencies and inconsistencies in communication between the various channels of communication, including the actual meaning of the words and the tone of voice in which they are spoken and the facial expressions and the tone of voice, on the communication of interpersonal attitudes, and in particular on judgements of degrees of liking. In the first study he selected three words judged to convey liking – 'honey', 'thanks' and 'dear'; three words judged to be neutral in this regard – 'maybe', 'really' and 'oh'; and three words that conveyed dislike – 'don't', 'brute' and 'terrible'. Two female speakers read each of the nine selected words using positive, neutral and negative vocal expressions and these communications were then played to sets of judges. In a second study, one neutral word was selected, the word 'maybe'. This time the facial expression was varied: it was positive, neutral or negative. Judges in this second study were presented with an audio recording of the message and a photograph of the person delivering the message. The judges had to rate the overall communication to determine how positive or negative it came across.

From these studies Mehrabian concluded that in the communication of interpersonal attitudes the facial and the vocal channels greatly outweigh the verbal channel and he estimated the relative contributions of the three channels as 55 per cent for the facial channel, 38 per cent for the vocal channel and 7 per cent for the verbal channel. Mehrabian's conclusion was 'when there is inconsistency between verbally and implicitly expressed attitude, the implicit proportion [the nonverbal component] will dominate in determining the total message'.

This is the first study that attempted to say exactly how much the verbal and nonverbal channels each contribute to the communication of interpersonal attitudes and it produced a set of figures that have been picked up and adopted within popular culture. Most of us have heard things such as nonverbal behaviour is thirteen times more powerful than language in the expression of interpersonal attitudes, and that facial expression is eight times more powerful than language. So at first sight we might conclude that nonverbal behaviour is very powerful here, and try to use it to support Bateson's theorising. But that is not how Mehrabian himself saw it. Mehrabian's conclusions about this research vis-à-vis the double bind were that

> Double bind theorists' basic assumption about the relationship between psychological disturbance and inconsistent messages was that the latter were ambiguous and difficult to interpret. However, we now know that this is not true. People do quite readily understand the true meaning when the verbal and implicit parts of a message are inconsistent – they rely on the implicit part and make their judgment accordingly.
>
> (Mehrabian 1971: 86)

In other words, the 'abstract' nonverbal channel might be critical in determining how an utterance like 'I love you' is perceived, but it does not generate any confusion on the part of the recipient.

But, of course, the problem with Mehrabian's basic paradigm is that it does not really consider *language* in the expression of interpersonal attitudes; at least not language as we normally understand it with meaningful sentences used to express how we feel. Only individual words, like 'honey', 'brute' and 'maybe' were used. Nobody talks in individual words in the real world for prolonged periods of time, when they can help it. 'Honey' as an expression on its own only gets you so far. Then when Mehrabian considered the effects of facial versus vocal cues, these different cues were not presented together on videotape but merely as a photograph accompanying a single word. In other words, the participants in this study were simply presented with a photograph of a particular facial expression and they heard the single word being said and then they had to integrate these two things in their mind and make their judgement. So this experiment made no real attempt to simulate anything approaching normal social behaviour or normal social judgement. Hence, we have to be a little wary about the conclusions that have been drawn from it.

However, two experiments carried out at Oxford in the early 1970s by Michael Argyle and his colleagues seem at first sight to address many of these issues. The experiments were published as two important studies, indeed 'citation classics', by Argyle et al. (1970) and by Argyle et al. (1971). The basic methodology of these experiments is quite straightforward. Three verbal messages, paragraphs this time rather than individual words (hostile, neutral or friendly in one experiment; superior, neutral or inferior in another), were delivered in each of three different nonverbal styles (the friendly style being 'warm, soft tone of voice, open posture, smiling face', the hostile style being 'harsh voice, closed posture, frown with teeth showing'). Care was taken at the outset to ensure that the verbal message and the nonverbal style had approximately the same effects on listener evaluation on certain specific dimensions. Here is an example of the types of message used in this experiment. This is the hostile message:

> I don't much enjoy meeting the subjects who take part in these experiments. I often find them rather boring and difficult to deal with. Please don't hang around too long afterwards and talk about the experiment. Some people who come as subjects are really rather disagreeable.

The combined communications, with the three verbal messages delivered in each of the three verbal styles, were then rated by judges to see how friendly or hostile the resultant messages were perceived as being. The results again apparently demonstrate quite clearly that the nonverbal channel greatly outweighs the verbal channel in the communication of interpersonal attitudes. For example, on a seven-point scale, where '7' means extremely friendly and '1' means extremely hostile, the hostile verbal message delivered in a friendly nonverbal style was rated as 5.17; in other words, it was perceived as being towards the friendly end of the scale and higher than the mid-point of 4. When the nonverbal style was friendly it didn't really seem to matter what was actually said; the overall communication was perceived as friendly. Similarly, when the nonverbal style was hostile, again it didn't really seem to matter what was said. The difference in perception of the friendly and hostile verbal messages delivered in the hostile nonverbal style was trivial, the scores being 1.60 and 1.80 respectively. Indeed, the hostile verbal message delivered in the hostile style was perceived as slightly friendlier than the friendly message in the hostile style. This latter form of communication was, of course, taken as a conflicting communication of the type Bateson termed a 'double bind'.

These results led Michael Argyle to the conclusion that nonverbal communication is twelve-and-a-half times more powerful than language in the communication of interpersonal attitudes, specifically on the friendliness – hostility dimension – and over ten times more powerful in the communication of a different interpersonal attitude, namely superiority – inferiority.

These figures are very similar to those of Mehrabian. This series of studies obviously struck a chord with the public and gave those who wished to discuss the importance of nonverbal communication precise figures to work with. The studies demonstrate that nonverbal communication is not just highly significant, but also that we can virtually dismiss verbal language if we want to understand how interpersonal attitudes are signalled, and interpersonal relations are built, in everyday life. It also means that we can ignore the connections between language and nonverbal communication because the judges in this experiment seem to do just that. But although they seem to demonstrate the power of nonverbal communication, again Argyle found no evidence of any confusion on the part of the recipient – 'there was no evidence of double bind effects – where verbal and non-verbal cues conflicted subjects simply disregarded the verbal signals' (Argyle et al. 1971: 401).

Much is built on these two sets of studies. But in my view these pioneering and very influential studies have fundamental weaknesses that really do limit the conclusions that can be drawn. Let's consider what these might be.

The Oxford studies involve judges having to watch a set of nine successive communications on videotape, all from the same person, tapes in which the language and nonverbal communication are systematically varied. The encoders were delivering scripts. Therefore, the whole point of the experiment would be immediately obvious to anyone who took part. Participants could quickly work out what the experimenter was getting at and therefore might decide to play along with him or her. This sometimes happens in psychological research and is called the 'demand characteristics' of the experiment. (Sometimes the opposite occurs: the participants work out what the experimenter wants and deliberately do not go along with it. This is known rather more colloquially as the 'f*** you' effect.) This is always a problem for psychological research where the point of the experiment is as obvious as it was here (Orne 1962).

Second, in order to try to measure the relative importance of language and nonverbal communication, the strength of the two channels had to be both measured and equated at the outset. They had to be equal in strength when measured independently. These studies therefore, at best, tell us about people's perceptions of a certain class of communication with the range of the strength of the components artificially set. The studies do not tell us anything about the range of effects produced by language and nonverbal communication in the world at large. Perhaps in the real world people do not use such explicitly friendly or unfriendly messages. Consider that hostile verbal statement again: 'I don't much enjoy meeting the subjects who take part in these experiments. I often find them rather boring and difficult to deal with.' Is that ever likely to be said directly to someone apart from as a joke? And when it is accompanied by a friendly verbal style ('warm, soft tone of voice, smile, open posture') how else is this supposed to be understood apart from as some sort of joke with the verbal statement to be dismissed? Don't forget that this is exactly what was found to happen in this experiment.

What would happen if we did not make the message quite as explicit as this? What would happen if we made the verbal message slightly more real and then used the same basic pattern of delivery? How would it then be perceived? Would the nonverbal component still make the verbal component seem completely unimportant? Let's do a quick mind experiment. Let's start with something pretty explicit but (in my experience) quite plausible: 'Would you mind leaving?'

This is delivered in the:

1   friendly nonverbal style 'warm, soft tone of voice, open posture, smiling face', or in the:
2   hostile nonverbal style 'harsh voice, closed posture, frown with teeth showing'.

You have to imagine both. Perhaps you could try delivering both messages in front of a mirror, or better still try delivering them to a friend. I am afraid that in both cases I think that I would get the message and go. The first message I imagine being delivered by 'the hostess with the mostest', you know the kind of person I mean. She is asking me to leave a posh party. The second I imagine being delivered by a nightclub bouncer. Both are clearly hostile but 'the hostess with the mostest', while hostile, is keeping it under control mainly for the benefit of the other guests (hence the friendly nonverbal style). The verbal message is, however, significantly more important in communicating her basic unfriendly attitude here than any accompanying behaviours. It may be explicit but it is a real request, heard many times, I would imagine, at many dinner parties (or is this just me?).

Or what about something that is a statement rather than a request or a command, something as basic as: 'You used to be such a nice person'?

Again this is delivered in the:

3   friendly nonverbal style 'warm, soft tone of voice, open posture, smiling face', or in the:
4   hostile nonverbal style 'harsh voice, closed posture, frown with teeth showing'.

My guess is that the nonverbal behaviour in message 3 will neither transform nor soften the basic message. It is not a friendly statement and the fact that it is being delivered in this style could make it even less friendly because it is as if the speaker is still trying to be understanding and yet, despite being understanding, she can still make the basic statement. In message 4 the person has started to lose control.

The point to be made here is that psychologists have never really been able to quantify the relative importance of language and nonverbal communication in interpersonal communication. It would be an extremely difficult and time-consuming experiment to do. I have made it seem easy with a few examples, but think of the generality of the conclusions that people are trying to draw from such an experiment. We would need a representative sample of an enormous variety of utterances, sampling all of the kinds of things that language can do and sampling different contexts as well. I have sketched out a few contexts above, but I am sure you can imagine some different contexts that might affect the basic interpretation of the utterances. Utterances, after all, only make sense in context.

If you don't believe me let's return to the first utterance, this time imagining slightly different contexts for the utterance: 'Would you mind leaving?' Imagine this being delivered at the very end of the evening by a bouncer in a nightclub and delivered in that friendly style 'warm, soft tone of voice, open posture, smiling face'. Suddenly it's quite friendly. Everyone has to leave, it's just that time of night. The bouncer is, after all, asking in a very friendly manner. I tried this experiment, believe it or not. I asked a doorman I knew to ask people to leave using this style of nonverbal behaviour. I then asked the poor innocent punter how he perceived the message. At the end of the night the punter said: 'Everything was fine, the bouncer was polite and friendly. Are you doing some research into customer satisfaction?' I also asked the doorman to say exactly the same thing in the same friendly manner early in the evening to a different punter. This second punter looked confused. He thought that it was a case of mistaken identity; bouncers don't just ask you to leave for no good reason. But how did the new punter perceive the overall message – the 'hostile' message in the 'friendly' style (at this point I really do need to rely on inverted commas)? Actually, he perceived it as very threatening. 'It was the understated way that he asked me,' the second punter explained. 'He was really hostile, as if he was looking forward to giving me a good thump if I didn't go immediately. But I hadn't done anything.'

He added, 'That was really the annoying thing.' He smiled when he was told that this was just a little test.

The picture is, as you can see, becoming a little more complicated. The conclusions, which are that interpersonal attitudes are signalled almost exclusively by nonverbal behaviour, are looking a little shakier. The general conclusion that 'humans use two quite separate languages, each with its own function' is looking somewhat less secure.

But to return to the studies of Michael Argyle, how could we make them more convincing? As a starting point we would want to make sure that the behaviours studied in the laboratory mirrored the kinds of behaviours shown in the real world. We can all be hostile using language without being quite as explicit as the speaker was in these experiments. When verbal statements become less explicit and more plausible, and more like the things that are said in everyday life, do they then become more powerful and significant as a consequence, and not so readily dismissed as some sort of joke in an experiment of this kind? The important point is that we do not know because unfortunately this experiment has never been carried out.

At this point you might be wondering how verbal language would function to signal friendliness in subtle and less direct ways in everyday life. (I came up with a couple of quite hostile utterances off the top of my head, again I wonder what this tells you about me.) Here are a few suggestions. You can perhaps add your own here because the range of ways verbal language might do this is potentially quite large. But I would suggest that opening up a conversation in the first place, the use of first names, compliments, disclosure, reciprocated disclosure, the asking of personal questions, verbal engagement, shared perspectives, sharing of childhood memories, offers of help, offers of support, all play some role in the communication of certain interpersonal attitudes by language itself.

How important are each of these verbal strategies compared with the appropriate forms of nonverbal communication like facial expressions, postures, smiles and frowns in the overall communication of interpersonal attitudes? We simply do not know, but my guess is that the verbal statements would not be dismissed quite so readily as they were in those pioneering but somewhat transparent experiments of the early 1970s. Again this is not to argue against the incredible significance of nonverbal communication, but merely represents an attempt to reinstate ordinary language and the connections between ordinary language and nonverbal communication in the heart of social relationships and the study of human communication.

Let me also add that there are other, rather more specific criticisms of these studies that are necessary given the incredible cultural weight which has come to rest on their conclusions. Only one person was used in these Oxford experiments to deliver the nine messages in the first place and she was described as 'an attractive female student'. In other words, we know nothing about the generality of the results. How do we know that the results were not specific to this one individual? Would the results have generalised to male students, to less attractive students, or to the population at large? We do not know. But a number of years ago I tried to replicate the original study using a male speaker, and the results were altogether a good deal less clear-cut. For example, the friendly verbal message in a hostile nonverbal style was rated as 3.90, essentially perceived as neutral rather than as very hostile, as in the original study (see Beattie 1983: 9).

In addition, in the original study the judges were watching the combinations of verbal and nonverbal communication on a video screen and were specifically requested to attend to the video clips. In real life, however, when we are engaged in social interaction we sometimes look at the other person, sometimes we do not. This shifting pattern of eye gaze depends upon interpersonal distance, relative status, seating or standing position, the content of what we are saying, the structure of what we are saying and emotions like shame, embarrassment, guilt, and so on. In real life we may miss a number of critical nonverbal signals for a variety of reasons. In the classic experiments by Michael Argyle there was never this possibility. Again, these experiments failed to simulate the complexities and patterns of everyday social life. For this and for the other reasons outlined we need to be extremely careful about how we interpret the results of these classic experiments.

But Argyle and his colleagues also thought that this experimental investigation of manipulated verbal-nonverbal messages could have implications for the double bind theory. In the study on the communication of inferior-superior attitudes, they found 'no evidence of double bind effects' (Argyle et al. 1971: 401). They found that participants simply ignored the verbal messages when there was an apparent conflict. But in the study on friendly-hostile attitudes they claimed to find some in that when there were inconsistent verbal-nonverbal signals of positive or negative affect the performer was 'judged unstable, insincere and confused' (p. 400). But. Of course, that is not really in line with the major prediction from the theory. If the individuals studied by Bateson had concluded that their ('schizophrenogenic') were 'unstable, insincere and confused', here presumably would be no major clinical problem with their children. These, after all, are dispositional attributions, presumably more than healthy in this situation. Presumably, it is much worse when you start to internalise these sorts of attributions, or blame the communicational system itself.

But there is another very important point to be made here about the nature of the various channels of communication and how they are built into the double bind theory. Bateson himself had said explicitly (as we have already seen) that 'It seems that the discourse of nonverbal communication is precisely concerned with matters of relationship. . . . From an adaptive point of view, it is therefore important that this discourse be carried on by techniques which are relatively unconscious and only imperfectly subject to voluntary control.' But at the same time he is saying that the 'framing and labelling of messages and meaningful actions reaches considerable complexity . . . and we rely preponderantly upon nonverbal media of posture, gesture, facial expression, intonation, and the context for the communication of these highly abstract, but vitally important, labels'. The obvious conclusion then is that *if* there are recurrent conflicting communications in the family dynamics with a schizophrenic offspring then the double binds are not being deliberately generated (at least not) through the mechanism of sending out the more powerful and 'abstract' nonverbal signals, which frame and label messages, because these are 'relatively unconscious' and 'only imperfectly subject to voluntary control'. This may make one very uncomfortable about labelling any individuals who might generate inconsistent communication as 'binders', with all the connotations of deliberative action. So is it still possible the other way round? Again, consider the classic example: the child hugs his mother, she stiffens, he withdraws his arm, she says: 'Don't you love me anymore?' Is the verbal utterance the deliberative action, the 'abstract' and powerful metacommunicative message that confuses the child to such a degree that madness is the only mechanism of adaptation? Possibly, but this flies in the face of everything that Bateson said about the operation of the two channels. The mother is not so much a 'binder' but a 'leaker'.

The logic of the double bind was, in my opinion, fatally flawed. It identified one possible moment in an interactional sequence and drew dramatic and damning conclusions from that moment in time. But consider the following. Assume for one second that the mother did stiffen when her schizophrenic son hugged her. How was the hug itself? Was it not loving enough? Is that why she reacted the way she did? Or what happens if we consider certain types of nonverbal behaviour as System 1 responses in Kahneman's terminology, more automatic, quicker and more unconscious than verbal behaviour? Was the mother leaking her true feelings through this behaviour and trying to compensate with her comment? Well, not necessarily. Nonverbal behaviour can be affected by situation as well as by interpersonal feelings. Perhaps her stiffening was occasioned by being observed by the psychiatrist or Bateson himself. Perhaps she didn't feel comfortable acting normally in his presence? But liked things even less when her son withdrew his affectionate hug (that's assuming that it was indeed affectionate; many hugs do not have this quality). Hugs are often part of a sequence of interaction that unfolds, but Bateson disregarded all of this in his analysis of the moment. And why would being on the receiving end of the mother's behaviour lead one to fail to understand meta-communication generally? Are human beings not natural dispositional theorists, keen to explain behaviour in terms of the personalities of the actors? Why wouldn't the son step back and think my mother has a problem with intimacy? To showing her affections in front of strangers? And why didn't Bateson, as the observer, gravitate naturally towards that type of explanation? Why would the son naturally assume that the communicational system was itself wrong rather than something to do with the mother (if indeed anything was wrong in the first place! It's really impossible to judge out of context). And what happens if the mother wanted a different sort of hug, a more affectionate hug, a full body hug, a hug with a kiss? What happens if that hug was not enough for her? She may have been signalling something, but not necessarily what Bateson assumes.

So what are we left with? Isolated observations of behaviour, extracted from their natural context, their sequential organisations disrupted, with gross interpretations of behaviour and intention. System 1 responses recoded in System 2 terms and a generation of mothers blamed, explicitly then implicitly, for every failing in their offspring. I caught my mother using double binds against me, or I thought I did as an undergraduate encouraged and goaded by my philosophy lecturer. Later, I was not so sure, in fact I was not sure at all. I think she wanted more love from me than I had time to give her, and a little understanding. No more, no less.

That's where I would have liked to leave it, but sometimes it's not that easy. I was in my spare room recently thinking about her, and all that psychology had taught me, and perhaps how I had used it against her. I found a bottle top, just where she had left it but I'd never noticed it before. It was in the top drawer in her bedroom. I say her bedroom but it was twelve years since she'd gone, and yet the room in my house still smelt of her, after all that time. It's odd the way that smells linger like that, like old memories that you can't quite shake off. I picked the bottle top up and sniffed it to see if the fragrance of the whisky was still there, but it just smelt of old metal, a rusty sort of smell, hardly anything really, just like old metal railings.

Of course, I remember the drinking, a few glasses in the evening, maybe more; convivial, that's what they say. 'I'm just being sociable,' she said, 'I never get out. When you live on your own you look forward to a wee drink with company.' And she would ask me what whisky I'd bought for her that night and then criticise my choice. Too cheap, too dear, too common, too unusual. Never right, never ever right. 'I'll have a drink with you, you go and get what you bought', and she always drank it anyway, after her initial ritualistic protestation, and she would start to cheer up by the second glass or so, once the glow had set in.

'I hope you didn't just get the one bottle. I worked in an off-license for a short time after I retired and we used to laugh at men with a bit of money about them coming in for their one wee lonely bottle. Sad, we called them, men with no friends, nobody to socialise with, auld bokes. Me and the other girls always said that those sort of men would be in bed at eleven, on their own. When you've got a couple of bottles in the house, at least you've got something to look forward to. The night is young; there's always possibilities.'

And you could see her glancing off into the distance, dreaming of those days of possibilities, when she was still young and on the town, when things might just happen, without willing them.

I assured her that I wasn't that sad.

'You drink awful fast,' she would say. 'I'm struggling to keep up with you.' But she always finished first and that was the cue for me to go downstairs for a refill. I poured her a large glass full of possibilities. 'I'm awful lonely,' she would say, 'ever since your father died. Awful lonely. Sitting on my own every night with my bad ankles, waiting for you to ring me. Then I get over to England to see you and you're always out, enjoying yourself, no time for me, just looking after number one. Is that what I worked for all those years in the mill? To get you an education so that you could just go out and gallivant around the place.'

The tears were starting to form; I couldn't bear to witness it.

'Let's have a good night,' I'd say, and I would drain my glass.

'So you're acting the big fella now, the money man, the fella in the big picture.'

'I drank that one a bit quick; it's made me feel a bit sick,' she would say, and I would pretend to boke all over her. And in those moments I would become a child again, back in the old mill house with the damp wallpaper coming off the walls before I left to get an education and come back 'a wee snob', her words, a wee frigging snob ashamed of his background, distracted by all that education, and all those new possibilities. I made more retching noises. She laughed for a moment or two, on that fine balance beam between up and down, good and bad, optimism and despair, before finally settling in that other darker place.

'All that education and you still talk bloody rubbish. You're only happy when you're acting the fool, at my expense, of course, poking fun at me,' she said. 'Don't think that I can't see it. That drink couldn't make you sick. You're acting all daft about nothing. Does that kind of wee show impress them up in the university? Because it certainly doesn't impress me. You'll regret this one day.'

It was, of course, just my little routine to distract her, to stop her thinking about Belfast and the Troubles and what might be happening back in her hometown while she was visiting me over in England, across the water; she called it 'way across the water'. It sometimes worked, that was the thing; my fooling around sometimes did the trick, that's why I had to persevere to cheer her up and overcome the guilt. I'd a lot to feel guilty about. I didn't just talk about Lorenz and learning theory and cognition in those vacations as a student, I brought back Eysenck's theory of racial differences in intelligence and why the blacks and the Irish are not as intelligent as the rest (always a good one for livening things up in Belfast), and how mothers uses double binds to drive their sons insane. I sat there, with my philosophy lecturer whispering in my ear, commenting on what she had said to me and her nonverbal behaviour; sometimes I used notes from the past, mentally encoded. I explained what a schizophrenogenic mother was, in this new undergraduate language of mine, and that slightly changing Belfast accent, and she sat looking back at me, with tears welling slowly in her eyes. 'Why do you hate me?' she said in her heavy Belfast accent, immutable, never changing. 'No Surrender!' to those social pressures from above telling her to speak differently. I'd surrendered alright.

'It's not you I hate; it's what mothers can do to you. It's obvious, they don't mean to; they just do it,' I stammered, that was my attack.

Of course, I grew up eventually and regretted it all so very, very much. I was using an unexamined and unsubstantiated theory in these skirmishes to deal with some deep longing inside for my father that neither of us could do anything about. Later I avoided saying anything significant in our conversations, but that was just me, I just tried to be funny (no doubt Bateson would have explained that as well). I was funny as fuck.

And back on that fateful night she said that she'd had enough. 'I'm away to bed. I thought that you might have something sensible to say to me, you with all that education and me living on my own. But no, you just like playing the bloody fool at my expense.'

She left the next morning, to go back home, and I only saw her once again. She lost consciousness in her sleep a few weeks after that and died in the hospital with me beside her. Her next door neighbour had found her. I went back home to arrange the funeral. Her neighbour sat on a floral cushion in her front room that smelt heavily of lavender spray. 'Your mother had a peaceful death the way she wanted it.'

I picked up the bottle top. She used to say that I always bought the wrong type. She said that it was deliberate. I sniffed the metal again, to try to remind myself about those nights sharing a bottle: that's what they say isn't it, *sharing* a bottle. But they weren't there. What would they know about sharing? What did we ever share except an unresolved sorrow that should have bound us together but didn't. And all that psychology, not only didn't help us in our relationship – it just seemed to hinder.

Postscript

But that was then; it's now quite a few years since she died, and the time has slipped effortlessly past. Time speeding along like a bullet train, I must have jumped on that train at some point, hurtling along now, occasionally with this abrupt stop in the middle of nowhere, and you just sit there staring out of the window, trying to work out where you've got to, trying to work out what you've seen.

She gave me far more than I could ever have recognised at the time. She gave me love and she gave me this insight into how we communicate with those we love most, and within that I came to understand how this communication can be so emotionally difficult because we're afraid to talk too openly. Terrified sometimes, fearing what we might say, fearing what we might hear.

I could see that I was trying to examine the things that meant most to me through the prism of psychology – that's what education does – it gives you a new way of viewing life. But it also gives you a way of critiquing what you read and hear and see; it makes you more sceptical and cynical. And with that slowly acquired cynicism you may well discover that the psychology itself, or the double bind, or the concept of the pathogenic mother, or this or that, are not up to scratch in its sum or in its parts. Inadequately observed, ideologically biased, fragmentary and incomplete. You can't just blame mothers like this to deflect attention from elsewhere, to occlude real understanding. Education can occasionally help put things right. I can see that now.

And in critiquing the double bind, I came to realise that all those years of micro-analysis of human behaviour in the low temperature building back in Cambridge, with long days and nights examining in detail the relationship between the explicit and implicit aspects of human behaviour, might well be relevant to real life after all. This research tells us something about how communication can unfold, and how it really is multimodal and that if you are ever going to blame mothers for a loss of reality in their children, because of aspects of this multimodality, as Bateson, Laing and others have tried to do, then it is best to start with some fundamental scientific understanding of how the various modalities actually operate together in everyday life. And even when these interactions occur in the observation room of a psychology department in Cambridge where you can film and analyse the multiple connections of this great complex and embodied computational machine that we call the human mind, you can still make some progress. Of course, you then still need to see how they operate outside, on the street, in the dives, in the clubs, in the gutter, wherever you think the action is, with all the inherent difficulties in this (Beattie 2018b). But, at least, you might know what you're looking for, you have a starting point. Then it is imperative to follow this up, to document the social world out there, in order to learn anything serious about the psychological and behavioural effects of unemployment, or understand violence, or masculine cultures, or job insecurity, or racism (Beattie 2013) or environmental indifference (Beattie 2010). I made some sort of start as you can see in this book. But when I read these accounts back, it's only the deficiencies I notice and how so much more needs to be done.

But my mother may also have helped me towards establishing some sort of concept of self. And maybe not even trapped between worlds as I had always thought, rather bridging these worlds (a different metaphor altogether – up high rather than down low), one foot in either camp, one big toe straining on each precarious plank (not as high as a bridge but higher than down below). Sure, the two floating fragments of the raft may drift further apart, and where does that leave you? But you can cling on, and dig your toes in and through time you don't have to think about it quite so much. It becomes automatic and routine, a habit – implicit and unconscious like so much else in life – both good and bad. I got used to it in the end.

It becomes who you are without that desperate attempt at reconciliation by Dostoevsky's narrator. 'I am a sick man . . . I am a wicked man.' I'm not that narrator from *Notes from Underground* anyway, I never have been, these aren't even my descriptors, not sick, not wicked. I have some alternatives, I always have had. But, importantly, there's no silent pause in the middle of these either.

Education has, at least, taught me something. It has taught me that silence can be very meaningful, sometimes even as meaningful as the speech itself. That, after all, is what I studied for three years at Cambridge so I should know. It's sometimes what's not said, that's the most significant.

References

Argyle, M. (1972). *Non-Verbal Communication in Human Social Interaction*. Oxford: Cambridge University Press.

Argyle, M., Alkema, F. and Gilmour, R. (1971). The communication of friendly and hostile attitudes by verbal and non-verbal signals. *European Journal of Social Psychology* 1: 385–402.

Argyle, M., Salter, V., Nicholson, H., Williams, M. and Burgess, P. (1970). The communication of inferior and superior attitudes by verbal and non-verbal signals. *British Journal of Social and Clinical Psychology* 9: 222–231.

Argyle, M. and Trower, P. (1979). *Person to Person: Ways of Communicating*. London: Harper Collins Publishers.

Bardon, J. (1992). *A History of Ulster*. Belfast: Blackstaff Press.

Bateson, G. (1968). Redundancy and coding. In Sebeok, T. A. (ed.), *Animal Communication: Techniques of Study and Results of Research*. Bloomington, IN: Indiana University Press, pp. 614–626.

Bateson, G. (1973/2000). *Steps to an Ecology of Mind: Collected Essays in Anthropology, Psychiatry, Evolution, and Epistemology*. New York: Paladin Books.

Bateson, G., Jackson, D. D., Haley, J. and Weakland, J. (1956). The double bind. *Behavioral Science* 1: 251–254.

Baudelaire, C. (1857/1995). *Les Fleurs du Mal*. New York: Dover Publications.

Beattie, G. (1977). The dynamics of interruption and the filled pause. *British Journal of Social and Clinical Psychology* 16: 283–284.

Beattie, G. (1978a). Sequential temporal patterns of speech and gaze in dialogue. *Semiotica* 23: 29–52.

Beattie, G. (1978b). Floor apportionment and gaze in conversational dyads. *British Journal of Social and Clinical Psychology* 17: 7–15.

Beattie, G. (1979a). The modifiability of the temporal structure of spontaneous speech. In Siegman, A. W. and Feldstein, S. (eds.), *Of Time and Speech: Temporal Speech Patterns in Interpersonal Contexts*. New York: Lawrence Erlbaum.

Beattie, G. (1979b). Planning units in spontaneous speech: Some evidence from hesitation in speech and speaker gaze direction in conversation. *Linguistics* 17: 61–78.

Beattie, G. (1979c). Contextual constraints on the floor-apportionment function of speaker-gaze. *British Journal of Social and Clinical Psychology* 18: 391–392.

Beattie, G. (1979d). Reflections on 'reflections on language' by Noam Chomsky. *Linguistics* 17: 907–923.

Beattie, G. (1981a). Interruption in conversational interaction, and its relation to the sex and status of the interactants. *Linguistics* 19: 15–35.

Beattie, G. (1981b). A further investigation of the cognitive interference hypothesis of gaze patterns during conversation. *British Journal of Social Psychology* 20: 243–248.

Beattie, G. (1981c). The regulation of speaker-turns in face-to-face conversation: Some implications for conversation in sound-only communication channels. *Semiotica* 34: 55–70.

Beattie, G. (1981d). Language and nonverbal communication: The essential synthesis? *Linguistics* 19: 1165–1183.

Beattie, G. (1982a). The dynamics of university tutorial groups. *Bulletin of the British Psychological Society* 35: 147–150.

Beattie, G. (1982b). Turn-taking and interruption in political interviews: Margaret Thatcher and Jim Callaghan compared and contrasted. *Semiotica* 39: 93–114.

Beattie, G. (1982c). Behaviour in the psychological laboratory. *New Scientist* 96: 181.

Beattie, G. (1983). *Talk: An Analysis of Speech and Non-Verbal Behaviour in Conversation*. Milton Keynes: Open University Press.

Beattie, G. (1986). *Survivors of Steel City*. London: Chatto & Windus.

Beattie, G. (1987). *Making It: The Reality of Today's Entrepreneurs*. London: Weidenfeld & Nicolson.

Beattie, G. (1988). *All Talk: Why It's Important to Watch Your Words and Everything You Say*. London: Weidenfeld & Nicolson.

Beattie, G. (1990). *England after Dark*. London: Weidenfeld & Nicolson.

Beattie, G. (1992). *We Are the People: Journeys through the Heart of Protestant Ulster*. London: Heinemann.

Beattie, G. (1996). *On the Ropes: Boxing as a Way of Life*. London: Victor Gollancz.

Beattie, G. (1998). *Head-to-Head: Uncovering the Psychology of Sporting Success*. London: Gollancz.

Beattie, G. (2002). *The Shadows of Boxing: Prince Naseem and Those He Left behind*. London: Orion.

Beattie, G. (2003). *Visible Thought: The New Psychology of Body Language*. London: Routledge.

Beattie, G. (2004). *Protestant Boy*. London: Granta.

Beattie, G. (2010). *Why Aren't We Saving the Planet? A Psychologist's Perspective*. London: Routledge.

Beattie, G. (2013). *Our Racist Heart? An Exploration of Unconscious Prejudice in Everyday Life*. London: Routledge.

Beattie, G. (2016). *Rethinking Body Language: How Hand Movements Reveal Hidden Thoughts*. London: Routledge.

Beattie, G. (2018a). *The Conflicted Mind: And Why Psychology Has Failed to Deal with It*. London: Routledge.

Beattie, G. (2018b). *The Body's Little Secrets*. London: Gibson Square.

Beattie, G. (2019). *Trophy Hunting: A Psychological Perspective*. London: Routledge.

Beattie, G. and Bradbury, R. J. (1979). An experimental investigation of the modifiability of the temporal structure of spontaneous speech. *Journal of Psycholinguistic Research* 8: 225–248.

Beattie, G., Cutler, A. and Pearson, M. (1982). Why is Mrs Thatcher interrupted so often? *Nature* 300: 744–747.

Beattie, G. and Ellis, A. (2017). *The Psychology of Language and Communication Classic Edition.* London: Routledge.

Beattie, G. and Sale, L. (2012). Do metaphoric gestures influence how a message is perceived? The effects of metaphoric gesture-speech matches and mismatches on semantic communication and social judgment. *Semiotica* 192: 77–98.

Beattie, G. and Shovelton, H. (1999a). Do iconic hand gestures really contribute anything to the semantic information conveyed by speech? An experimental investigation. *Semiotica* 123: 1–30.

Beattie, G. and Shovelton, H. (1999b). Mapping the range of information contained in the iconic hand gestures that accompany spontaneous speech. *Journal of Language and Social Psychology* 18: 438–462.

Beattie, G. and Shovelton, H. (2002). What properties of talk are associated with the generation of spontaneous iconic hand gestures? *British Journal of Social Psychology* 41: 403–417.

Berger, A. (1965). A test of the double bind hypothesis of schizophrenia. *Family Process* 4: 198–205.

Berger, J. (1972). *Ways of Seeing.* Harmondsworth: Penguin.

Bernstein, B. (1974). *Class, Codes and Control* (Vol. 1). London: Routledge and Kegan Paul.

Bugental, D. E., Love, L. R., Kaswan, J. W. and April, C. (1971). Verbal-nonverbal conflict in parental messages to normal and disturbed children. *Journal of Abnormal Psychology* 77: 6–10.

Butterworth, B. L. and Beattie, G. (1978). Gesture and silence as indicators of planning in speech. In Smith, P. T. and Campbell, R. (eds.), *Recent Advances in the Psychology of Language: Formal and Experimental Approaches.* New York: Plenum.

Chomsky, N. (1957). *Syntactic Structures.* The Hague: Mouton.

Chomsky, N. (1959). Review of B.F. Skinner's 'Verbal Behavior'. *Language* 35: 26–58.

Chomsky, N. (1965). *Aspects of the Theory of Syntax.* Cambridge, MA: MIT Press.

Chomsky, N. (1972). *Problems of Knowledge and Freedom.* London: Fontana.

Chomsky, N. (1976). *Reflections on Language.* Glasgow: Fontana.

Ciotola, P. V. (1961). *The Effect of Two Contradictory Levels of Reward and Censure on Schizophrenics.* Doctoral dissertation. Columbia, MO: University of Missouri.

Cohen, D., Beattie, G. and Shovelton, H. (2010). Nonverbal indicators of deception: How iconic gestures reveal thoughts that cannot be suppressed. *Semiotica* 182: 133–174.

de Saussure, F. (1916/2000). The nature of the linguistic sign. In Burke, L., Crowley, T. and Girvin, A. (eds.), *The Routledge Language and Cultural Theory Reader.* London: Routledge, pp. 21–32.

Dostoevsky, F. (1864/1993). *Notes from Underground.* New York: Alfred A. Knopf.

Duncan, S. (1972). Some signal and rules for taking speaking turns in conversation. *Journal of Personality and Social Psychology* 23: 283–292.

Ekman, P. (1992a). An argument for basic emotions. *Cognition and Emotion* 6: 169–200.

Ekman, P. (1992b). Facial expressions of emotion: New findings, new questions. *Psychological Science* 3: 34–38.

Eysenck, H. (1960). *Uses and Abuses of Psychology.* London: Pelican.

Eysenck, H. (1961). *Sense and Nonsense in Psychology.* London: Pelican.

Freud, S. (1910/2001). *Leonardo da Vinci: A Memoir of His Childhood.* London: Routledge.

Fromm-Reichmann, F. (1948). Notes on the development of treatment of schizophrenics by psychoanalytic psychotherapy. *Psychiatry* 11: 263–273.

Garfinkel, H. (1967). *Studies in Ethnomethodology*. Englewood Cliffs, NJ: Prentice Hall.

Goffman, E. (1963). *Behavior in Public Places*. Glencoe, IL: Free Press.

Goffman, E. (1976). *The Presentation of Self in Everyday Life*. Harmondsworth: Penguin.

Goffman, E. (1981). *Forms of Talk*. Pennsylvania: University of Pennsylvania Press.

Goldin-Meadow, S., McNeill, D. and Singleton, J. (1996). Silence is liberating: Removing the handcuffs on grammatical expression in the manual modality. *Psychological Review* 103: 34–54.

Goldman-Eisler, F. (1967). Sequential temporal patterns and cognitive processes in speech. *Language and Speech* 10: 122–132.

Goldman-Eisler, F. (1968). *Psycholinguistics: Experiments in Spontaneous Speech*. London: Academic Press.

Hartwell, C. E. (1996.) The schizophrenogenic mother concept in American psychiatry. *Psychiatry* 59: 274–297.

Hawkins, P. R. (1969). Social class, the nominal group and reference. *Language and Speech* 12: 125–135.

Hawkins, P. R. (1973). The influence of sex, social class and pause location in the hesitation phenomena of seven-year-old children. In Bernstein, B. (ed.), *Class, Codes and Control* (Vol. 2). London: Routledge and Kegan Paul.

Heaney, S. (1975/1992). *North*. London: Faber and Faber.

Helion, C., Helzer, E. G., Kim, S. and Pizarro, D. A. (2020). Asymmetric memory for harming versus being harmed. *Journal of Experimental Psychology: General* 149: 889–900.

Holler, J. and Beattie, G. (2003a). Pragmatic aspects of representational gestures: Do speakers use them to clarify verbal ambiguity for the listener? *Gesture* 3: 127–154.

Holler, J. and Beattie, G. (2003b). How iconic gestures and speech interact in the representation of meaning: Are both aspects really integral to the process? *Semiotica* 146: 81–116.

Huxley, A. (1956/2004). *The Doors of Perception*. London: Harper & Row.

James, W. (1890). *The Principles of Psychology*. New York: Holt.

Jordan, R. and Beattie, G. (2003). Understanding male interpersonal violence: A discourse analytic approach to accounts of violence on the door. *Semiotica* 144: 101–142.

Kahneman, D. (2011). *Thinking, Fast and Slow*. London: Penguin.

Karon, B. P. and Rosberg, J. (1958). Study of the mother-child relationship in a case of paranoid schizophrenia. *American Journal of Psychotherapy* 12: 522–533.

Kasanin, J., Knight, E. and Sage, P. (1934). The parent-child relationship in schizophrenia. *The Journal of Nervous and Mental Disease* 79: 249–263.

Labov, W. (1972a). Rules for ritual insults. In Sudnow, D. (ed.), *Studies in Social Interaction*. New York: Oxford.

Labov, W. (1972b). *Sociolinguistic Patterns*. Oxford: Basil Blackwell.

Laing, R. D. (1960). *The Divided Self: A Study of Society and Madness*. London: Tavistock.

Lee, V. and Beattie, G. (1998). The rhetorical organization of verbal and nonverbal behavior in emotion talk. *Semiotica* 120: 39–92.

Levy, D. M. (1931). Maternal over-protection and rejection. *Journal of Nervous and Mental Disease* 73: 65–77.

Lidz, T., Cornelison, A. R., Fleck, S. and Terry, D. (1957). The intrafamilial environment of schizophrenic patients: II. Marital schism and marital skew. *American Journal of Psychiatry* 114: 241–248.

Lidz, T., Cornelison, A. R., Singer, M., Schafer, S. and Fleck, S. (1965/1985). The mothers of schizophrenic patients. In Lidz, T., Fleck, S. and Cornelison, A. R. (eds.), *Schizophrenia and the Family*. New York: International Universities Press.

Loeff, R. G. (1966). Differential discrimination of conflicting emotional messages by normal, delinquent, and schizophrenic adolescents. *Dissertation Abstracts* 26: 6850–6851.

McNeill, D. (1992). *Hand and Mind: What Gestures Reveal about Thought*. Chicago: University of Chicago Press.

Mehrabian, A. (1971). *Silent Messages*. Wadsworth: Belmont.

Mehrabian, A. and Ferris, S. R. (1967). Inference of attitudes from nonverbal communication in two channels. *Journal of Consulting Psychology* 31: 248–252.

Mehrabian, A. and Wiener, M. (1967). Decoding of inconsistent communications. *Journal of Personality and Social Psychology* 6: 109–114.

Merton, R. K. (1948). The self-fulfilling prophecy. *The Antioch Review* 8: 193–210.

Nietzsche, F. (1889/1974). *Twilight of the Idols*. Harmondsworth: Penguin.

Orne, M. T. (1962). On the social psychology of the psychological experiment: With particular reference to demand characteristics and their implications. *American Psychologist* 17: 776.

Petrie, W. M. F. (1895). *Race and Civilization*. Report of the Smithsonian Institution for 1895, Washington, DC. p. 597.

Pevear, R. (2004). *Introduction to Notes from Underground*. London: Everyman's Library.

Popper, K. (1945/1983). *The Autonomy of Sociology*. Reprinted in *Popper* (D. Miller, Ed.). London: Fontana.

Potash, H. (1965). *Schizophrenic Interaction and the Double Bind*. Doctoral dissertation. East Lansing, MI: Michigan State University.

Pushkin, A. (1829/1997). *Alexander Pushkin: Everyman's Poetry*. London: J.M. Dent.

Reichard, S. and Tillman, C. (1950). Patterns of parent-child relationships in schizophrenia. *Psychiatry* 13: 247–257.

Ringuette, E. L. and Kennedy, T. (1966). An experimental study of the double bind hypothesis. *Journal of Abnormal Psychology* 71: 136–141.

Roosevelt, T. (1889/2004). *The Winning of the West. Volume 1. From the Alleghanies to the Mississippi, 1769–1776*. New York: G. P. Putnam's Sons.

Schegloff, E. and Sacks, H. (1973). Opening up closings. *Semiotica* 8: 289–327.

Schuham, A. I. (1967). The double-bind hypothesis a decade later. *Psychological Bulletin* 68: 409–416.

Sears, D. O. (1986). College sophomores in the laboratory: Influences of a narrow data base on social psychology's view of human nature. *Journal of Personality and Social Psychology* 51: 515–530.

Shepherd, I. L. and Guthrie, G. M. (1959). Attitudes of mothers of schizophrenic patients. *Journal of Clinical Psychology* 15: 212–215.

Skinner, B. F. (1957). *Verbal Behavior*. New York: Appleton-Century-Crofts.

Skinner, B. F. (1974). *Beyond Freedom and Dignity*. Harmondsworth: Penguin.

Sullivan, H. S. (1927). The onset of schizophrenia. *American Journal of Psychiatry* 84: 105–134.

Thatcher, M. (1995). *The Path to Power*. London: Harper Collins.

Trower, P., Bryant, B., Argyle, M. and Marzillier, J. (1978). *Social Skills and Mental Health*. London: Methuen.

Vygotsky, L.S. (1965). *Thought and Language*. Cambridge, MA: MIT Press.

Watzlawick, P. (1963). A review of the double bind theory. *Family Processes* 2: 132–153.

Watzlawick, P., Beavin, J. H. and Jackson, D. D. (1967). *Pragmatics of Human Communication: A Study of Interactional Patterns*. London: Faber and Faber.

Whorf, B. L. (1956/1967). *Language, Thought and Reality*. Cambridge, MA: MIT Press.

Wittgenstein, L. (1922). *Tractatus Logico-Philosophicus*. London: Kegan Paul.

Yeats, W. B. (1900/1990). *Selected Poetry*. London: Pan.